Application Development Using OS/2 REXX

Anthony S. Rudd

A Wiley–QED Publication

John Wiley & Sons, Inc.

New York • Chichester • Brisbane • Toronto • Singapore

Designations used by companies to distinguish their products are often claimed as trademarks. In all instances where John Wiley & Sons, Inc. is aware of a claim, the product names appear in initial capital or all capital letters. Readers, however, should contact the appropriate companies for more complete information regarding trademarks and registration.

This text is printed on acid-free paper.

© 1994 by John Wiley & Sons, Inc.

ISBN 0 471-60691-X

Printed in the United States of America

10 9 8 7 6 5 4 3 2 1

Contents

Preface

The title of this book *Mastering OS/2 REXX: The Practical Usage of OS/2 REXX* reveals the purpose I had in writing it: a concise, but complete, source of information necessary to master the REXX language for applications in the OS/2 environment.

Practical means that the information is presented in such a form to be easy to find and use – lists and diagrams are used where possible. Consequently, the book does not read like a novel. My personal experience is that books on such topics are not read from cover to cover, rather only those items of interest are read. With this in mind, I have structured the book with numbered sections, and used self-contained syntax diagrams. The widespread acceptance of REXX in many different environments is good for the language, but creates difficulties for an author. Which implementation should be described? Unfortunately, each implementation has its differences (in the form of implementation-specific function libraries). If all implementations were described in detail, the book would no longer be a compact reference. I have chosen to describe the most widely-available REXX implementation, namely IBM's OS/2 2.x. In this way *Mastering OS/2 REXX* is hopefully of use to the widest possible range of readers.

And who should these readers be? The answer: both beginners and experts. Beginners are lead through the steps required to develop REXX applications; complete worked examples, large enough to be practical, but devoid of superfluous detail, enable the REXX novice to see what is necessary to write a simple application. Experts have a compact reference. Special emphasis is given to the programming interfaces, a topic that is not usually given the treatment it warrants – the easy expansibility of REXX is one of the most powerful features of the language.

The book itself is divided into three parts: Part 1 – Basic REXX; Part 2 – Advanced REXX; Part 3 – REXX Applications. Part 1 describes the basic features of the language. Part 2 describes the advanced features of the language: the REXXUTIL function library, and the Application Programming Interfaces (APIs), both of which can be used to implement OS/2-specific applications. Part 3 describes the use of REXX in conjunction with a number of third-party applications. The first two parts both end with a comprehensive worked example that serves to illustrate the use of a wide range of facilities described in the preceding chapters. Each section also has explanatory examples.

At this point I would like to thank Charles Daney, Brian Honour, Detlef Insel, and Steve Price for their help in the preparation of this book.

Part 1

Basic REXX

1

Introduction

1.1 WHAT IS REXX?

REXX is the acronym derived from **Re**structured Extended Executor, and is IBM's Systems Application Architecture (SAA) procedural language. The name REXX gives several clues as to its origin. Extended Executor: an extension of the EXEC procedure language implemented for the VM/CMS operating system; Restructured: as the word says. As all good acronyms, REXX itself has a meaning; it is derived from the Latin word *rex, regis* (king) – REXX is namely the King of Programming Languages.

Procedural language in this context means a language used to create *procedures* or *commands*; a procedure being a named series of statements to perform some particular task. REXX procedures are also known as *execs, programs, macros, shells* and *scripts* – this book uses the term exec. These names show some of the uses of REXX execs.

Procedures are common in data processing, although they may be given different names. Examples from various environments are:

- DOS or OS/2, a batch file (extension .BAT or .CMD);
- VM/CMS, an EXEC or EXEC2 procedure;
- MVS-TSO, a CLIST (command procedure).

The preceding definition of a procedure is essentially that of a program. Indeed, REXX can be used for programming tasks. However, REXX offers more, as it also interfaces with other system components, and allows applications to use system services. For example, in the OS/2 environment, a REXX program can use OS/2 facilities to obtain directory information.

1.2 REXX'S ORIGIN

REXX was originally implemented for the IBM VM/CMS environment. Those readers interested in the historical background of the development of the REXX language should read the book *The Rexx Language, A Practical Approach to Programming* written by M.F.Cowlishaw, the original author of the language.

Several experimental versions followed the VM/CMS implementation. However, these implementations were only of limited general interest. More important implementations were the porting of the language to the IBM Personal Computer (PC) in the form of Quercus Systems' (originally Mansfield Software Group's implementation) *Personal REXX*, and IBM's implementations for MVS TSO/E Version 2 and OS/2 Version 1.2. REXX is now available for almost all hardware and software platforms.

1.3 REXX FEATURES

REXX is a structured language with a limited number of basic *instructions*. These instructions are supplemented by a library of *functions*. The library functions are especially suited to character-string processing. These standard (SAA) REXX components (instructions and functions) are supplemented by routines particular to the operating environment: *host commands* (.*service routines*) and *programming interfaces* – these extensions are implementation dependent. Figure 1.1 illustrates the scope of a REXX implementation, and Appendix E contains tables showing the degree to which the various implementations are compatible with each other. The language is simplified by removing the need to perform housekeeping functions, for example, field definition.

The standard components can be augmented by user routines; written either in REXX or in a conventional programming language. REXX also interfaces with host operating system components.

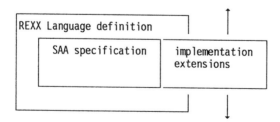

Figure 1.1.Scope of a REXX implementation.

To summarize:

- The limited number of instructions makes REXX an easy, yet complete, language to learn.
- The extensive library of powerful functions greatly reduces the amount of coding necessary to write applications.

- The availability of implementations in a wide range of environments simplifies the writing of applications to run under different hardware and operating systems.
- Applications can use open-interfaces to access REXX services.

1.4 WHERE CAN REXX BE USED?

REXX is a general purpose language. The wide availability of REXX simplifies the porting of applications among the various operating environments. Unfortunately, the host environment extensions are often needed for input/output operations, and these extensions are not always identical in all operating environments.

REXX is usually an interpreted language, although compilers are becoming available in some platforms. In the interpreted form REXX is not particularly suitable to be used for long-running applications, although it may well be used to create a prototype for such an application.

The interfaces from REXX with other components (for example, Database Manager) make it well suited to be used as an intelligent link between the various components of an application. These programming interfaces also enable REXX to be used from conventional programming languages; for example, REXX parsing facilities are useful for string processing applications.

To summarize, REXX is especially useful for:

- prototyping
- front-end for dialogue applications
- macro language
- one-off jobs
- teaching tool.

However, REXX is not limited to such tasks. Its power will often avoid the necessity of having to write a program in a conventional language.

1.5 FUTURE DEVELOPMENTS

Currently two sources determine the REXX language specification:

- M.F.Cowlishaw's language definition (currently at version 4.00)
- IBM's SAA Procedures Language definition (currently at level 2).

Except for DBCS (double-byte character set) processing, only supported in the SAA definition, these two specifications are equivalent. OS/2 2.x Procedures Language implements the SAA definition of REXX (this implementation is known as OS/2 REXX).

In the future a third body will influence the definition of the REXX language. The ANSI X3J18 committee was formed in 1991 to standardize the REXX language. The founding of this Standards Committee confirms the importance of REXX, and should serve to popularize the language.

There is a marked trend to implement compiler versions of REXX on various platforms (e.g., VM, MVS). These compilers reduce the time overhead inherent in interpreted languages, and so make REXX usable for an even wider range of applications. The availability of both an interpreter and a compiler combines the benefits of the two: the interpreter with its improved diagnostics during the implementation phase, and the compiler to produce optimized execution code.

In concordance with the trend towards object-oriented languages, there is an experimental object-oriented version of REXX.

An increasing number of products use REXX as their script language, or offer interfaces to REXX (e.g., Borland's ObjectVision). This welcome trend gives users a powerful standardized customising tool without requiring them to learn proprietary languages.

1.6 THE OS/2 IMPLEMENTATION

REXX as implemented in OS/2 2.x (**OS/2 REXX**) supports the full language definition. In addition, a standard function package contains interfaces to many utility functions, such as file searching, and access to the Workplace Shell.

OS/2 REXX has a wide range of Application Programming Interfaces (APIs) to enable conventional programs to make use of REXX services. These APIs offer support for:

- external environments
- external functions (written in a conventional programming language)
- system exits
- macrospaces
- shared variables.

The facility to use **external environments (commands)** is included in the language, but which commands are supported is implementation-specific. User command environments, together with external functions, offer the principal means of extending the language. User command environments are applications not included with the operating system, written either by the user or by a thirdparty.

The default command environment interfaces to the standard operating system commands, such as DIR, TIME. However, REXX, being such a rich language, usually offers better alternatives; for example, the TIME function.

External functions are extensions to the standard set of functions. As for command environments, external functions may be written by the user or be part of a third-party application. The OS/2 Extended Services function library supplied with Database Manager is probably the best-known example of external functions.

System exits are programmed functions that replace the standard routines for certain instructions and exec processing. System exits, when used, are activated when the REXX interpreter is explicitly invoked with the RexxStart function. For example, a user exit routine can be invoked when the exec is initiated.

A **macrospace** is one or more execs preloaded into main-storage. Such macrospaces can be stored as an external file. Macrospaces can significantly improve performance by avoiding disk access when execs are called; for example, as editor macros.

The **variable pool interface** allows programs to access the variables of the currently active REXX exec.

In addition to IBM's OS/2 REXX implementation described in this book, Quercus Systems offers an OS/2 version of *Personal REXX*. A particular feature of *Personal REXX* is its powerful function package.

2

REXX Concepts

2.1 INTRODUCTION

The general concepts of a REXX exec are best demonstrated by developing a simple program. This exec illustrates many of the features available in REXX.

The REXX equivalent of the renowned C "hello world" program consists of just two lines:

```
/* demonstration program */
SAY Hello World
```

The first line is a commentary that the command processor requires to distinguish a batch procedure from a REXX exec (with commentary). The second line displays the Hello World message. Hello and World are two variables, which in REXX have their uppercase name as initial content. So this program would actually display HELLO WORLD. This REXX feature may simplify the writing of text strings, but is a major cause of error in REXX programs. It is better to write explicit alphanumeric constants; e.g., SAY 'Hello World' or SAY "Hello World".

The use of variables can be illustrated by adding a request that the user's name be input.

```
SAY "enter name"
PULL name
SAY "Hello" name
```

The PULL instruction places the terminal input in the name variable (the PULL instruction is actually an abbreviated form of the PARSE instruction that converts the input data to uppercase). Variables are not explicitly declared – a variable is implicitly created on its first reference. The SAY instruction outputs the constant Hello and the contents of the name variable. REXX automatically places a single blank between the tokens, irrespective of how many blanks have been specified, unless the tokens are contiguous.

Like most modern programming languages, REXX has structured programming constructions (DO, SELECT, etc.). The DO statement starts a program block that is terminated with an END statement (program blocks can be nested). The DO instruction has several forms: unconditional, conditional, infinite, iterative. This example uses the iterative form.

```
DO i = 1 TO 5
  SAY "enter address line" i
  PULL line.i
  IF line.i = '' THEN LEAVE
  i0 = i
END
```

The PULL instruction shows the other form for variables: an array (stem variable). There are no theoretical limits to either the number of dimensions or the size of each dimension, nor do the array element numbers need to be numeric.

The IF instruction tests whether null input has been made, in which case the LEAVE instruction terminates the DO loop. The I0 variable is set to contain the number of lines read.

Larger programs are often easier to write (and understand) when the mainline routine controls the processing logic and invokes routines for the detailed processing. REXX has two means of invoking such routines: with an explicit CALL or as a function (which must return a value).

Here the StoreLine routine is passed a single argument: the number of lines read.

```
CALL StoreLine i0
```

The StoreLine routine is defined as a procedure (PROCEDURE keyword). A routine may have the form: function, procedure, or subroutine. Procedures, in contrast with nonprocedures, impose data hiding – variables must be explicitly exposed to be visible outside the routine.

The ARG instruction is used to retrieve the passed argument, which is stored as variable n. The QUEUE instruction places the line.i variables at the end of the current queue (stack). The RETURN instruction terminates the routine, and returns to the point of invocation.

```
StoreLine: PROCEDURE EXPOSE line.
  ARG n
  DO i = 1 TO n
    QUEUE line.i
  END
RETURN
```

REXX has a number of forms for constants: numeric (e.g., 5), alphanumeric (e.g., "Hello"), hexadecimal (e.g., "1a"x), binary, and so on. Hexadecimal and binary literals are suffixed with X or B, respectively.

```
QUEUE "1a"x /* ^z (Ctrl-Z) */
```

REXX has a large library of standard functions. Additional functions can be implemented in either REXX or as programmed functions (written in a conventional programming language, such as C). Functions are directly invoked with their name, and zero or more arguments enclosed within parentheses. QUEUED is a standard function that returns the number of elements in the queue (stack). The SAY instruction can be used to display this count.

```
SAY queued()
```

REXX execs have direct access to the command environment (command processor). Statements that are not recognized as REXX instructions are passed to the command processor. The standard OS/2 command processor CMD.EXE is the default processor. Application-specific command processors can be programmed in a conventional programming language using the ADDRESS instruction to specify the name of the current environment (and, by inference, the associated command processing program).

The copy command as used here takes its input from the console (terminal input). In the REXX environment, the queue (unless nonempty) preempts the terminal input. Hence the copy command will use the data previously stored in the queue as its input.

```
"copy con: c:file.dat"
```

The EXIT instruction terminates the exec. If this instruction were not included in the following example, the following procedure would be (erroneously) invoked. The omission of an EXIT (or some equivalent) instruction before the routine definitions is a frequent error in REXX execs.

The complete sample exec follows:

```
/* REXX demonstration program */
SAY "Hello World"
SAY "enter name"
PULL name
SAY "Hello" name
DO i = 1 TO 5
  SAY "enter address line" i
  PULL line.i
  IF line.i = '' THEN LEAVE
  i0 = i
END
CALL StoreLine i0
```

```
QUEUE "1a"x /* ^z */
SAY queued()
"copy con: c:file.dat"
EXIT
StoreLine: PROCEDURE EXPOSE line.
  ARG n
  DO i = 1 TO n
    QUEUE line.i
  END
RETURNT
```

Note: The coding in REXX execs is case-insensitive (except for literals).

2.2 REXX COMPONENTS

REXX **execs** (programs), like most programs, are comprised of **statements** (*Note*: The REXX literature does not have a term for statements.) Statements are:

- keyword instructions (including assignment),
- host commands, or
- comments, and

are, in turn, comprised of **clauses**.

Clauses can use **REXX built-in functions** and **external functions**. Both keyword instructions and REXX built-in functions are part of the SAA definition, and so standard to all REXX implementations, whereas host commands are implementation-specific. The availability of host environment command functions depends on the **host environment** being used.

Statements that are not recognized as being keyword instructions are passed to the current host environment.

Because, in almost all environments, REXX was not the initial procedural language, there must be some means of identifying a REXX exec to the command processor. A comment as the first statement serves as explicit identification of a REXX exec (*note*: some implementations require that this comment contains the word REXX).

2.3 STATEMENT FORMAT

REXX statements can generally be written free format as described in Section 2.3.1. The hexadecimal notations used in this section (e.g., '0D'X) refer to the coding and not how the character is actually written.

Statement syntax:

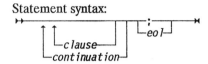

continuation

> A continuation indicator. The end-of-line character (see **eol**) terminates the current statement, unless continuation is set (*explicit continuation* is a comma) or implied (the instruction is not complete; e.g., IF must be followed by THEN, or the final literal delimiter has not yet been specified).

eol

> '0D'X (carriage-return) is the **end-of-line character** – the line-feed character ('0A'X) may optionally follow the carriage-return character. A semicolon explicitly terminates a statement, except in the cases where it can terminate a clause (DO, IF and SELECT instructions).

Clause syntax:

token

> Tokens are described in Section 2.4.

2.3.1 Free Format Considerations

Free format means:

- Individual tokens in a clause are separated by one or more delimiters – normally a blank, comment or horizontal-tab ('09'X) – but may be any nonalphanumeric character allowed in the expression.

  Example:
  ```
  a = b * 12;
  a  =  b  *   12;
  a=b*12;
  ```
  are all equivalent.

  Note: In character expressions, tokens separated by one or more blanks are concatenated together with a single blank between each token. For example,
  ```
  SAY "alpha"    "beta";
  ```
  displays
  ```
  alpha beta
  ```

- The tokens in a clause are, in general, case-insensitive. This means that the tokens may be written in either uppercase or lowercase, or mixed. This rule does not apply to character literals, which are case-sensitive. Despite the flexibility that REXX allows, it helps to make programs easier to read and understand if some convention is adopted – for example, I have used uppercase notation in this book to denote instructions and noninternal functions.

- The end-of-statement (clause) delimiter (;) is usually optional and is only needed when the meaning would otherwise be ambiguous. The end-of-line character implies the end of the statement, unless continuation is implied from the syntax of the statement.

  Example:
  ```
  IF a = b THEN SAY "equal"; ELSE SAY "not equal"
  ```
  requires a semicolon at the end of the THEN clause when the statement is written in a single line; otherwise ELSE SAY "not equal" would be taken as part of the text to be displayed when the condition is satisfied.

  Note: It is good programming practice to end each statement with an end-of-statement delimiter – this can avoid certain program errors caused by inadvertent continuations.

- Statements can be written on one or more lines, but a comma (,) must be used to indicate *explicit continuation*.

  Example:
  ```
  IF a = b
    THEN SAY "equal"
    ELSE SAY "not equal";
  ```
  does not require a **continuation comma** (,) at the end of each line because the continuation is implicit (IF is followed by THEN, which may itself be followed by ELSE), conversely;
  ```
  a = b,
  * c;
  ```
  requires an explicit continuation at the end of the first line, as the line in itself is complete, and so no continuation is expected.

  If the comma is required in the continued statement, it must be repeated.

  Example:
  ```
  CALL alpha beta,,
    gamma;
  ```
  is equivalent to CALL alpha beta, gamma;.

- A line can contain one or more statements, although this approach is usually not good programming practice.
  Example:
  ```
  a = b; SAY "this is a second statement";
  ```

2.4 REXX TOKENS

REXX clauses are comprised of the following tokens:

- numbers
- literals
- symbols
- constants
- operators
- special characters (delimiters)
- comments

There are three types of literals:

- literal string (alphanumeric literal)
- hexadecimal literal
- binary literal

This book, and indeed most books on programming languages, uses syntax diagrams to define the language elements. Although syntax diagrams may at first appear complex, they are easier to understand than long-winded prose. Familiarity with syntax diagrams is a prerequisite to understanding this book. Three simple examples to define elementary concepts are used as an introduction to syntax diagrams (Appendix B contains a detailed explanation on how to read syntax diagrams):

- digit;
- integer;
- signed integer

Figure 2.1 defines a digit as being one (and only) of the characters 0, 1, 2, 3, 4, 5, 6, 7, 8, 9. Figure 2.2 defines an integer as being a string of one or more of the characters 0, 1, 2, 3, 4, 5, 6, 7, 8, 9; the arrow indicates that the character can be repeated. The individual characters are written without any intervening blanks.

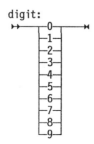

Figure 2.1. Syntax diagram for the definition of a digit.

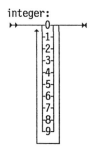

Figure 2.2. Syntax diagram for the definition of an integer.

The syntax diagram for an integer could also have been simplified to use the previous definition of a digit, as follows:

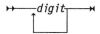

Digit written in italics indicates that it is defined elsewhere.

Figure 2.3 specifies the syntax of a signed integer. The sign here is optional; the underlined operand (+) is the default.

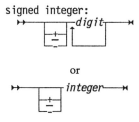

Figure 2.3. Syntax diagram for the definition of a signed integer.

2.4.1 Number

REXX does not explicitly subdivide numerical values into integers; floating-point numbers, and so on, rather it has the concept of *number*. The *precision* of a number is determined by the value specified in the NUMERIC DIGITS instruction (the default precision is 9 digits). There is no theoretical limit to the size of a number, although there may be a practical limit (computational time, main-storage, etc.).

Numbers larger or smaller than the precision are automatically converted to REXX floating point representation (the default format is SCIENTIFIC, but this may be changed with the NUMERIC FORM instruction).

The form of a number as shown in Figure 2.4 is somewhat simplified in that the following three conditions are omitted:

- The exponent 0 is not allowed; e.g., `1.2E0` is invalid.
- A number must contain at least one digit.
- A number may not start with an E (or e). For example, `1e2` rather than `e2`, otherwise the floating-point number could not be distinguished from the symbol E2.

E (or e) in a number represents the power 10. For example, E2 is 100, and E-2 is 0.01.

number:

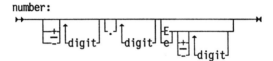

Figure 2.4. Syntax diagram for the definition of a number.

Examples of numbers:
```
123
12.3
12.3E-2  (equivalent to 0.123)
.123
0.123
-0.123
```

2.4.2 Literal

A literal is a string of characters contained within single quotes (') or double quotes ("), which are called the *delimiting quotes*. Although either single or double quotes may be used as delimiting quotes, the same quote-character must be used in a given literal. An individual literal has a maximum length of 250 characters; longer literals can be formed by concatenating shorter literals. A string that does not contain any characters (e.g., ' ') is a *null string*. Figure 2.5 shows the syntax for a literal – the *suffix operator* X (x) or B (b) defines a hexadecimal or binary literal, respectively.

literal:

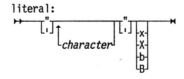

Figure 2.5. Syntax diagram for the definition of a literal.

Example:
    'alpha BETA gamma', "alpha BETA gamma" and "alpha" "BETA gamma"
are all equivalent, and define the 16 characters alpha BETA gamma.

If the delimiting quotes are required within the literal, then they must be paired. For example,
    'O''Brien'
represents O'Brien.
    However, it is usually better to use the other delimiter, which is then not paired. For example,
    "O'Brien"

Data within a literal are case-sensitive. For example,
    "alpha"
    "ALPHA"
    "Alpha"
are three distinct literals representing alpha, ALPHA and Alpha, respectively.

A literal can be continued onto the next line by placing a comma after the literal to be continued. Both the literal to be continued and the continuation literal must be enclosed within quotes. A single blank is inserted between the individual literals. For example,
    "alpha beta",
        "gamma"
defines the literal "alpha beta gamma".

If the continuation literal is to be placed immediately after the first literal, i.e., without the intervening blank, then the *abuttal ;operator* (||) must precede the continuation comma. For example,
    "alpha beta"||,
        "gamma"
defines the literal "alpha betagamma".

2.4.2.1 Hexadecimal literal. The X (or x) suffix operator specifies that the preceding alphanumeric literal has a hexadecimal value, and so defines a *hexadecimal literal*. The suffix operator must be written immediately following the terminating '. The individual characters in the literal may only be valid hexadecimal digits: 0 through 9, A through F, or a through f. Literals whose length is not a multiple of 2 will be left-padded with a 0. For example

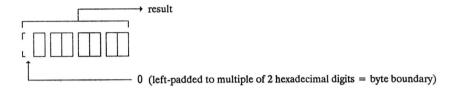

Example:

    "4142303132"x

defines the literal containing the hexadecimal digits, 41, 42, 30, 31 and 32, or the ASCII string "AB012".

To improve readability, pairs of hexadecimal digits can be separated by one or more blanks. For example, the previous hexadecimal string could have been written as:

    "41 42 30 31 32"x

2.4.2.2 Binary literal. The B (or b) suffix operator defines the preceding numeric literal as having binary values, and so defines a *binary literal*. The suffix operator must be written immediately following the terminating '. The literal may contain only digits 0 and 1, and any blanks used to improve the readability must be placed between groups of 4 (or 8) digits . Each 8 binary digits represents a byte. Literals whose length is not a multiple of 8 will be left-padded with 0's. For example,

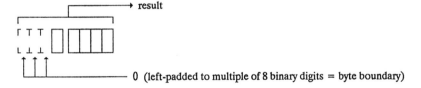

Example:

    "1100 0001"b

defines the literal containing the hexadecimal digits C1.

2.4.3 Symbol

REXX has two types of symbol:

- simple symbol
- compound symbol

A symbol name has a maximum length of 250 characters.

simplesymbol:

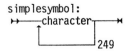

Character must be one of the following:
- a – z
- A – Z
- 0 – 9
- ! ? _

Note: The first character of a simple symbol may not be a digit (0 through 9).

Important: A **symbol** has initially its own name (uppercase) as content; e.g.,
alpha contains ALPHA
a1   contains A1

compoundsymbol:
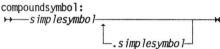

A **compound symbol** is a special form of symbol consisting of one or more simple symbols each separated by a period. The first variable in a compound symbol is called the **stem**; the rest of the compound symbol is called the **tail**. The stem is always an alphanumeric literal. Even if the simple symbol has been assigned a different value, the stem remains unchanged. Tail variables may be assigned values. The stem cannot start with a digit, although the subsequent simple symbols may be numeric.

When the stem is used to reference all the associated compound variables, it is written with an appended point; e.g., alpha.. *Note*: Many programmed utility functions allow the period to be omitted.

Example:
```
alpha = "BETA";
alpha.alpha = "GAMMA";
```
assigns the value GAMMA to the compound symbol ALPHA.BETA (BETA has been assigned to the second alpha in the compound symbol alpha.alpha; the stem (first alpha) remains unchanged).

The stem can be used to assign a value to all compounds of that stem. This applies even to compound variables that have not yet been used. For example,
```
alpha. = 0;
```
assigns 0 to all compounds having alpha. as stem.

2.4.3.1 Declaration of symbols. Symbols are not declared. Each symbol has its own name (in uppercase) as initial content. For example, the symbol Alpha has initial content ALPHA. Similarly, symbols have no implicit attribute (numeric, character, etc.). The attribute is determined by the current content, and may change during the course of execution.

2.4.3.2 Length of symbol data. Symbols, with the exception of those containing numeric data, have no explicit length. The length of data that can be stored in a symbol is limited only by the amount of main-storage available.

The length (precision) of numeric data is determined by the NUMERIC DIGITS setting. The default length is 9, which means that a number is stored with a precision of 9 digits. The NUMERIC DIGITS setting does not necessarily apply to the whole program; rather, it may be set where required.

2.4.3.3 Array. An array is a logical grouping of compound symbols that have the same stem. The indices are the second, third, and subsequent variables in the compound symbol. These indices need not be numeric. For example, arrays can be used as *associative storage*. There is no limit to the number of dimensions.

Arrays have no implicit sequence. This means, for example, that an array can have elements a.1 and a.5, with other elements undefined.

Example:
The C array alpha[i][j] could be written as the REXX compound variable alpha.i.j, or using self-explanatory terms, alpha.month.day.

2.4.3.4 Symbol locality. Symbols are local to the exec in which they are used. Within an exec, variables are hidden in internal routines defined with the PROCEDURE instruction, except for those variables that have been specified in the EXPOSE clause. The VALUE built-in function with the OS2ENVIRONMENT selector uses the system environment pool, within the constraints of the command processor, for limited access to global variables.

2.4.4 Constant

REXX has several forms of constants:

- explicit literals (enclosed within single or double quotes)
- tokens starting with a digit or a period (.)
- tokens used as explicit instruction operands

Constant examples:
```
'alpha'
"beta"
123
.1
CALL gamma
```

In the last example, the INTERPRET instruction must be used if a call modification is required. For example,

```
gamma = 'delta'
x = 'CALL' gamma
INTERPRET x
```

These statements cause the routine DELTA to be invoked; whereas, the following statements cause the routine GAMMA to be invoked:

```
gamma = 'delta'
CALL gamma
```

2.4.5 Operator

There are two forms of operators:

- unary (one operand)
- binary (two operands)

A unary operator operates on the token that immediately follows it. A binary operator operates on the tokens that come immediately before and after it. Table 2.5 lists the REXX operators.

The individual operators in multisymbol operators (e.g., >=) may be separated by one or more blanks (e.g., as > =), although this form should be avoided as it reduces readability. *Note*: The comment delimiters (/* and */) are not operators, and so may not be separated.

Example:

```
x = (\a); /* unary operator */
x = ((a / b) / c); /* binary operator */
```

The parentheses are introduced to show the processing sequence – the processing is not affected if they are omitted.

Important: The operators used in an expression determine the type of the expression. There are four classes of operators (described in section 2.5):

- character
- arithmetic
- comparison
- logical (Boolean)

Example:

a||b   is a character expression ("||" is a character operator);
a+b   is a numeric expression ("+" is an arithmetic operator);
a=b   is a comparison expression ("=" is a comparison operator);
a&b   is a logical expression ("&" is a logical operator).

A single expression cannot contain mixed operators, although an expression can be comprised of subexpressions, which themselves contain different classes of operators; subexpressions are expressions contained within parentheses.

Example:
        x=2+(b>c)-(d&1);
is a valid numeric expression; the second subexpression (b>c) evaluates to either 1 or 0, depending on whether the expression is true or false, respectively; the third subexpression (d&1) is the value of performing a Logical Or with 1 on the content of the symbol d (d must contain either 0 or 1).

Note: This is an example of what *can* be done, not necessarily of how it *should* be.

2.5 REXX SYNTAX

The general syntax for REXX statements is shown in Figure 2.6. The syntax for instructions, host commands, and comments is described in Chapter 9.

A *label* is the target for a SIGNAL instruction, or the name of an internal routine that is invoked with the CALL instruction or as a function call. Labelled statements can also be traced with the TRACE LABELS instruction. In the following syntax diagram **instruction** is a REXX instruction, and **hostcommand** is any statement that is neither an instruction nor a comment (and is passed to the current command processor, which is set with the ADDRESS instruction − CMD.EXE is the default command processor).

statement:

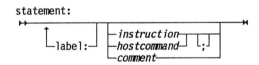

Figure 2.6. − Syntax diagram for the definition of a statement.

Many instructions contain *expressions*, the syntax of which is shown in Figure 2.7. The *operator* determines the expression type; e.g., a character operator forms a character expression.

expression:

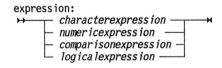

Figure 2.7. − Syntax diagram for the definition of an expression, part 1 of 2.

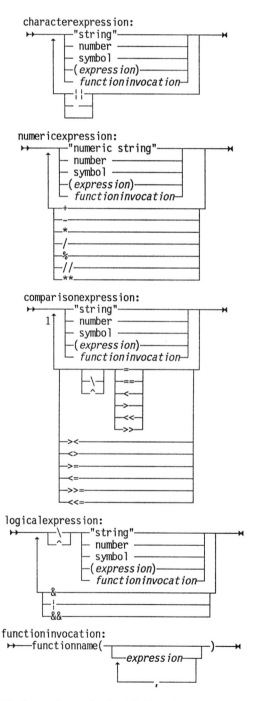

Figure 2.7. – Syntax diagram for the definition of an expression, part 2 of 2.

2.5.1 Character Operators

REXX has only one character operator – *concatenation*, which has two forms:

- implicit
- explicit

Those operands (terms) in a character expression that are separated by one or more blanks (*blank operator*) will be concatenated together with one blank between each term (*implicit concatenation*). Those operands in a character expression that are not separated will be concatenated together without any intervening blanks (*abuttal concatenation*). Abuttal concatenation requires that the operands be distinguishable as such; e.g., a symbol followed by a literal. The *abuttal operator* (||) may also be used for *explicit concatenation*. Table 2.1 illustrates concatenation (a is assumed to contain alpha, b is assumed to contain beta).

Operation	Result
a b	alpha beta
"c"b	cbeta
a ¦¦ b	alphabeta

Table 2.1. Concatenation examples.

2.5.2 Arithmetic Operators

Arithmetic operators are used to define the processing to be performed on the operands of a numeric expression. A numeric expression yields a numeric result, the precision of which is determined by the value set with the instruction NUMERIC DIGITS (the default is nine digits precision). Table 2.2 illustrates the results of various arithmetic operations.

Operation	Result
5 + 2	7
5 − 2	3
5 * 2	10
5 / 2	2.5
5 % 2	2
5 // 2	1
5 ** 2	25
5 ** -2	0.04

Table 2.2. Typical arithmetic operations.

REXX has the arithmetic operators:

+   add
-       subtract
*   multiply
/   divide (return full-precision quotient)
%   divide (return integer quotient)
//   divide (return integer remainder)
**   exponentiation (may only be an integral value)

The operators "+" and "-" may also be used as prefix operators.

2.5.3 Comparison Operators

Comparison operators are used to compare two operands with each other. The operands being compared will be padded if necessary. The accuracy of the comparison of numeric operands is determined by the NUMERIC FUZZ instruction, which specifies how many least-significant digits are to be ignored from the comparison (the default is 0 – the complete operands are used). Table 2.3 illustrates the results of various comparison operations.

A comparison expression is processed from left to right, and yields a numeric result:

- 1   The comparison condition is *true*.
- 0   The comparison condition is *false*.

Similarly, a binary value (0 or 1) can be used in place of a comparison expression.

REXX has the comparison operators:

==   strictly equal
=   equal (padded, if necessary)
><   greater or less than (unequal)
<>   less or greater than (unequal)
>   greater than
<   less than
>>   strictly greater than
<<   strictly less than
> =   greater than or equal
< =   less than or equal
>> =   strictly greater than or equal
<< =   strictly less than or equal

The adverb *strictly* includes padding characters (nonsignificant blanks and 0's) in the comparison (refer to Table 2.3 for examples).

Operation	Result
"5 " == "5"	false
"5 " = "5"	true
"5 " \== "5"	true
"5 " \= "5"	false
"6 " > "5"	true
"5 " > "5"	false
"5 " >> "5"	true
"6 " < "5"	false

Table 2.3. Typical comparison operations.

The prefix ^ or \ (NOT) can be used with the =, ==, >, <, >> and << operators. For example, \= and ^= both mean not equal. Refer to the syntax diagram in Figure 2.7 for the allowed uses of the NOT prefix-operator.

2.5.4 Logical (Boolean) Operators
Logical operators perform a Boolean operation on binary operands, which may contain only 0 or 1 – logical operations on operands containing any other value will cause an error. The NOT operator (\ or ^) is right-associative, and takes a single operand. The other logical operators have two operands, and are left-associative (the second operand operates on the first operand). The built-in functions BITAND, BITOR and BITXOR can be used to perform a bit-by-bit logical operation. Table 2.4 illustrates the results of various logical operations.

REXX has the Boolean operators:

&	And
|	Inclusive Or
&&	Exclusive Or
\	Not
^	Not

2.5.5 Operator Associativity
Associativity expresses to which operand the operator applies. Unary operators (one operand) are right-associative. Binary operators (two operands) are left-associative.

Operation	Result
\"0" \"1"	"1" "0"
"0" & "0" "1" & "0" "0" & "1" "1" & "1"	"0" "0" "0" "1"
"0" | "0" "1" | "0" "0" | "1" "1" | "1"	"0" "1" "1" "1"
"0" && "0" "1" && "0" "0" && "1" "1" && "1"	"0" "1" "1" "0"

Table 2.4. Result of logical operations.

The diagrams in this section use the notation:

☐ intermediate result

(*n*) sequence

Example (right associativity):

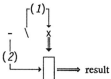

or, using parentheses:
  (- (\ x))

Example (left associativity):

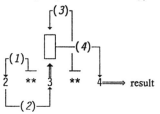

or, using parentheses:

```
( (2 ** 3) ** 4)
```

2.5.6 Operator Precedence

Statements are generally processed from left to right. This priority can be affected:

- by the explicit use of parentheses, which divide the clause into one or more sub-clauses contained within parentheses – the innermost sub-clause is evaluated first, then the next innermost, and so on.
- by the inherent processing sequence (priority) of operators (see Table 2.5).
- by the inherent associativity of operators.

Within a priority level, the operators have the same priority, and are evaluated from left to right.

Examples:

```
1 - 6 * -2 / 3
```

yields 5.

```
6 * -2 -> -12 (the "-" in -2 is a prefix operator)
-12 / 3 -> -4
1 - -4 -> 5 (the "-" in -4 is an implicit prefix operator)
```

```
(1 + 5) * 2 / 3
```

yields 4.

```
1 + 5 -> 6
6 * 2 -> 12
12 / 4 -> 3
```

Priority Associativity	Operator	Comment
1 right	+ − ^ \	prefix operator
2 left	**	exponential (power) operator
3 left	* / % //	multiplication, division
4 left	+ −	addition, subtraction
5 left	¦¦	concatenation (also implicit)
6 left	= == > < >< <> >> << >= <= >>= <<=	comparison
7 left	&	And
8 left	¦ &&	Or, Exclusive Or

Table 2.5. Operator precedence and associativity.

2.6 INVOCATION OF A REXX EXEC

A REXX exec can be invoked in the following ways:

- by entering the exec name and any arguments in the OS/2 window or full-screen command line (such REXX execs must have .CMD as their extension, and a comment in the first line to distinguish them from normal batch procedures – the SYS1041 error will be issued if this requirement is not satisfied).
- with the START command (see Section 15.3).
- from the REXXSTART function (see Section 16.4).
- with the PMREXX command (see Section 12.2).

2.6.1 Direct Invocation of a REXX Exec

The direct invocation of a REXX exec is done in two phases:

- tokenize the source (and store the *tokenized image* in an extended attribute associated with the source);
- run this tokenized image.

The tokenized image is an intermediate code that can be processed more efficiently than the original source.

Invocation syntax:

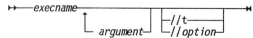

execname
> The name of the REXX exec (together with path information) to be executed. REXX execs have .CMD as extension.

argument
> An argument to be passed to the exec.

//t
> Tokenize the REXX exec without executing it.

//option
> Options prefixed with // are reserved.

Example:
```
A:\REXXLIB\BETA GAMMA DELTA
```
The exec BETA.CMD contained in the REXXLIB directory on drive A is to be invoked. The argument string "GAMMA DELTA" is to be passed to the exec.

3

REXX Program Elements

3.1 INTRODUCTION

The REXX programming language has instructions for:

- structured programming constructions:
  ```
  DO
  ITERATE
  LEAVE
  SELECT
  ```
- sequence control:
  ```
  IF - THEN - ELSE
  ```
- subroutine control and invocation:
  ```
  CALL
  EXIT
  PROCEDURE
  RETURN
  ```
- assignment:
  ```
  =
  ```
- error processing:
  ```
  SIGNAL
  ```
- queue (stack) processing:
  ```
  PULL
  PUSH
  QUEUE
  ```
- parsing:
  ```
  PARSE
  ```
- debugging:
  ```
  TRACE
  ```

- miscellaneous instructions:
  ADDRESS
  ARG
  DROP
  INTERPRET
  NOP
  NUMERIC
  SAY.

REXX also has a direct interface to user-specified command processors (the subcommand environment), which handle all statements not recognized as REXX instructions. The standard operating system command processor (CMD.EXE) is the default subcommand environment.

These basic program elements are augmented by a comprehensive library of functions that can be used in instructions.

This chapter describes the use (semantics) of the instructions; the detailed syntax is described in Chapter 9.

3.2 ROUTINES

A series of REXX statements can be grouped together (called a **routine**) and assigned a name. A routine has one of the forms:

- subroutine
- procedure
- function

A self-contained, executable routine is most commonly called an **exec** (other names are: program, macro, script, shell, etc.). REXX execs must have a comment as their first statement to distinguish them from conventional batch procedures. This restriction is not necessary for execs that are explicitly invoked with the REXX interpreter – see Chapter 16.

There are three kinds of functions:

- built-in functions
- internal functions
- external functions

Built-in functions are the standard functions belonging to the REXX repertoire; they are described in Chapters 10 and 11. **Internal functions** are contained in the current REXX exec. **External functions** are defined external to the current REXX exec, and may be written either in REXX or as **programmed external functions** in a conventional programming language (e.g., C). Chapter 16 contains the specifications for programmed external functions.

Each explicitly invoked routine receives the standard environment (ADDRESS, NUMERIC, SIGNAL and TRACE, and elapsed time) settings on entry. The original settings are restored on return to the point of invocation. However, the queue is common to all routines in the current environment.

Arguments can be passed to routines using the following methods:

- explicit
- implicit
- queue.

The passed arguments are received as *parameters*. *Explicit arguments* are passed at the point of invocation. *Implicit parameters* are those parameters referred to by name in the routine. Procedures must declare such parameters with the EXPOSE clause in the PROCEDURE instruction. Implicit parameters should be avoided if possible, as they increase the danger of modifications to the program affecting the processing.

Section 3.2.6 describes the use of arguments. Figures 3.1 through 3.3 illustrate subroutines, procedures and functions. Brackets ([ ]) indicate optional entries in these figures.

3.2.1 Subroutine
A subroutine can be invoked:

- with the CALL instruction
- as a function
- by being dropped through to

```
name:
    statements

RETURN;
```

Figure 3.1. Subroutine.

Example:
```
CALL alpha beta gamma;
  ...
EXIT;
alpha:
  PARSE ARG parm1 parm2;
  SAY "subroutine 'alpha' called with:" parm1 parm2 "arguments";
RETURN;
```

The subroutine alpha is called with one argument that contains two subarguments: beta and gamma. The subroutine displays the contents of these two parameters.

3.2.2 Procedure

A procedure is a routine identified with the PROCEDURE instruction, and is invoked in the same way as a subroutine. A procedure differs from a subroutine in that:

- Global variables used in a procedure must be explicitly declared with the EXPOSE clause in the PROCEDURE instruction – this is the concept of *information hiding*.
- A procedure can only be invoked with the CALL instruction or as a function.

```
name: PROCEDURE [EXPOSE parameters]
    statements

    RETURN;
```

Figure 3.2. Procedure.

Example:
```
CALL alpha;
    ...
EXIT;
alpha: PROCEDURE EXPOSE beta gamma;
    SAY "subroutine 'alpha' called with:" beta gamma "arguments";
    RETURN;
```
The procedure alpha is called with two global parameters (variables): beta and gamma. The procedure displays the contents of these two parameters.

3.2.3 Function

A function may be either a subroutine or a procedure. A function is invoked with the function name (e.g., function()) or with the CALL instruction (e.g., CALL function).

Functions must always return a value in the RETURN instruction, even if this is the null value. This returned value replaces the explicit function invocation (and may be used in an expression), or is set into the RESULT special variable if invoked with the CALL instruction. Functions may be invoked recursively; see Example 2.

```
name: [PROCEDURE]
    statements

    RETURN expression;
```

Figure 3.3. Function.

Example 1:

```
x = alpha(beta,gamma);
...
EXIT;
alpha:
  PARSE ARG parm1,parm2;
  SAY "function 'alpha' called with:" parm1 parm2 "arguments";
RETURN "";
```

The function alpha is called with two arguments (variables): beta and gamma. The function displays the contents of these two parameters and returns the null value to the point of invocation.

Example 2 (recursive function):

```
PARSE ARG x;
SAY "fact" x fact(x);
EXIT;
fact:
PARSE ARG n;
IF n < 1 THEN RETURN 1;
RETURN n * fact(n-1);
```

The function fact is called recursively to calculate the factorial of the number passed as argument.

3.2.4 Search Order

The normal search order for routines is:

- internal routine
- built-in function
- external routine

This search order can be influenced in two ways:

- A routine name written within quotes is assumed to be either a built-in function or an external routine.
- Macrospace external routines (see Chapter 16) may be placed either before or after other external routines.

3.2.5 Invocation

Functions can be invoked in two ways:

- directly using the function name
- indirectly using the CALL instruction with the function name as routine name.

A function call is not a REXX instruction, and so must be contained in an instruction. For example, in the assignment (=) instruction (the CALL instruction should be used if no result is returned).

Example:
```
x = alpha();
```
The function name must be immediately followed by parentheses, without any intervening blanks. Arguments to be passed to the function are included within these parentheses; the individual arguments are separated by a comma. A maximum of 20 arguments can be passed to a function. The parentheses must always be written, even when no arguments are passed to the function.

Nonfunction procedures and subroutines are invoked with the CALL instruction.

Example:
```
CALL time;
```
invokes the routine with the name time

whereas
```
CALL 'TIME';
```
invokes the external time routine.

The first method, with a nonliteral name, invokes an internal routine, if present, or else the external routine. A routine invoked with a literal name is always an external routine. In this way user versions of standard functions can be tested.

3.2.6 Arguments
Routines may receive parameters in two ways:

- explicit arguments at the point of invocation (arguments for a function invocation are set within the parentheses)
- arguments contained in variables (such variables for a procedure or procedural function must be defined with the EXPOSE keyword).

Either a single argument or multiple arguments, separated by commas, may be passed. The individual arguments may have subarguments.

Examples:
Passing a single argument consisting of two subarguments to a subroutine or procedure:
```
CALL alpha "beta" gamma;
```

Passing two arguments to a subroutine or procedure:
```
CALL alpha "beta", gamma;
```

Passing two arguments to a function:

```
x = alpha("beta", gamma);
```

The parameters are retrieved in the invoked routine using the ARG function, or the ARG or PARSE ARG instruction:

- The function ARG() returns the number of parameters.
- The function ARG(n) returns the nth parameter.

The ARG function has the advantage in that it returns explicitly the number of parameters. The usual parsing operations can be used to obtain the subparameters.

Example 1:

```
CALL alpha "beta" gamma;
...
alpha:
  n_parm = ARG();
  parm1 = ARG(1);
    ...
RETURN;
```

yields the results:

```
n_parm        1
parm1         'beta' gamma
```

Example 2:

```
CALL alpha "beta", gamma;
...
alpha:
  n_parm = ARG();
  parm1 = ARG(1);
  parm2 = ARG(2);
    ...
RETURN;
```

yields the results:

```
n_parm        2
parm1         'beta'
parm2         gamma
```

Example 3 (using the PARSE ARG instruction):
```
CALL alpha "beta", gamma;
...
alpha:
  PARSE ARG parm1, parm2;
  ...
RETURN;
```
yields the results:
```
parm1        'beta'
parm2        gamma
```

3.2.7 Return

Routines use the RETURN instruction to return to the statement immediately following the point of invocation. If a routine is not invoked with the CALL instruction, or implicit call in case of a function, the RETURN instruction is processed as an EXIT instruction, and the REXX exec is terminated.

Functions must return a value in the RETURN instruction, even if no value is required by the invoking statement. This returned value is used in place of the function invocation in the invoking statement.

The value of the expression specified in the RETURN instruction is set into the RESULT special variable. The RESULT variable is noninitialized if no expression is specified.

Examples:
```
x = alpha();
SAY x;
...
alpha:
RETURN 4;
```
and
```
CALL alpha;
SAY RESULT;
...
alpha:
RETURN 4;
```
both display 4.

3.3 DO-GROUP

The DO instruction introduces one or more statements terminated by the END instruction. These statements are known as a *Do-group*. The DO instruction has several forms:

- simple Do
- repetitive Do

- endless Do
- controlled repetitive Do

A Do-group can contain other Do-groups, forming what is called a *nested Do-group*. Nested Do-groups constitute a *hierarchy* of Do-groups; the DO and END statements of a Do-group are at a *hierarchy level*, as illustrated in Figure 3.4.

The forms of a Do-group – other than the simple Do (repetitive Do, endless Do, and controlled repetitive Do) – constitute a *Do-loop*.

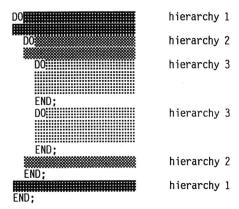

Figure 3.4. Do hierarchy example.

Two conditions control whether the Do-loop is performed:

- An *iteration condition* is specified. The iteration condition has a *control variable*, which is assigned an *initial value*, and is incremented on each pass through the loop. An *end value* (limit) must be specified for the control variable. The *increment* to be added to the control variable for each pass through the loop is optional – the default value is 1. The initial value, end value, and increment can be negative. Any changes made within the Do-loop to the end value or increment have no affect on the loop control.
- A *conditional expression* determines whether the loop is terminated. The conditional expression can be influenced from within the Do-loop.

These two conditions may be specified alone or in combination.

3.3.1 Simple Do

A simple Do is a group of statements that belong together and can be used instead of a single statement; such as in the WHEN clause of a SELECT instruction.

Example:
```
DO;
  alpha = 1;
  SAY alpha "beta";
END;
```

3.3.2 Repetitive Do
A repetitive Do is a group of statements performed several times.

Example:
```
DO 3;
  alpha = 1;
  SAY alpha "beta";
END;
```
performs the two statements between the DO and END three times.

3.3.3 Endless Do
The endless Do is a special form of the repetitive Do; the FOREVER operand is used instead of a number. Some means must be provided to leave the Do-group; otherwise an unending loop will result.

Example:
```
DO FOREVER;
  PULL num;
  IF num = 0 THEN LEAVE;
  SAY num;
END;
```
performs the statements between the DO and END until a 0 is input.

3.3.4 Controlled Repetitive Do
A controlled repetitive Do uses a variable called the *control variable*, which is assigned an initial value(= keyword), an end value (TO keyword), and an increment value (BY keyword). The control variable is incremented by this increment value each time the Do-group is performed. The Do-group is terminated when the control value is greater than the end value for a positive increment, or less than the end value for a negative increment. Alternatively, the BY keyword may be replaced by the FOR keyword, which specifies the number of times the Do-group is to be performed. The control variable can be specified in the corresponding END instruction. This technique can help avoid having unbalanced DO-END instructions and assist in the writing of robust programs.

Example:
```
DO i = 1 TO 4 BY 2;
  SAY i;
END i;
```
This code displays 1 and 3.

Note: The END instruction contains the control variable associated with it (in this case, i); this is not strictly necessary, but it clarifies the structure within nested Do-groups.

3.3.5 Iteration Condition

The iteration condition can also be augmented with a conditional expression, which specifies under what conditions the iteration is to be performed. There are two forms of conditional expression:

- Do-group is performed while the condition is satisfied; the test is made at the start of the Do-group (WHILE keyword).
- Do-group is performed until the condition is satisfied; the test is made at the end of the Do-group (UNTIL keyword). This means that a Do-group controlled by UNTIL is always performed at least once.

Example:
```
j = 0;
DO i = 1 TO 10 WHILE j < 21;
  j = i * 7;
  SAY i j;
END;
```
performs three cycles. *Note*: The variable j should be initialized before the loop, otherwise the initial condition (j < 21) may fail.

In contrast,
```
j = 0;
DO i = 1 TO 10 UNTIL j > 21;
  j = i * 7;
  SAY i j;
END;
```
performs four cycles. Both of these examples are illustrated in Figures 3.5 and 3.6.

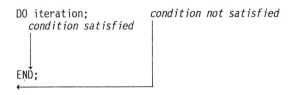

Figure 3.5. WHILE processing.

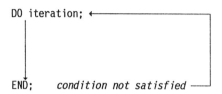

Figure 3.6. UNTIL processing.

3.3.6 Modification of Processing Within a Do-Loop
Processing within Do loops can be modified in the following ways:

- The current cycle is terminated (ITERATE instruction); i.e., an implicit branch is made to the END instruction.
- The current Do-group is terminated (LEAVE instruction); i.e., an implicit branch is made to the statement following the END instruction.
- The program is terminated (EXIT instruction).
- The routine is terminated (RETURN instruction).
- The current Do-group is exited by passing control to some routine outside the Do-group (CALL or SIGNAL instruction) – this is dirty programming and is not recommended, as it results in an unstructured program.

3.3.6.1 ITERATE – Terminate Cycle of a Do-loop. The ITERATE instruction terminates the current cycle in the Do-loop having the same hierarchy; all statements following the ITERATE instruction up to the next END instruction at the same hierarchy are bypassed. The control variable is incremented, and the iteration condition tested as usual. This process is illustrated in Figure 3.7.

Example:
```
DO i = 1 TO 4;
  IF i = 3 THEN ITERATE;
  SAY i;
END;
```
displays 1, 2 and 4.

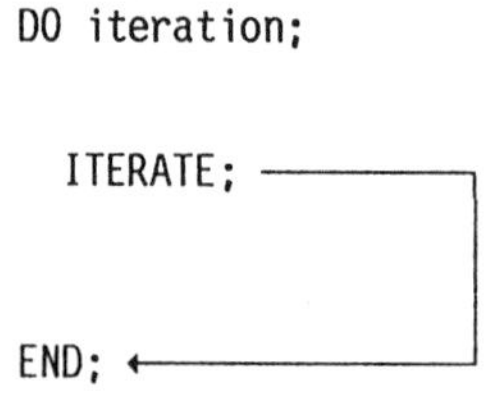

```
DO iteration;

    ITERATE; ────────┐
                      │
                      │
    END; ◄────────────┘
```

Figure 3.7. ITERATE processing.

3.3.6.2 LEAVE – Terminate a Do-loop. The LEAVE instruction, illustrated in Fig 3.8, terminates the Do-loop; processing continues at the statement following the next END instruction at the same hierarchy.

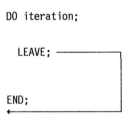

```
DO iteration;

    LEAVE;

END;
```

Figure 3.8. LEAVE processing.

Example:
```
    DO i = 1 TO 4;
       IF i = 3 THEN LEAVE;
       SAY i;
    END;
```
displays 1 and 2.

3.3.6.3 Modification of the Conditional Expression from Within the Do-Loop. The conditional expression controlling a Do-loop can be changed from within the Do-loop.

Example:
```
    j = 5;
    DO i = 1 TO j WHILE j = 5;
       SAY i j;
       IF i = 2 THEN j = 3;
    END;
```
This example performs two cycles.

3.4 SELECT – SELECT ONE CONDITION FROM A SERIES OF CONDITIONS

The SELECT instruction is used to perform one (and only one) statement from a series of conditions defined with the WHEN keyword. The THEN statement applying to the first satisfied WHEN condition is executed.

A Do-group can be used if more than one statement is to be performed in the THEN-clause. Processing always continues after the END instruction, even if a subsequent condition would have been satisfied.

The statements introduced by the OTHERWISE keyword are performed if none of the conditions are satisfied.

A SELECT instruction must have at least one WHEN-THEN clause. An error results if no OTHERWISE clause is present for the case in which none of the WHEN conditions has been satisfied. The NOP instruction can be used for the WHEN-THEN clause if no processing is to be performed; the OTHERWISE clause does not require any statements. Figure 3.9 illustrates SELECT processing.

```
SELECT
   WHEN condition;
     THEN statement;
       ...
     WHEN condition;◄─────── first condition satisfied
       THEN statement;──┐
     WHEN condition;     │
       ...               │
     WHEN condition;     │
       THEN statement;   │
     OTHERWISE;◄──────── ├── no condition satisfied
       statement;        │
       statement;        │
         ...             │
       statement;        │
   END;                  │
 ◄─────────────────────┘
```

Figure 3.9. SELECT processing.

Example 1:
```
    a = 2;
    SELECT
      WHEN a < 2;
        THEN SAY "a lt 2";
      WHEN a > 1;
        THEN SAY "a gt 1";
      OTHERWISE
        SAY "a not gt 1";
    END;
```
This code displays the message "a gt 1".

Example 2:
```
a = 2;
SELECT
  WHEN a < 2;
    THEN SAY "a lt 2";
  WHEN a > 1;
    THEN DO;
      SAY "a gt 1";
    END;
  OTHERWISE;
    SAY "a not gt 1";
END;
```
This code uses a Do-group to display the message "a gt 1".

3.5 CALL – INVOKE ROUTINE

The CALL instruction invokes a routine, and is illustrated in Figure 3.10. The invoked routine returns to the statement following the CALL instruction with the RETURN instruction. The calling instruction can pass arguments to the called routine; these parameters are retrieved with the ARG function or the ARG (or PARSE ARG) instruction. The CALL instruction may be used to invoke a function whose return value is not required. The RESULT special variable contains the return value for functions invoked with the CALL instruction.

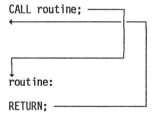

Figure 3.10. CALL processing.

Example:
```
CALL alpha;
SAY "beta";
...
alpha:
SAY "gamma";
RETURN;
```
This code displays beta and gamma, in that sequence.

3.6 SIGNAL – CONTROL PROCESSING FLOW

The SIGNAL instruction can be used in each of the following three ways:

- enable a trap to be taken should the specified condition arise (ON parameter)
- disable a trap (OFF parameter)
- pass control to a specified label

The statement number of the statement that caused the SIGNAL to be invoked (not the statement number where the SIGNAL instruction was enabled) is set into the SIGL special variable.

Tip: Reserve the CALL instruction for invoking routines, unless the RETURN instruction is used to return control to the point of invocation.

Example:
```
SIGNAL ON NOVALUE;
  ...
NOVALUE:
SAY "novalue exit taken at statement" SIGL;
EXIT
```
This displays the text 'novalue' exit taken at statement nnnn if a noninitialized variable has been used (nnnn is replaced by the number of the statement in error).

3.7 ASSIGNMENT (=)

Unfortunately, the REXX language does not entirely conform to the good software engineering principles of having a unique meaning for all operators. In particular, the = operator is used in several ways:

- assignment
- assignment of initial value for the control variable in a Do-group
- comparison for equality (the == operator tests for strict equality)

This potential conflict is resolved by the following rule.

Rule
The sequence:
- symbol
- =

as the first two items in a statement (ignoring any labels) is interpreted as being an assignment of the expression following this = operator to the symbol preceding the = operator.

Example 1:

```
alpha = (a = "b") + 1;
```

→ equality (comparison) operator
→ assignment operator

Example 2:

```
c = b = a;
```

This example is related to Example 1, and shows one of the few REXX statements that does not behave as expected. This statement does not assign the contents of a to ɒ and c, rather it assigns either 1 or 0 to c, depending on whether a equals b, or not, respectively; in all cases b remains unchanged.

3.8 QUEUE (STACK) PROCESSING

A useful feature of the REXX language is *queue processing*. The queue is also called the **stack**. The queue can be used for the following purposes:

- terminal input buffer
- general data storage (intraprogram communication)
- passing data between programs (interprogram communication)

There are three instructions used for explicit operations on the queue:

- PARSE PULL or PULL (obtain entry from the head of the queue)
- PUSH (put entry at the head of the queue)
- QUEUE (put entry at the tail of the queue)

PUSH and QUEUE processing are also called LIFO (last-in, first-out) and FIFO (first-in, first-out) processing, respectively. However, these terms lead to confusion when the operations are used in combination in the same queue. It is better to visualize where each entry is to be stored. Queue processing is illustrated in Figure 3.11.

Although more than one (named) queue can concurrently exist, only a single queue is active at any one time. The RXQUEUE service function (see Chapter 12) is used for logical queue manipulation (create named queue, set current queue, and so forth). Named queues provide only limited data security, as any application that knows the queue name can access it. In particular, applications are responsible for queue synchronization – for example, by using semaphores. *Personal REXX* (see Chapter 20) contains a function package that supplies semaphore support.

Note: The REXX queue is distinct from the OS/2 queue.

Example (illustrated in Figure 3.12):

```
QUEUE "alpha";
PUSH "beta";
QUEUE "gamma";
n_elements = QUEUED();
DO i = 1 TO n_elements;
  PARSE PULL x;
  SAY x;
END;
```

This code displays in the order given: beta; alpha; gamma.

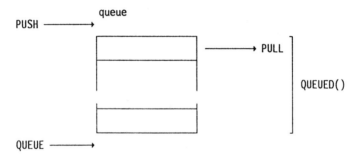

Figure 3.11. Queue processing.

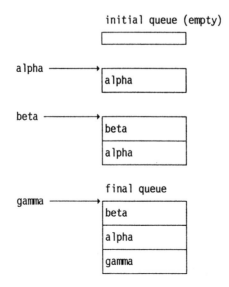

Figure 3.12. Queue processing from the previous example.

3.8.1 Queue as Terminal Input Buffer

The queue is the primary buffer for terminal input. This has three consequences:

- Data for programs or commands awaiting terminal input can be stored in the queue.
- Any data remaining in the queue after the completion of the program will be used as terminal input; i.e., commands for the command processor.
- Any request for queue data from an empty queue will await (nonprompted) terminal input.

Tip: Clear the queue before the program terminates, unless the remaining entries in the queue are to be used as commands for the command processor. The RXQUEUE filter can be used to clear the queue.

3.8.2 Queue for General Data Storage

The queue can be used for the storage of data items; for example, to pass data to a routine.

Tip: Use the queue for data that are to be processed sequentially. Compound symbols are more suitable for data that are to be accessed in a random manner.

3.8.3 Queue for Passing Data Between Programs

The queue can be used to pass data items between programs running in the same host environment. This facility is related to the use of the queue to pass commands to the command processor described in Section 3.8.1.

3.9 DATA SHARING

REXX has three direct methods of sharing data:

- the shared variable pool
- queues
- explicit argument passing

REXX also has three indirect methods of sharing data:

- The VALUE function can use the selector operand to access data from a non-REXX source (OS/2 environment variables).
- The SysIni function provides access to the profile variables (the programmer can create and use application-specific profiles).
- Files.

Each exec has its own shared variable pool that contains named variables. These items can be either simple or compound variables. Compound variables are similar to arrays in other programming languages, but may also be used as associative storage. All routines within an exec, other than procedures, share the same variable pool. Each procedure must explicitly name (expose) those variables that it is to share. Invoked routines return (optionally) their result in the RESULT special variable in the shared variable pool of the invoking routine.

The other two methods of passing data (queues and explicit arguments) use copies of the variables.

3.10 SPECIAL VARIABLES

REXX has three reserved words for use as control variables:

- RC   the return code set by commands
- RESULT   the value of the expression set in the RETURN instruction
- SIGL   the number of the source line that caused the current exception to be raised.

3.11 DEBUGGING

The REXX language offers many facilities for debugging:

- trace statements
- trace intermediate results
- trace final results
- trace statements causing an error return
- trace labels
- disable the execution of host commands
- pause after the execution of selected types of statement (equivalent to single-step).

The required level of debugging can be specified in the REXX exec, or set interactively after interrupting the execution. Chapter 7 describes debugging in detail.

4

Parsing

4.1 INTRODUCTION

Parsing, list analysis, is one of the most powerful REXX facilities. There are two forms of parsing:

- lists of words
- strings of characters

Words, in the REXX sense, are strings of characters delimited by one or more blanks. Strings of characters can be parsed in the following ways:

- at a particular position (absolute or relative)
- at a particular delimiter
- at a word boundary (blank)

The parsing pattern is known as the **template**. The parsed data are assigned to variables or to **placeholders**; the placeholder, represented by a period, takes the place of a variable. The same variable may appear more than once in the list of variables.

4.2 PROCESSING OF WORDS

REXX has several functions concerned with the processing of words:

SUBWORD	Extract the specified number of words from a list of words
WORD	Extract the specified word (number) from a list of words
WORDINDEX	Return the character position of the specified word (number) from a list of words
WORDLENGTH	Return the length of the specified word (number) from a list of words
WORDPOS	Return the word number of the specified word in a list of words
WORDS	Return the number of words in a list of words

These functions are described in Chapter 10.

4.3 PARSING OF CHARACTER STRINGS

Character strings to be parsed have several sources:

- arguments passed to a REXX exec
- data obtained from the input device (terminal)
- data from the queue
- data contained in a variable
- various control data (e.g., current REXX version)

REXX has three instructions concerned with parsing:

ARG   Process the argument (string) passed to the REXX exec or internal routine

PARSE   Process the specified string

PULL   Process the next entry from the queue (or standard input device)

The ARG and PULL instructions are subsets of the PARSE instruction. The parsing instructions may specify the UPPER keyword, which returns the parsed results in upper-case

4.3.1 Parsing at a Particular Position

This processing is equivalent to extracting a substring from the specified data source, and is shown in Figure 4.1.

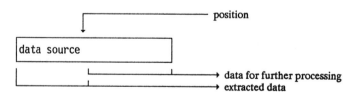

Figure 4.1. Parsing using position as parameter.

Example:
```
a = 'alpha, beta  gamma';
PARSE VAR a b 4 c;
```
This example splits the content of variable a at position 4; alp is set into the variable b and the remainder of the input (ha, beta gamma) is set into variable c.

4.3.2 Parsing at a Particular Delimiter

The source data are scanned, starting at the left, for the specified delimiter. The data before this delimiter are set into the specified variable, and the data after the delimiter are further processed. The delimiter is not restricted to being a single character. The delimiter may be either a literal or a character expression (specified within parentheses). Figure 4.2 illustrates this processing.

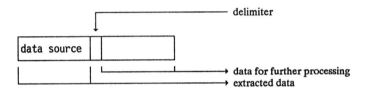

Figure 4.2. Parsing using delimiter as parameter.

Example:
```
a = "alpha, beta  gamma";
PARSE VAR a b ',' c;
```
and
```
dlm = ",";
a = "alpha, beta  gamma";
PARSE VAR a b (dlm) c;
```
These two code fragments are equivalent, and use ',' as delimiter; alpha is set into the variable b and the remainder of the input (beta gamma) set into variable c.

4.3.3 Parsing at Words

The words in the source data are delimited by one or more blanks. The processing of words and blanks depends on their position in the source data (see Figure 4.3):

- Any blanks preceding the first word are ignored.
- For the last word in the source data only the *first* blank preceding the word is used as delimiter, any blanks following this first blank and any blanks following the last word are assigned to the specified variable.
- Blanks between words (except the last word) are not passed to the output variables.
- If only one word is present, it is processed as a last word; i.e., all leading and trailing blanks are passed to the output variable.

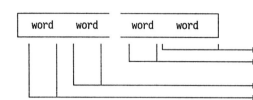

Figure 4.3. Word parsing.

Example 1:
```
a = "alpha, beta  gamma";
PARSE VAR a b c;
```
The word alpha, is set into the variable b and the remainder of the input (beta gamma) set into variable c.

Example 2:
```
a = "  alpha,  beta    gamma  ";
PARSE VAR a b c d;
```
The word alpha, is set into the variable b, the word beta is set into the variable c and the last word ' gamma ' set into variable d. *Note*: beta and gamma are separated by three blanks; the first blank serves as word delimiter, and the other two blanks are passed with the following word to the specified variable.

4.3.4 Parsing for an Embedded String
The word parsing facility described in Section 4.3.3 cannot be used to parse for embedded character strings. The presence of an embedded character strings can be determined by parsing for the particular character string, and testing whether the extracted string is the same as the original string. If the two strings are identical, the required string is not present.

Example:
```
str = "alphabetagamma";
PARSE VAR str a "beta" .;
IF str <> a THEN SAY "string contains 'beta'";
```
This example parses the specified string STR to determine whether it contains the character string beta.

4.3.5 Parsing at a Relative Position
A variation of positional parsing (Section 4.3.1) is the use of a relative position. The relative position is addressed by specifying the plus or minus sign (+ or -) followed by the numeric displacement from the last parsing operand that was located.

This option yields meaningful results only when it is used after either positional parsing (Section 4.3.1) or parsing with a delimiter (Section 4.3.2). When used after a delimiter, the parsing delimiter is assigned to the specified variable – this is illustrated in the following example.

Example:
```
a = "  alpha,  beta    gamma  ";
PARSE VAR a b ',' c +4 d;
```
The string alpha is assigned to b (',' is the parsing delimiter); the next parsing position is at displacement 4 from the comma; the string starting at the comma and having length 4 (the displacement) is assigned to c; the remainder is assigned to d.

4.3.6 Parsing Using Placeholders
If not all parsing results are required as variables, a **placeholder** may be used instead of a variable. A placeholder is indicated by using a period (".") instead of a variable name.

Tip. Use placeholders when the number of parsing elements is not known or could change.

Example:
```
a = "  alpha,  beta    gamma  ";
PARSE VAR a . b .;
```
The word beta is set into the variable b; the first and last words are parsed as usual, but are not assigned to any variables.

4.3.7 Parsing of Arguments
Normally parsing is performed on a single expression. The processing of multiple arguments (parameters) passed to a routine is simplified by allowing the PARSE ARG (or ARG) instruction to parse the individual arguments; the names of the variables to contain the parsed items are separated by commas.

Example:
```
CALL alpha beta, "gamma";
   ...
alpha:
  PARSE ARG b, c;
    ...
  RETURN;
```
assigns beta to b and 'gamma' to c.

4.3.8 Composite Parsing

The parsing described in Sections 4.3.1 through 4.3.3 can be combined to form a composite parsing on an input source string. The form of the symbol following the current output variable determines the current parsing to be performed. For example, if a variable is followed by a number, then parsing by position is to be performed for that variable.

Example:
```
a = "  alpha,  beta    gamma   ";
PARSE VAR a b 5 c ',' d;
```
This example assigns '   al' to b , 'pha' to c and ' beta   gamma ' to d.

4.3.9 Parsing Using Variables

In addition to numeric and literal values, the template can use REXX variables to control the parsing process. Such variables are written within parentheses. These parsing variables are treated as either a string pattern or a position specification (absolute or relative), depending on whether the parenthesized variable is prefixed with = (absolute position), or + or - (relative position).

Example:
```
alpha = "beta gamma delta";
pos1 = 2;
pos2 = 6;
PARSE VAR alpha =(pos1) p1 +(pos2) p2 p3;
SAY 'p1:'p1 'p2:'p2 'p3:'p3;
```
This example displays p1:eta ga p2:mma p3:delta. Figure 4.4 illustrates the processing.

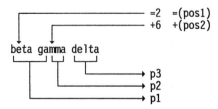

Figure 4.4. Parsing using variables.

4.3.10 Dynamic Parsing

A flexible form of parsing is to use information from the parsed string to alter the subsequent parsing of the string. In particular, data extracted from the input string can be used as the delimiter for the following data (see Example 1). Similarly, the parsed result can be recursively used as subsequent input (see Example 2).

Example 1:

```
alpha = "%abc % ghi";
PARSE VAR alpha dlm 2 b (dlm) c;
SAY b c; /* abc    ghi */
```

The first character of the input string (alpha) is the delimiter to be used for subsequent parsing; i.e., the input string is to be split at the second character. This delimiter character is parsed into the variable dlm, which is then used as delimiter for the next operands.

Example 2:

```
beta = "a: c: f:"
DO i = 1 TO 99999 /* high-value */
  IF beta = '' THEN LEAVE /* end of input */
  PARSE VAR beta p.i ':' beta
END
```

The compound variables p.1,..., are set to contain the parsed values.

5

Arithmetic

5.1 INTRODUCTION

The concepts of a number and of arithmetic operators were introduced in Sections 2.4.1 and 2.5.2, respectively. The processing of arithmetic expressions in REXX follows the general rules one expects. However, as in all programming languages, there are special rules with regard to:

- precision
- representation
- sequence of operations

5.2 PRECISION AND REPRESENTATION

Precision is determined by the value specified with the NUMERIC DIGITS instruction (the default precision is 9 digits). This precision specifies how many digits are to be retained as the result of a numeric operation, and is also directly concerned with how the result is represented in external format (e.g., how the number is displayed with the SAY function).

Tip: Do not set the precision higher than need be, because:

- Increasing the precision increases the storage allocated, even when the higher precision is not used.
- Increasing the precision increases the computation time.

Rule
If the number of digits before the decimal place is greater than the value specified for DIGITS, then the number is represented in exponential format. If the number of digits after the decimal place is greater than twice the value specified for DIGITS, then the number is represented in exponential format.

This rule is best illustrated with an example. If DIGITS has been set to 2 (e.g., x = NUMERIC DIGITS 2), then the following results of multiplying 12.5 by 3 (to various numbers of decimal places) are displayed:

30 * 12.5	3.8E2
3 * 12.5	38
0.3 * 12.5	3.8
0.03 * 12.5	.38
0.003 * 12.5	.038
0.0003 * 12.5	.0038
0.00003 * 12.5	3.8E-4

Exponential format is a mathematical way of representing both very large and very small numbers. The "E" (or "e") represents in REXX the power ten, and the number following is the exponent.

Example:
E2 represents 10^2 = 100
E-2 represents 10^{-2} = 1/100 = 0.01

The mantissa, the number preceding the "E", is multiplied by this power of ten to give the end result.

Example:
3.8E2   represents $3.8 \cdot 10^2$ = $3.8 \cdot 100$ = 380
3.8E-2   represents $3.8 \cdot 10^{-2}$ = $3.8 \cdot 0.01$ = 0.038

5.3 SEQUENCE OF OPERATIONS

General mathematics has the rule that multiplicative operations (which include division) are performed before additive operations (which include subtraction). REXX also obeys this rule.

Example:
        x = 10 + 4*2; /* assign 18 to x */

As in general mathematics, the order in which operations are performed can be specified by using parentheses; the expression in parentheses is calculated first.

Example:
        x = (10 + 4)*2; /* assign 28 to x */

If the parenthesized expression itself contains parentheses, then the innermost parentheses are resolved first.

Example:

    x = (2+(10 + 4)*2);

is calculated in the following manner:

$10 + 4 = 14$; $14 \cdot 2 = 28$; $2 + 28 = 30$

Table 2.5 in Chapter 2 specifies the order of precedence of the arithmetic operators.

6

Input/Output

6.1 INTRODUCTION

The REXX I/O facilities can be classified into five groups:

- simple terminal operations (PULL and SAY instructions)
- operations at the character (byte) level (CHARIN, CHAROUT and CHARS functions)
- operations at the line (record) level (LINEIN, LINEOUT and LINES functions)
- operations at the file level (STREAM function)
- external data queue processing

REXX has two file (stream) types:

- persistent
- transient

Persistent files are stored on an external medium (e.g., a disk). Transient files are terminal data, print output, and so on.

This chapter describes the general I/O facilities. Subsequent chapters contain detailed descriptions of the I/O operations:

- Chapter 9: I/O terminal instructions (PULL, SAY)
- Chapter 11: I/O functions (CHARIN, CHAROUT, CHARS, LINEIN, LINEOUT, LINES, and STREAM functions)

6.2 DATA BUFFERING

The data buffering is related to the level (character, line, or file) at which the I/O operation is performed. Input terminal data can be buffered in the queue. REXX variables contain the data for character and line operations.

6.3 OPENING AND CLOSING THE DATA FILES

REXX files are automatically opened when they are first used. They are also automatically closed when the REXX exec terminates. Files may also be explicitly opened and closed with the STREAM function.

In general, a file should be closed when it is no longer needed. This has two advantages:

• Main-storage used for buffers is freed.
• If the file has been reserved for exclusive use by the processing exec, it is then available for use by other programs.

6.4 TERMINAL OPERATIONS

The PULL and SAY instructions are used for basic data transfer from and to the terminal, respectively – the STDIN: and STDOUT: devices are implicitly used. However, the I/O functions (CHARIN, LINEIN, etc.) can also be directed to the terminal.

Terminal input is taken by default from the queue. This means that a request for terminal input is first satisfied by taking data from the queue; if the current queue is empty, the program awaits input from the terminal.

This use of the queue has two consequences:

• Responses can be prestored with the PUSH or QUEUE instruction. This can be useful to provide information for host environment commands and functions.
• When the REXX exec terminates, any entries remaining in the queue will be interpreted as commands (the RXQUEUE function or filter can be used to remove the queue).

Tip: Always precede a request for terminal input data with a message to the terminal. This avoids the application program seeming to wait for no apparent reason.

6.5 CHARACTER-MODE OPERATIONS

In character-mode the input data stream is read character by character, including any delimiters for end-of-line, end-of-file, and so on.

Either persistent or transient files can be processed. A *current position pointer* is maintained for persistent files. Character-mode and line-mode processing can be combined for persistent files.

The REXX character-mode I/O functions are:

CHARIN	Read series of characters.
CHAROUT	Write series of characters.
CHARS	Return stream information.

6.6 LINE-MODE OPERATIONS

In line-mode the input data stream is read line by line. Any delimiters for end-of-line, end-of-file, and so forth are ignored on input and generated for output.

Either persistent files or transient files can be processed. The same *current position pointer* as for character-mode operations is maintained for persistent files. Character-mode and line-mode processing can be combined for persistent files.

The REXX line-mode I/O functions are:

LINEIN	Read a line.
LINEOUT	Write a line.
LINES	Return line information.

6.7 FILE-LEVEL OPERATIONS

The STREAM function performs file-level operations:

- explicitly open a file
- explicitly close a file
- position within a file
- retrieve (persistent) file information (size, date last changed, etc.)

6.8 FILE NAMES

OS/2 file names may be either an explicit file name or a standard device name. Explicit file names may include path information (e.g., a:\alpha\beta.txt). If no path information is specified, the usual OS/2 access rules apply.

The standard device names are:

COMn:	communications port (n = 1, 2, etc.)
CON:	console terminal (both input and output)
KBD:	keyboard input
LPTn:	printer (n = 1, 2, etc.)
PRN:	current printer
STDERR:	standard error message output
STDIN:	standard input stream
QUEUE:	REXX external data queue

Example:
```
x = LINEIN("QUEUE:");
```
This statement retrieves the next entry from the active queue.

6.9 EXTERNAL DATA QUEUE

The external data queue is external to REXX execs, and can be used to transfer data linewise to REXX execs that have access to it. Although only one queue can be active at any one time, more than one (named) queue can coexist.

The operations to process at queue and element level are:

RXQUEUE	Create, delete, set and query queue (function).
RXQUEUE	Redirect terminal output to a queue (filter).
PULL	Retrieve element from the head of the queue (instruction).
PUSH	Place element at the head of the queue (instruction).
QUEUE	Place element at the tail of the queue (instruction).

6.10 ERROR HANDLING

The NOTREADY condition of the CALL ON and SIGNAL ON instructions can be used to trap input/output errors. The REXX exec is not terminated if an error occurs when the NOTREADY condition has not been trapped.

7

Debugging

7.1 INTRODUCTION

Debugging described in this chapter deals with the mechanics involved in the tools that REXX makes available. The techniques used for debugging are largely an art, which can only be learned to a limited degree – a good debugger (the person who debugs) does it largely by intuition. For those people who do not fall into this category, the best help is information. This chapter describes the REXX facilities available to supply this information.

REXX supports two forms of debugging:
- signal processing to be performed if a specified exception condition occurs
- trace statement execution

REXX offers two means of obtaining information:
- statically
- dynamically (interactively)

Static means build the debugging statements into the REXX exec. *Dynamic* or *interactive* means interrupt the REXX exec while it is executing, and invoke the appropriate debugging statements from the terminal. All REXX statements are available in interactive debugging mode (for example, the SAY instruction can be used to display the contents of a variable). REXX supplies two utility commands that can be used to assist in debugging: PMREXX and REXXTRY.

7.2 EXCEPTION CONDITIONS

Exception conditions are:

- error   A nonzero return code has been returned from a host command.
- failure   A negative return code has been returned from a host command
- halt   The interpretation of the REXX exec is halted (for example, with the HI command).
- novalue   A symbol has been used that has not been initialized (i.e., has not received data).
- notready   An error has occurred during input/output operations.
- syntax   An invalid REXX statement has been invoked (this may mean invalid syntax, or an operand contains invalid data, such as nonnumeric data in an arithmetic expression).

These exception conditions are trapped by the SIGNAL instruction. If exception conditions are not trapped, then messages are displayed only under the following circumstances:

- a host command returning the failure condition
- syntax error (and processing is terminated)

Tip

To avoid unexpected processing, the NOVALUE exception condition should always be set, even though this may increase the program coding to some extent.

One feature of the REXX language that makes coding easier is that each symbol is initialized by default to have its own name as content (in uppercase). The hidden danger is that when such symbols, rather than explicit literals, are used as parameters, their value may be altered somewhere in the program – possibly when modifications are made at some later point in time.

7.3 TRACING OPTIONS

One of the following tracing options can be set:

- all
- commands
- error
- failure
- intermediate
- labels
- results

These options specify what tracing is to be performed, and under what circumstances a trace message is to be displayed. Only one tracing option can be active at any one time. However, the setting of the trace option may be altered during the course of running the REXX exec.

REXX also has a prefix operator:

- ?

that may be prefixed before any of the options specified above.

The prefix ? invokes interactive debugging, which means that execution pauses when the set option occurs. For example, TRACE ?ALL stops before each statement is executed, and is equivalent to operating in single-step mode.

    The prefix operator (?) is a binary switch (toggle). Each setting reverses the previous setting.

7.3.1 ALL – Display All Expressions Before Execution
The ALL option is used to display all expressions before they are executed.

7.3.2 COMMANDS – Display All Commands Before Execution
The COMMANDS option is used to display all commands before they are executed.

7.3.3 ERROR – Display All Commands that Return an Error Condition
The ERROR option is used to display all commands that return a nonzero code after being executed.

7.3.4 FAILURE – Display All Commands that Return a Negative Error Condition
The FAILURE option is used to display all commands that return a negative code after being executed. This is the default setting.

7.3.5 INTERMEDIATE – Display All Expressions (with Intermediate Results) Before being Executed
The INTERMEDIATE option is used to display all expressions before being executed. This is the option usually used for general debugging.

7.3.6 LABELS – Display All Labels as they are Reached
The LABELS option is used to display the names of labels as they are reached. This option is useful for tracing the program flow. The displayed labels are automatically nested; that is, each hierarchy is indented.

7.3.7 RESULTS – Display All Expressions (with End Results) Before being Executed
The RESULTS option is used to display all expressions before being executed.

7.4 TRACE OUTPUT

Trace output is prefixed with a three-character code that identifies the content of the following trace line. There are two forms of prefixes:

- those used for trace data
- those used for (intermediate) results

7.4.1 Trace Data Prefixes
Prefixes used for trace data:

-	the program source line
+++	trace message
>>>	result
>.>	value assigned to a placeholder

7.4.2 Trace Intermediate Data Prefixes
The following prefixes are used only when TRACE INTERMEDIATES has been specified:

>C>	Data are the name of a compound variable.
>F>	Data are the result of a function invocation.
>L>	Data are a literal.
>O>	Data are the result of an operation.
>P>	Data are the result of a prefix operation.
>V>	Data are the contents of a variable.

The displayed data are shown in character form within double quotes. The symbol "?" denotes noncharacter data.

7.4.3 Trace Output Example
Sample REXX exec

```
1       /* REXX trace */
2       TRACE I;
3       i = 1;
4       PARSE VALUE DATE('E') WITH day.i '/' .;
5       x = day.1 * -2;
6       SAY x;
7       BETA();
```

The corresponding (annotated) output follows. The number in the left-hand column refers to the statement number in the REXX exec. Annotations are written in italics and immediately follow the trace output to which they refer.

```
      3 *-*   i = 1;
```
source statement 3
```
        >L>     "1"
```
content of numeric literal
```
        >>>     "1"
```
result
```
      4 *-*   Parse Value DATE('E') With day.i '/' .;
```
source statement 4
```
        >L>     "E"
```
content of character literal, parameter for DATE function
```
        >F>     "09/11/92"
```
result of evaluating the DATE function
```
        >>>     "09/11/92"
```
result
```
        >C>     "DAY.1"
```
resolved name of compound variable; "1" has been substituted for "i" in
"day.i"
```
        >>>     "09"
```
first parsed operand from the evaluated DATE('E'), "/" has been used as
delimiter
```
        >.>     "11/92"
```
remainder after parsing to the "/" delimiter, this has been assigned to a
placeholder
```
      5 *-*   x = day.1 * - 2;
```
source statement 5
```
        >V>     "09"
```
content the variable "day.1"
```
        >L>     "2"
```
content of numeric literal
```
        >P>     "-2"
```
result of performing the prefix operator (-) on 2
```
        >O>     "-18"
```
result of the operation of multiplying 12 by -2
```
        >>>     "-18"
```
result
```
      6 *-*   Say x;
```
source statement 6
```
        >V>     "-18"
```
content the variable "x"
```
        >>>     "-18"
```
result

```
-18
```
output from the SAY instruction
```
      7 *-*    BETA();
```
source statement 7
```
      7 +++    BETA();
```
trace message
```
REX0043: Error 43 running XTRACE.CMD, line 7: Routine not found
```
REXX error message REX0043 specifies that the routine (function) BETA() has not been found, i.e., invalid.

7.5 INTERACTIVE DEBUG

Interactive debug mode is invoked in one of two ways:

- with the TRACE ?option instruction (option is one of the trace options; e.g., TRACE ?ALL);
- by interrupting the REXX exec while it is executing; for example, by pressing the Ctrl-C key.

On entry to interactive debug mode, a message similar to the following is displayed:
```
+++ Interactive trace. 'Trace off' to end debug
```

In interactive debug mode one of the following actions can be performed:

- Enter a null line (i.e., press the ENTER key without having entered any input data). This causes the REXX exec to proceed to the next trace point, when it will again pause. For example, the TRACE ?COMMAND will stop at the next command.

   Tip: TRACE ?ALL (TRACE ?A) stops at each statement, single-stepping through the REXX exec.

- Enter a single equals sign ("=") to reexecute the last statement traced. Processing will pause after this statement has been reexecuted, irrespective of the setting of trace option.

- The TRACE OFF instruction terminates interactive tracing.

- The EXIT instruction terminates the REXX exec.

- Any other input data will be interpreted as a REXX statement and will be immediately processed as if it were contained within a Do-End group. This means that the input can be multiple REXX statements, each separated by ";" (semicolon).

7.5.1 Interactive Debugging Example

Sample REXX exec to invoke interactive debug when an error condition arises. Note that the statement numbers at the start of each line are for identification purposes only, and are not present in the actual code.

```
1       /* REXX debug */
2       SIGNAL ON SYNTAX;
        ...

3       EXIT;
        ...
4       SYNTAX:
5       SAY "debug invoked";
6       SAY "condition" CONDITION('C');
7       TRACE ?a;
8       SAY "source line" SIGL " " SOURCELINE(SIGL);
9       SAY "debug end"
10      EXIT;
```

Interpretation:

2   The SIGNAL instruction specifies that the SYNTAX exception condition is to be set.

3   Terminate normal processing.

4   The entry point for the interactive debug routine.

5   Display a message to the user indicating that an exception condition has arisen.

6   Display the name of the condition that has arisen. The CONDITION built-in function with operand 'C' supplies this information.

7   Activate interactive trace. This enables the user to input debugging commands, if required. The text specifying that interactive trace has been invoked is displayed after the next text line is output.

8   Display the line number (contained in the SIGL special variable) and source data (obtained with the built-in SOURCELINE function) in error.

9   Display a message to indicate that debugging has terminated.

10   Terminate error processing.

Typical output arising from a syntax error using the preceding interactive debug processing follows.

```
debug invoked
condition SYNTAX
    9 *-*   Say 'source line' sigl ' ' SOURCELINE(sigl);
source line 3   x = beta();
```

```
   +++    Interactive trace. "Trace Off" to end debug, ENTER to Continue.

   10 *-*  Say 'debug end';
debug end
```

7.6 ADVANCED DEBUGGING TECHNIQUES

REXX offers three advanced debugging techniques:

- the RXTRACE environment variable
- the PMREXX command
- the REXXTRY command.

The first two techniques can also be used to obtain debugging information for execs that cannot be augmented with trace code (e.g., for an exec that is read-only).

7.6.1 RXTRACE Environment Variable

Interactive debugging for a REXX exec can be activated by setting the RXTRACE environment variable to ON (or on), which is equivalent to the TRACE ?R instruction. This enables trace information for an exec to be obtained without having to set debugging code into the exec. The RXTRACE setting is checked only on initiation of the exec.

The RXTRACE environment variable can be set by entering the SET RXTRACE = ON command in OS/2 Full Screen or Window, etc. Any value other than ON (on) deactivates the trace mode, and is equivalent to the TRACE 0 instruction.

The current setting of the environment variables can be displayed by entering the SET command without any operands.

7.6.2 PMREXX Command

The PMREXX command executes the specified exec as a PM (Presentation Manager) application. The exec's trace output is placed in a scrollable window. PMREXX options can be set to activate (or deactivate) interactive tracing. Section 12.2 contains a detailed description of PMREXX.

7.6.3 REXXTRY Command

The REXXTRY command simulates the processing of REXX instructions (try the instructions). This can be useful when an instruction performs complex processing; for example, parsing instructions. Section 12.3 describes the REXXTRY command in more detail.

8

Programming Practices

8.1 INTRODUCTION

Good programming practices are related to the debugging discussed in Chapter 7. A well written program can, to a large extent, preclude the need to debug.

This discussion of good programming practices is of necessity subjective. Such recommendations as the use of structured programming techniques can, but need not, assist in the readability, reliability, and maintainability of a program. However, they cannot guarantee that the program is free from errors. An example from one of my courses serves to show that a structured program is more than just a theoretical nicety. The results of my putting structure into a nonstructured program, without changing the functionality, are shown in Table 8.1.

The aspects of performance and compatibility can also be of importance for a program.

	Original Version	Revised Version
lines of code	299	241
GoTos	87	0
labels	44	0
errors	3	0

Table 8.1. Example of the benefits of a structured program.

The programming practices discussed in this chapter are principally concerned with their use with REXX. A specialized text should be consulted for the more general aspects of good programming.

Although the REXX language allows much flexibility, the programmer is responsible for how this flexibility is used. In many cases it is advantageous not to use all the facilities that are available.

8.2 READABILITY

Readability, as the word says, is the ease with which a program can be read; i.e., a physical characteristic. A program that is not easy to read is not easy to understand. However, the converse does not necessarily apply – a program that is easy to read may be difficult to understand.

Readability can be influenced in a number of ways:

- Format the program in a structured manner. Devise some consistent method to format structured constructions (DO-groups, SELECT-blocks, etc.). For example, indent at least two positions for each hierarchy in a DO-group, and start related THEN and ELSE clauses in the same column. Modularization, splitting the program into distinct (self-contained) routines, is the most common method of logically structuring a program.

- Do not use uppercase exclusively. It is well known that text written in uppercase is more difficult to read than text written in mixed case. I use the convention: instructions, noninternal functions and keywords are written in uppercase, and all other entries written in lowercase. Similarly, double quotes (") are used for normal literals, and single quotes (') are used to delimit parametric operands, unless a quote-delimited operand is to be passed to some environment, or the literal itself contains the delimiting quote; for example, "O'Brien".

- The actual conventions adopted are not so significant. Consistency is more important.

8.2.1 Modularization
Modularization is the splitting of a program into smaller units that are easier to understand, and so make the complete program easier to understand (*"divide and conquer"*). Although modules are uniquely named files, the concept of modularization can also be made within program. Internal modularization is accomplished by coding named routines (sections of code): functions, procedures, and subroutines. Each routine should have a distinct purpose. This method also facilitates the technique of stepwise refinement.

Modularization also enforces information-hiding. The variables used within a module are not accessible outside that module; internal PROCEDURES have similar information-hiding.

8.2.2 Stepwise Refinement

Stepwise refinement is a form of top-down programming. Initially only dummy routines are implemented (the RETURN instruction, with the return value simulating the normal processing). This enables the program logic to be tested without being concerned with the details of the individual routines. The routines can be successively implemented.

8.3 RELIABILITY

A program can be regarded as reliable when it behaves in a controlled fashion under both normal and exception conditions. Certain features that make it easy to write REXX programs pose potential problems, because they conflict with the aims of reliability.

Potential errors:

- A noninitialized symbol has its name (in uppercase) as content. For example, the symbol Alpha has ALPHA as its initial content. Although this simplifies the writing of alphanumeric literals, there is the danger that the content of the symbol is inadvertently altered in the program. This potential problem can be solved as follows:

  1. Write alphanumeric literals explicitly; e.g., "ALPHA"
  2. Set the SIGNAL ON NOVALUE instruction to trap the use of noninitialized symbols.

- A REXX program is interpreted. The syntax is checked only when the statement is executed. This means that latent syntax errors may be present in sections of the code that are not normally executed; for example, error processing routines.

- Input data should be checked for validity if the possibility exists that they may be invalid; for example, numeric data entered from the keyboard. As a rule, error messages should be displayed as near as possible to the source of error.

- Terminate a program with an explicit EXIT instruction.

- Terminate each statement (clause) with a ";" (semicolon). This can avoid unexpected continuations.

- Use control variables on END statements. This can help in the detection of unbalanced blocks.

8.4 MAINTAINABILITY

Maintainability is the ease with which a program can be maintained. Maintenance is not restricted to removing errors, but also includes **expandability** (extension to include new functionality). Observance of readability and reliability is a necessary requirement for a maintainable program.

8.5 COMPATIBILITY

The major significance of compatibility arises when a REXX program is to be used in various environments; for example, in OS/2 and MVS/TSO. Full compatibility is possible only for those applications that do not use components specific for the particular host environment – such components include input/output (other than simple terminal operations using the SAY and PULL instructions). The porting of applications can be simplified by isolating environment-specific features in subroutines. Appendix E contains a table of the compatibilities among the various implementations.

Certain implementations, including OS/2 REXX, demand a commentary as first line in a REXX program. In some cases this comment must also include the word REXX to distinguish REXX execs from other procedures. It is in any case a good practice to begin every REXX exec with a comment that describes its purpose.

8.6 PERFORMANCE

OS/2 REXX execs are interpreted. An interpreted program has advantages such as flexibility, ease of debugging (errors can be corrected on the spot), speed of implementation (compilation, etc., is not required). However, the execution time of a REXX program will of necessity be longer than a that of compiled program. The size of this time-overhead is influenced by optimising measures built into the REXX interpreter (for example, the OS/2 REXX implementation uses preprocessed intermediate code as input, which saves the conversion of the source program to this code), and how the REXX program is written. Frequently-used execs can be rewritten as programmed routines (see Chapter 16).

The best way to influence the speed of execution is not to execute unnecessary statements. For example, use a SELECT instruction rather than a series of IF statements, when not more than one condition can apply.

The macrospace facility (see Chapter 16) can be used to optimize performance by loading execs into internal storage.

9

REXX Instructions

9.1 INTRODUCTION

The REXX instructions constitute the framework with which a REXX program is written.

The REXX instructions can be grouped into:

- REXX keyword instructions
- commands
- comments, which includes a null (empty) instruction

9.2 INSTRUCTION DEFINITIONS

REXX has the instructions:

=	assignment
ADDRESS	set environment
ARG	fetch argument
CALL	invoke routine
DO	define start of block
DROP	free variable
EXIT	terminate exec
IF	conditional execution
INTERPRET	interpret statement
ITERATE	terminate the current cycle in the Do-loop
LEAVE	terminate Do-loop
NOP	no-operation
NUMERIC	define numeric formats
OPTIONS	pass special parameters to the language processor
PARSE	assign data

PROCEDURE	define internal procedure
PULL	fetch data element from the head of the queue
PUSH	set data element at the head of the queue
QUEUE	set data element at the tail of the queue
RETURN	return from routine
SAY	display
SELECT	conditional execution of one statement from a group of statements
SIGNAL	enable (or disable) an exception condition, or cause control to be passed to a routine
TRACE	set debugging options

Note: The syntax diagrams in this chapter show the instructions terminated with a semicolon (;). This delimiting semicolon is optional, unless more than one statement is written in a single line.

9.2.1 = – Assignment
The assignment instruction, represented by the = keyword, assigns an expression to the specified symbol.

Syntax:
▸▸——*symbol=expression;*——◂

symbol
> The name of the target variable.

expression
> The expression which, after evaluation, is assigned to **symbol**.

Example:
```
alpha = beta; /* assign content of beta variable to alpha */
alpha = "beta"; /* assign the string beta to alpha */
alpha = 3*4; /* assign 12 to alpha */
```

9.2.2 ADDRESS – Set Environment
The ADDRESS instruction sets the system component environment to which the non-REXX instructions are to be passed.

An ADDRESS instruction without an expression sets the global environment, which applies, until changed, to all subsequent non-REXX instructions. An ADDRESS clause prefixed to an expression sets the local environment only for that statement. CMD is the initial ADDRESS environment.

The ADDRESS built-in function returns the current environment name.

Syntax:

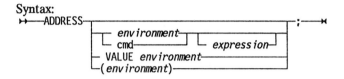

environment

>   The name of the new subcommand environment. The environment setting may
>   be either temporary or permanent (until it is changed), depending on whether
>   an **expression** is specified or not. If the subcommand environment is not
>   unique, it may be prefixed with its associated library name (see Chapter 16 for
>   further information on subcommand environment registration).
>
>   *Note*: The ADDRESS instruction does not check the environment name for
>   validity.

expression

>   The expression that is to be passed to the specified local **environment**.

If no operands are specified, then the global environment is set back to what it was
before the last change was made (see Example 3).

Example 1:

```
ADDRESS 'CMD';
ADDRESS 'CMD' 'TIME';
```

The first instruction sets the global environment for CMD. The second instruction
passes the "TIME" command to the local CMD environment.

Example 2:

```
env = 'CMD';
ADDRESS (env);
```

This example has the same effect as the first instruction in example 1, namely to set
the global environment to CMD.

Note: At least one blank must follow the ADDRESS keyword, otherwise the ADDRESS function would have been invoked.

Example 3:

```
SAY ADDRESS(); /* display current environment */
ADDRESS 'USER'; /* set USER environment */
SAY ADDRESS(); /* display current environment */
ADDRESS; /* set previous environment */
SAY ADDRESS(); /* display current environment */
```

This example displays: CMD, USER, and CMD, respectively.

9.2.3 ARG – Fetch Argument

The ARG instruction parses the argument passed with the CALL instruction or function invocation. The ARG instruction is a subset of the PARSE ARG instruction.

Note: This instruction largely duplicates the ARG function.

Syntax:

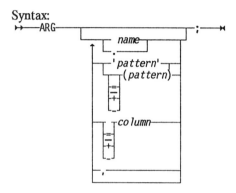

name

> The symbol to be assigned the parsed data.

.

> A placeholder. The data are parsed but no assignment is made.

'pattern'

> The delimiter that is to be used as search argument for the source data; **pattern** is not restricted to being a single character.

(pattern)

> If prefixed, pattern is a column specification.
> =   specifies an absolute position,
> + or -   specifies a relative position.
> Otherwise, **pattern** is an expression that is to be used as a delimiter for the source data.

column

> The position at which the source data is to be split. Position 1 is first in the source data.
> If **column** is prefixed with either a + or - sign, then this **column** is relative to the last location parsed.

,

> A comma specifies that the next argument in the source data is to be processed.

Example:
```
alpha = "beta ** gamma";
CALL delta alpha;

  ...
delta:
  ARG a b;
  ARG a '**' b;
  ARG a '*' b;
  ARG a 3 b;
RETURN;
```

returns the following results:

a	b
"BETA"	"** GAMMA"
"BETA "	" GAMMA"
"BETA "	"* GAMMA"
"BE"	"TA ** GAMMA"

9.2.4 CALL – Invoke Routine

The CALL instruction invokes the specified routine, and can optionally pass one or more arguments. The called routine returns with a RETURN instruction.

Note: The OS/2 CALL command, which invokes a batch procedure, must be invoked as a command; for example: "CALL alpha".

Syntax:

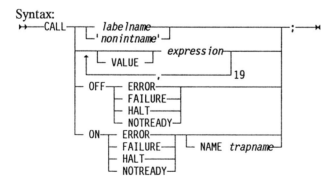

labelname
>   The name of the routine to which control is to be passed.

'nonintname'
>   The name of the external routine or built-in function that is to be invoked.

expression

The argument to be passed to the called routine. The individual arguments are separated by commas. Each argument may contain subparameters, which can be parsed in the usual way.

OFF

The following trap condition is disabled.

ON

The following trap condition is enabled. If the trapped condition is raised, control is passed to the label having the condition name, unless a **trapname** is explicitly specified. For example, if the NOVALUE condition is enabled, control is passed to the label NOVALUE if this condition is raised. A syntax error is signalled if the required label does not exist.

ERROR

The error condition (positive, nonzero return from host command) is disabled or enabled, according to whether OFF or ON has been specified.

FAILURE

The failure condition (negative return from host command) is disabled or enabled, according as to whether OFF or ON has been specified.

HALT

The halt condition is disabled or enabled, according to whether OFF or ON has been specified. The halt condition can be raised in several ways; for example, with the HI command.

NOTREADY

The stream raised the not ready condition.

trapname

The name of the statement to which control is to be passed if the set condition arises. If **trapname** is omitted, the statement having the name of the raised condition receives control.

Example:

```
CALL alpha beta;
SAY RESULT;
 ...
alpha:
gamma = ARG(1); /* fetch argument */
SAY gamma;
 ...
RETURN delta;
```

The routine alpha is invoked with argument beta.

9.2.5 DO – Define Start of Block
The DO instruction defines the start of a block, which is terminated with an END instruction.

Syntax:

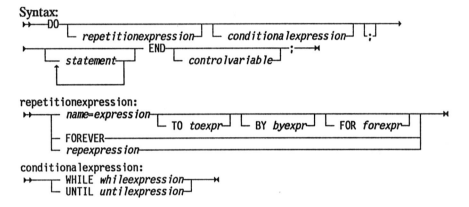

name = expression

> Assignment of the initial value (**expression**) to the control variable (**name**) used for the DO-loop.

toexpr

> Definition of the final value (**toexpr**) of the control variable used for the DO-loop. Default: high-value.

byexpr

> Definition of the increment value (**byexpr**) to be added to the control variable for each cycle through the DO-loop. The increment may be either positive or negative. Default: 1

forexpr

> Definition of the number of cycles (**forexpr**) to be performed in the DO-loop. The **forexpr**, if present, takes priority over any other loop counts specified. Default: high-value.

FOREVER

> This keyword specifies that an endless Do-loop is to be performed. Normally such a DO-loop will be terminated with a LEAVE or EXIT instruction.

repexpression
>   Assignment of the repetitive expression (**repexpression**) to be used for the DO-loop. This expression specifies the number of cycles to be performed.

whileexpression
>   Definition of the expression (**whileexpression**) used as additional condition for the execution of the DO-loop. The DO-loop is performed only when this condition, in conjunction with any other conditions for the DO-loop, is satisfied. The WHILE condition is tested before the DO-loop is performed.

untilexpression
>   Definition of the expression (**untilexpression**) used as additional condition for the execution of the DO-loop. The DO-loop is performed only until this condition, in conjunction with any other conditions for the DO-loop, is satisfied. The UNTIL condition is tested at the end of the DO-loop; this means that the DO-loop is always performed at least once.

Example 1:
```
DO i = 1 TO 10;
 ...
END;
```
performs 10 iterations.

Example 2:
```
J = 3
DO i = 1 TO 10 FOR J;
 ...
END;
```
performs 3 iterations.

Example 3:
```
DO FOREVER;
 ...
END;
```
performs an endless iteration.

9.2.6 DROP – Free Variable

The DROP instruction frees the specified variables. This means that the said variables no longer have any value and revert to their uninitialized state. The NOVALUE condition is signalled if a dropped variable is used without having been assigned a value.

Tip: A DROP instruction can be used to release storage that has been allocated to a variable. The storage allocated to compound variables (arrays) can be extensive.

Syntax:

name

> The name of the variable to be freed.

namevar

> The name of the variable that contains a list of variable names to be freed. Each variable name is separated by one or more blanks.

Example:
```
alpha = "beta gamma";
DROP beta gamma;
DROP (alpha);
```

These two DROP instructions are equivalent.

9.2.7 EXIT – Terminate Exec

The EXIT instruction (logical end) terminates the execution of the current REXX exec, and returns control to the invoking program. A REXX exec may have more than one EXIT. An EXIT is automatically generated at the physical end of the REXX exec; i.e., after the last statement.

Tip: It is good programming practice to explicitly specify the program EXIT. This is especially true before internal routines, which could be inadvertently executed by being dropped through to.

Note: The OS/2 EXIT command, which terminates the invoking session, must be invoked as a command; for example: "EXIT".

Syntax:
```
►►──EXIT──┬──────────────┬──;──►◄
          └─ expression ─┘
```

expression

> Value to be returned to the point of invocation.

Example:
```
EXIT 8;
```

9.2.8 IF – Conditional Execution

The IF instruction specifies the processing to be performed based on the result of the condition tested. The IF instruction has two branches: the THEN-branch is taken when the condition is satisfied; the ELSE-branch, if present, is taken when the condition is not satisfied.

Syntax:

```
►►──IF  expression───┬─── THEN  thenstatement──┬────────────────────────────────┬──;──►◄
                     └─;┘                       └─;┘  └─ ELSE  elsestatement─┘
```

expression

> The condition to be tested. The **expression** must evaluate to either 1 (true) or 0 (false).

thenstatement

> The statement to be performed if **expression** evaluates to 1 (true). A NOP instruction can be used as that statement if no processing is to be performed.

elsestatement

> The statement to be performed if **expression** evaluates to 0 (false). The ELSE clause is optional. A NOP instruction can be used as that statement if no processing is to be performed.

Note: The statements may be DO-groups, if more than one statement is to be performed.

Example:

```
IF alpha < 2
  THEN NOP;
  ELSE DO;
    SAY "alpha ge 2";
    SAY "line 2";
  END;
```

This example uses a DO-group as the ELSE clause.

9.2.9 INTERPRET – Interpret Statement

The specified expression is interpreted at runtime; i.e., perform dynamic processing.

Syntax:

```
►►──INTERPRET  expression;──►◄
```

expression

> The statement to be performed. The **expression** must be a valid REXX statement – the final semicolon (";") is not specified.

Example:
```
alpha = "SAY 'beta'"
INTERPRET alpha;
```
is equivalent to:
```
SAY 'beta';
```

9.2.10 ITERATE – Terminate the Current Cycle in the Do-Loop
The ITERATE instruction causes control to be passed to the END instruction of the current Do-loop.

Syntax:

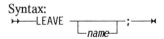

name

> The name of the control variable for the DO-loop. The use of the control variable assists in detecting unbalanced DO-groups.

Example:
```
DO i = 1 TO 4;
   IF i = 2 THEN ITERATE;
   SAY i;
END;
```
displays 1, 3 and 4. The example could also have been written as:
```
DO i = 1 TO 4;
   IF i = 2 THEN ITERATE i;
   SAY i;
END i;
```

9.2.11 LEAVE – Terminate Do-Loop
The LEAVE instruction causes the current DO-loop to be terminated; i.e., control is passed to the statement following the END instruction of the current DO-loop.

Syntax:
```
►►──LEAVE ─┬──────┬─;──►◄
           └─name─┘
```

name

> The name of the control variable for the DO-loop. The use of the control variable assists in detecting unbalanced DO-groups.

Example:
```
DO i = 1 TO 4;
  IF i = 2 THEN LEAVE;
  SAY i; /* display 1 */
END;
```

9.2.12 NOP – No-Operation
The NOP instruction serves as statement placeholder. It is principally used in the THEN clause, when no processing is required but the clause must be present to satisfy the syntax requirements.

Syntax:
```
►►──NOP;──►◄
```

Example:
```
SELECT;
  WHEN alpha < 2;
    THEN SAY "alpha lt 2";
  WHEN alpha = 2;
    THEN NOP;
  OTHERWISE
    SAY "alpha gt 2";
END;
```
In this example processing is required only when alpha is not equal to 2.

9.2.13 NUMERIC – Define Numeric Formats
The NUMERIC instruction is used to define the format of numeric values. The DIGITS, FORM, and FUZZ functions complement the NUMERIC instruction by returning the current format settings.

Syntax:

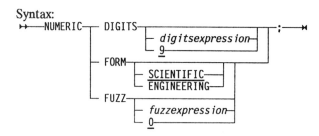

digitsexpression
    A numeric value that specifies the precision of numeric values. Default: 9.

FORM

> The FORM keyword specifies the external (display) form of numeric values whose size exceeds the DIGITS value. Such large, or very small, values are represented in exponential notation. There are two forms of exponential notation:

SCIENTIFIC

> Only one nonzero appears before the decimal point of the mantissa; e.g., 1.2E+4.

ENGINEERING

> The exponent is always a power of three; e.g., 12E+3, 2.4E-6.

fuzzexpression

> A **fuzzexpression** is a numeric value that specifies the number of digits to be ignored (rounded) during numeric comparisons. Default: 0.

Example 1:
```
n = 123456;
NUMERIC DIGITS 4;
NUMERIC FORM ENGINEERING;
SAY n*2; /* displays 246.9E+3 */
NUMERIC FORM SCIENTIFIC;
SAY n*2; /* displays 2.469E+5 */
NUMERIC DIGITS 6;
SAY n*2; /* displays 246912 */
```

Example 2:
```
NUMERIC DIGITS 4;
SAY 2.004 = 2; /* displays 0 (= false) */
NUMERIC FUZZ 1;
SAY 2.004 = 2; /* displays 1 (= true) */
SAY 1.998 = 2; /* displays 0 (= false) */
```

FUZZ is equivalent to:
```
ABS(value1-value2) = 0
```

9.2.14 OPTIONS – Pass Special Parameters to the Language Processor

The OPTIONS instruction is used to pass special parameters to the language processor. The form of these parameters is implementation dependent, and usually concerned with DBCS (double-byte character set) processing.

Note: This book does not discuss DBCS processing.

Syntax:
▸▸───OPTIONS *expression;*───◂

OS/2 REXX supports the options:

    ETMODE
    NOETMODE
    EXMODE
    NOEXMODE

9.2.15 PARSE – Assign Data

The PARSE instruction assigns the source data to the specified variables. The assignment is made according the following criteria:

- words
- delimiter
- position

Syntax:

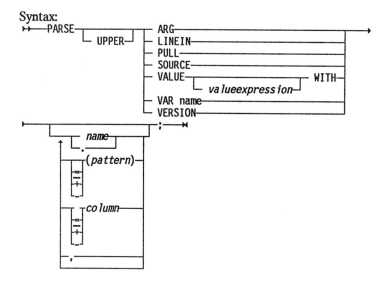

UPPER

> The assigned data are converted to uppercase.
> Default: The case of the source data is retained.

ARG

> The current argument is used as the source data. The argument is set in one of the following ways:
> - argument passed to the REXX exec
> - argument passed to a routine (subroutine, procedure, or function)

LINEIN

The next line from the default input stream is read and parsed.

PULL

The entry at the head of the queue (or the input data stream, if the queue is empty) is fetched and used as the source data.

SOURCE

The current program source is used as the source data. Table 9.1 shows the program source format. Each entry is separated by a blank (* – COMMAND, FUNCTION, or SUBROUTINE).

name

The symbol containing the source data.

valueexpression

The evaluation of **valueexpression** is used as the source data.

name

The symbol to be assigned the parsed data.

A placeholder. The data are parsed but no assignment is made.

OS/2
invocation *
path

Table 9.1. Program source.

'pattern'

The delimiter that is to be used as search argument for the source data. The delimiter is not restricted to being a single character.

(pattern)

If prefixed, **pattern** is a column specification.

=   specifies an absolute position

+ or -   specifies a relative position

Otherwise **pattern** is an expression that is to be used as a delimiter for the source data.

column

> The position at which the source data is to be split. Position 1 is first in the source data. The column may also be a displacement; i.e., prefixed with either a + or - sign. This column is then relative to the last location parsed.

,

> A comma specifies that the next argument in the source data is to be processed. This operand may only be used in conjunction with the ARG keyword.

VERSION

> The identifier containing REXX version information is used as the source data. Table 9.2 shows the version format (5 words).

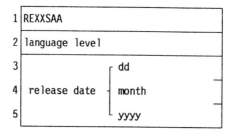

1	REXXSAA
2	language level
3	release date ⌐ dd
4	⌐ month
5	⌐ yyyy

Table 9.2. Version format.

Example 1:
```
CALL alpha "beta gamma";
EXIT;
alpha:
PARSE ARG a b;
SAY a b; /* displays alpha beta */
PARSE UPPER ARG a b;
SAY a b; /* displays ALPHA BETA */
RETURN;
```

Example 2:
```
alpha = "beta gamma";
PARSE VALUE alpha WITH a b;
SAY a b; /* display beta gamma */
```

9.2.16 PROCEDURE – Define Internal Procedure

The PROCEDURE instruction defines the start of an internal procedure. A procedure differs from a subroutine in that it can only be invoked explicitly, and global variables used in the procedure must be defined with the EXPOSE keyword.

Syntax:

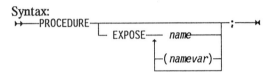

name

    The name of a global variable.

namevar

    The name of the variable that contains a list of global variable names. Each variable name is separated by one or more commas.

Example:

```
beta = "gamma";
CALL alpha;
EXIT;
alpha: PROCEDURE;
   SAY beta; /* displays BETA */
RETURN;
```

BETA is displayed, because the variable beta has not initialized for the procedure alpha.

```
beta = "gamma";
CALL alpha;
EXIT;
alpha: PROCEDURE EXPOSE beta;
   SAY beta; /* displays gamma */
RETURN;
```

The variable beta has been exposed for procedure alpha, hence its content is available in the procedure.

9.2.17 PULL – Fetch Data Element from the Head of the Queue

The PULL instruction is equivalent to the PARSE UPPER PULL instruction. The entry at the head of the queue (or the input data stream, if the queue is empty) is fetched and used as the source data.

Syntax:

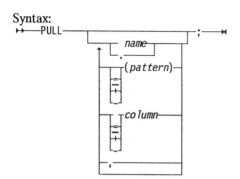

name

> The symbol to be assigned the parsed data.

> A placeholder. The data are parsed but no assignment is made.

'pattern'

> The delimiter that is to be used as search argument for the source data. The delimiter is not restricted to being a single character.

(pattern)

> If prefixed, **pattern** is a column specification.
> =   specifies an absolute position
> + or -   specifies a relative position
> Otherwise **pattern** is an expression that is to be used as the delimiter for the source data.

column

> The position at which the source data is to be split. Position 1 is first in the source data. If **column** is prefixed with either a + or - sign, then this column is relative to the last location parsed.

Example:

```
PULL . alpha .;
```

assigns the second word from the head of the queue to the variable alpha. Two place-holders (".") are used; one for the first word, and one for all words after the second word.

9.2.18 PUSH – Set Data Element at the Head of the Queue

The PUSH instruction places the specified data element at the head of the queue.

Syntax:

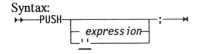

expression
> The data element to be put into the queue. If **expression** is omitted, a null
> string is put into the queue.

Example:
```
PUSH "alpha";
PUSH "beta";
```
sets two entries into the queue.

9.2.19 QUEUE – Set Data Element at the Tail of the Queue
The QUEUE instruction places the specified data element at the tail of the queue.

Syntax:

expression
> The data element to be put into the queue. If **expression** is omitted, a null
> string is put into the queue.

Example:
```
QUEUE "alpha";
QUEUE "beta";
```
sets two entries into the queue.

9.2.20 RETURN – Return from Routine
The RETURN instruction either:

- returns to the statement following the invoking statement, or
- exits from the exec, if the issuing routine was not invoked with a CALL instruction

Syntax:

expression
> The numeric value to be passed back to the point of invocation. If **expression**
> is omitted, the RESULT variable becomes dropped (uninitialized).

Example:
```
CALL alpha;
  ...
alpha:
  ...
  RETURN 4;
```
The value 4 is passed back to the statement following CALL alpha.

9.2.21 SAY – Display
The SAY instruction displays the specified data as terminal output.

Syntax:
```
►►──SAY──┬────────────┬──;──►◄
         └ expression ┘
```

expression

The data to be displayed. The **expression** is evaluated before being displayed.

Example:
```
alpha = 10;
SAY "value of alpha is:" alpha;
```
displays the message value of alpha is: 10.

9.2.22 SELECT – Conditional Execution of One Statement from a Group of Statements
The SELECT statement executes one (and only one) statement from a group of state-ments. A WHEN condition is specified for each statement in the group. The following THEN statement is executed if the condition is satisfied (yields a true result). The OTHERWISE group of statements is executed if none of the previous conditions has been satisfied. At least one WHEN condition must be specified. An error will be signalled if no OTHERWISE clause is present when none of the previous conditions has been satisfied.

Syntax:

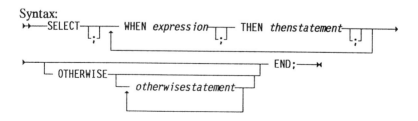

expression
> The condition to be tested. The **expression** must evaluate to either 1 (true) or 0 (false).

thenstatement
> The statement to be performed if the WHEN **expression** evaluates to 1 (true). If more than one statement is to be performed, then a Do-group must be used.
> A NOP instruction can be used if no processing is to be performed.

OTHERWISE

> The keyword OTHERWISE introduces the statements to be performed if none of the conditional clauses was true. The following **otherwisestatement**(s) (up to the Select END) are performed if the OTHERWISE clause is executed – this is an implicit DO.
> The OTHERWISE clause must be present if none of the previous WHEN clauses have been satisfied, even when no processing is to be done. However, the OTHERWISE not need have any entries – in such a case a NOP instruction can be used to emphasize that no processing is to be performed.

Example:
```
SELECT;
  WHEN alpha < 2;
    THEN SAY "alpha lt 2";
  WHEN alpha = 2;
    THEN NOP;
  OTHERWISE;
    SAY "alpha gt 2";
END;
```
This example performs processing only when alpha is not equal to 2.

9.2.23 SIGNAL – Enable (or Disable) an Exception Condition, or Cause Control to be Passed to a Routine (or Label)

The SIGNAL instruction can be used in one of three ways:

- pass control to a routine or labelled statement
- enable an exception condition
- disable an exception condition

If an exception condition has been enabled, control is passed to the specified routine should the particular exception condition occur; multiple exception conditions can be active at any one point of time. The setting of any particular exception condition over-rides any previous setting for that condition.

Syntax:

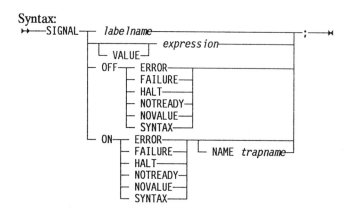

labelname

> The name of the statement to which control is to be passed.

expression

> The evaluated **expression** is the name of a label to which control is to be passed.

OFF

> The following trap condition is disabled.

ON

> The following trap condition is enabled. If the trapped condition is raised, then control is passed to the label having the condition name, unless a **trapname** has been specified. For example, if the NOVALUE condition is enabled, then control is passed to the label NOVALUE if this condition is raised. A syntax error is signalled if the required label does not exist.

ERROR

> The error condition (positive, nonzero return from host command) is disabled or enabled.

FAILURE

> The failure condition (negative return from host command) is disabled or enabled.

HALT

> The halt condition is disabled or enabled. The halt condition can be raised in several ways, for example, with the HI command.

NOTREADY

> The stream not ready condition is disabled or enabled.

NOVALUE
The no value condition (noninitialized variable used in a statement) is disabled or enabled.

SYNTAX
The syntax condition is disabled or enabled. The syntax-error condition can be raised in several ways; for example, a nonnumeric value is used in an arithmetic expression.

trapname
The name of the statement to which control is to be passed if the set condition arises. If **trapname** is omitted, the statement having the name of the raised condition receives control.

Example:
```
SIGNAL alpha;
SAY "beta";
alpha: SAY "gamma";
SIGNAL ON NOVALUE;
SAY delta;
EXIT;
NOVALUE: SAY "novalue raised";
EXIT;
```
displays:
```
gamma
no value raised
```
in this sequence. The **novalue** exception condition is raised by the statement SAY delta; (the variable delta has not been initialized).

9.2.23.1 SIGNAL Used as GoTo. The SIGNAL instruction can be used as a GoTo, but it should not be used to branch into a DO or SELECT construction, because this will cause an error. See the following code segment.
```
DO i = 1 TO 5;
    IF i = 3 THEN SIGNAL a1;
a2: END;
    ...
a1: SIGNAL a2;
```
The first SIGNAL (to a1) functions correctly, whereas the second SIGNAL (to a2) results in an error situation, because the END is misplaced.

The SIGNAL target can also be a character expression, similar to a computed Goto.

Example:
```
target = "alpha";
SIGNAL (target||1);
```
causes control to be passed to the label alpha1.

Warning: A SIGNAL instruction having the function of an implicit branch should be used with caution. Where possible, the SIGNAL instruction should be reserved for setting (or disabling) trap conditions.

9.2.24 TRACE – Set Debugging Options
The TRACE instruction is used to set the debugging option. Because of its frequent use in interactive debugging, the TRACE instruction has a compact syntax.

Syntax:

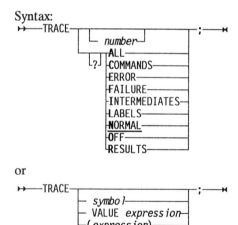

or

number
>   The value of **number** must be an integer.
> > 0 – this is the number of pauses to be bypassed;
> < 0 – this is the number of trace outputs to be suppressed.

Only the first character of the following alphabetic keywords is significant.

ALL
>   All expressions are displayed before being executed.

COMMANDS
>   Host commands are displayed before being executed.

ERROR

Host commands that return a nonzero code are displayed after being executed.

FAILURE

Host commands that return a negative code are displayed after being executed. This is the same as the **Normal** setting.

INTERMEDIATE

All expressions, with the intermediate results, are displayed before being executed.

LABELS

Labels are displayed as they are reached.
Tip: This setting is useful for following the program paths.

NORMAL

Host commands that return a negative code are displayed after being executed. This is the default.

OFF

Stop trace.

RESULTS

All expressions and end results are displayed before being executed.
Tip: This setting is recommended for general debugging purposes.

?

Turn on interactive debugging.

Note: "?" is a binary switch (toggle): each setting reverses the current setting of the option.

The second instruction form offers an alternative method of specifying the trace option.

symbol

symbol is treated as being a literal, and must have the same name as a trace option.
For example, i = x; TRACE i; is equivalent to TRACE I.

expression

An expression that evaluates to a valid trace option.
For example, x = 'i'; TRACE (x); is equivalent to TRACE I.

Example:
```
TRACE ?R;
```
single-steps through the program.

9.3 NON-REXX INSTRUCTIONS

In addition to the REXX instructions described in section 9.2, there are two statements
that can be used in REXX execs:

- command invocation
- comment

9.3.1 Command Invocation

A command is any instruction (**subcommand**) that is neither a REXX instruction nor a
comment. The subcommand is passed to the current command environment. The
initial command environment is CMD, which is the operating system command processor. The ADDRESS instruction changes the command environment. The REXX language
supports user-specific subcommand handlers (see Chapter 16).

The OS/2 commands that have the same names as REXX instructions and functions
(CALL, DATE, ENDLOCAL, EXIT, FOR, IF, SETLOCAL, TIME and TRACE) must be written within
quotes (see Example 2).

Example 1:
```
/* REXX */
"DIR" /* invoke the DIR command */
ADDRESS "alpha" /* set new command environment */
"beta gamma" /* pass subcommand beta gamma to alpha command handler */
```

Example 2:
```
"TRACE" /* invoke the OS/2 TRACE command */
TRACE ?R /* invoke the REXX TRACE instruction */
```


9.3.2 Comment

A comment is zero or more characters enclosed within the **comment delimiter
characters**. The character pairs /* introduce and terminate a comment */, respectively. Comments may be written over more than one line without the continuation
comma. Comments may be nested to a maximum of 10 levels.

Comments used within clauses have the same syntactical significance as a blank;
.i.e., serve as a delimiter.

REXX execs that are directly invoked with the standard command processor
(CMD.EXE) must have a comment at the start of the first line. This is necessary so that

the command processor can distinguish a REXX exec from a batch procedure (see Example 2).

Example 1:
```
/* this is a one line comment */
/* this is a two
   line comment */
/* this is a
   /* nested */
comment */
SAY/* */123 /* comment used as delimiter */
```

Example 2:

a1.cmd is a batch procedure:
```
TIME
```

a2.cmd is a REXX procedure:
```
/* */
SAY TIME()
```

The comment in a REXX exec is required to distinguish the exec from a batch procedure. TIME, as used in the batch procedure, displays the current system time and prompts for a new setting. The TIME function in the REXX exec displays the current system time.

9.4 EXAMPLE

The following example shows the use of REXX instructions as a simple exec that displays the first 10 Fibonacci numbers.

The algorithm for the computation of the Fibonacci numbers is:

$$\text{Fibonacci}(n) = \text{Fibonacci}(n-1) + \text{Fibonacci}(n-2)$$

(starting with $n = 2$).

9.4.1 Sample Exec
```
/* REXX - Fibonacci numbers */
f0 = 1 /* initialize */
f1 = 1
DO i = 1 TO 10 /* start loop */
  f = f1 + f0
  f0 = f1
  f1 = f
  SAY f /* display */
END /* end loop */
```

This sample exec displays: 2, 3, 5, 8, 13, 21, 34, 55, 89 and 144.

10

REXX Built-In
Functions (SAA)

10.1 INTRODUCTION

The REXX language has an extensive library of functions known as **built-in functions**. There are two classes of built-in functions:

- those that are part of SAA (Systems Application Architecture) specification
- implementation-specific functions.

This chapter describes the SAA (Level 2) built-in functions. The non-SAA functions are described in Chapter 11. The functions can be grouped into the categories:

- arithmetic (ABS, MAX, MIN, SIGN)
- bit manipulation (BITAND, BITOR, BITXOR)
- comparison and validation (ABBREV, COMPARE, DATATYPE, SIGN, SYMBOL, VERIFY)
- data conversion (B2X, C2D, C2X, D2C, D2X, TRANSLATE, X2B, X2C, X2D)
- data generation (COPIES, RANDOM, XRANGE)
- date and time (DATE, TIME)
- error handling (CONDITION, ERRORTEXT, SOURCELINE, TRACE)
- format (DIGITS, FORM, FORMAT, FUZZ)
- input/output (CHARIN, CHAROUT, CHARS, LINEIN, LINEOUT, LINES, STREAM)
- string processing (CENTRE (CENTER), DELSTR, INSERT, LASTPOS, LEFT, LENGTH, OVERLAY, POS, REVERSE, RIGHT, STRIP, SUBSTR, TRUNC)
- word processing (DELWORD, SPACE, SUBWORD, WORD, WORDINDEX, WORDLENGTH, WORDPOS, WORDS)
- miscellaneous (ADDRESS, ARG, QUEUED, VALUE)

Operands remain unchanged during the execution of the REXX function. This means that the same variable may be used as both an operand and as the result; the result is set only on completion of the function. *Note*: this does not apply to exposed variables used in user-written functions.

Example:

```
alpha = COPIES(alpha,2);
```

creates an intermediate field containing two copies of alpha, and then assigns the content of this intermediate field to alpha, as depicted in the following diagram.

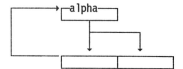

Many functions have keyword operands, of which only one letter, usually the initial letter, is significant – the significant letter is shown in boldface. These keyword operands may be written in either uppercase or lowercase, or may be a variable that contains the keyword value. For example, the uppercase operand for the DATATYPE function can be written as either 'Uppercase' or 'U', or even U. The last form (U) should not be used, because there is always the possibility that the symbol has been used as a variable somewhere else. This recommendation is not restricted to functions, because all keyword operands should be written as literals.

A direct function invocation must include the parentheses, even when no arguments are to be passed to the function. This open-parenthesis ("(") must immediately follow the function name without any intervening blanks. If this requirement is not met, then the function name is interpreted as a symbol. The CALL instruction is an alternative method of invoking functions that do not return a value.

REXX adopts the following conventions:

- The first position of a string is position 1.
- A word is a string of characters delimited by one or more blanks.

This book normally uses literals to simplify the examples, although variables could also have been used. For example, the following three function calls are all equivalent:

```
alpha = "translate";
beta = "trans";
x = ABBREV(alpha,beta);
y = ABBREV(alpha,"trans");
z = ABBREV("translate",beta);
```

10.1.1 Arithmetic
REXX has four arithmetic functions.

ABS	Return absolute value.
MAX	Determine the maximum of a series of numeric values.
MIN	Determine the minimum of a series of numeric values.
SIGN	Determine numeric sign.

10.1.2 Bit Manipulation
The bit manipulation functions process bit by bit, and return the result of processing the first operand with the second operand. REXX also has logical operators that perform Boolean operations on complete operands.

BITAND	logical And
BITOR	logical Or
BITXOR	logical Exclusive-Or

10.1.3 Comparison and Validation
The comparison and validation functions test either the content of a variable or the variable type.

ABBREV	Test whether string is an abbreviation.
COMPARE	Compare.
DATATYPE	Determine data type.
SYMBOL	Determine the status of a symbol.
VERIFY	Test whether only characters in a phrase are present in string.

10.1.4 Data Conversion
The conversion functions convert a variable to some other form. Whereas the other conversion functions are field-oriented, the TRANSLATE is table-driven, and processes characterwise.

B2X	Convert binary data to hexadecimal.
C2D	Convert character data to decimal.
C2X	Convert character data to hexadecimal.
D2C	Convert decimal data to character.
D2X	Convert decimal data to hexadecimal.
TRANSLATE	Translate.
X2B	Convert hexadecimal data to binary.
X2C	Convert hexadecimal data to character.
X2D	Convert hexadecimal data to decimal.

10.1.5 Data Generation

The data generation functions create a variable with the specified content. COPIES replicates an existing variable (or literal). RANDOM creates a pseudo-random number within specified bounds. XRANGE creates a variable that contains the complete range of characters whose hexadecimal code lies within the specified range.

COPIES	Duplicate data.
RANDOM	Generate a (pseudo-)random number.
XRANGE	Create a range of hexadecimal values.

10.1.6 Date and Time

The date and time functions return the current date or time, respectively. Both of these functions have a wide range of options to specify the required form.

DATE	Return current date.
TIME	Return the current time-of-day.

10.1.7 Error Handling

The error handling functions can be used to obtain information should an error occur. Chapter 7 (Debugging) contains general information.

CONDITION	Return condition.
ERRORTEXT	Return message text.
SOURCELINE	Return "program line".
TRACE	Return (and set) the current trace mode.

10.1.8 Format

The format functions are used to control both the internal (precision) and external formats.

DIGITS	Return the NUMERIC DIGITS setting.
FORM	Determine NUMERIC FORM setting.
FORMAT	Format numeric value.
FUZZ	Determine NUMERIC FUZZ setting.

10.1.9 Input/Output
Chapter 6 provides a detailed discussion of the REXX input/output model.

CHARIN	Read a string of characters.
CHAROUT	Write a string of characters.
CHARS	Interrogate the status of the input stream (character mode).
LINEIN	Read a line (record).
LINEOUT	Write a line (record).
LINES	Interrogate the status of the input stream (line mode).
STREAM	Return status of character stream.

10.1.10 String Processing
The string processing functions form the largest group of REXX built-in functions.

CENTRE (CENTER)	Centralize data.
DELSTR	Delete substring.
INSERT	Insert substring.
LASTPOS	Determine last position of phrase.
LEFT	Left-align string.
LENGTH	Determine length of string.
OVERLAY	Overlay part of a string with a phrase.
POS	Search for substring.
REVERSE	Reverse the sequence of data.
RIGHT	Right-align string.
STRIP	Remove padding-characters at the start or end of a string.
SUBSTR	Extract substring.
TRUNC	Truncate numeric value.

10.1.11 Word Processing
A word in the REXX sense, is one or more characters delimited by one or more blanks. REXX has a powerful set of functions to process such items. A frequent use of word lists is for control tables.

DELWORD	Delete one or more words.
SPACE	Insert fill-character between words.
SUBWORD	Extract series of words from word-string.
WORD	Fetch word.
WORDINDEX	Determine the character position of a word in a string of words.
WORDLENGTH	Determine word length.
WORDPOS	Determine word-number of a word in word-string.
WORDS	Determine number of words in word-string.

10.1.12 Miscellaneous Functions

The miscellaneous functions are those that do not belong in any other category.

ADDRESS	Return name of current environment.
ARG	Return argument.
QUEUED	Determine the number of entries in the queue.
VALUE	Return the content of a symbol.

10.1.13 DBCS Functions

The following DBCS (double-byte character set) built-in functions are available but not discussed in this book:

DBADJUST	EBCDIC function to adjust string with regard to the SI/SO characters.
DBBRACKET	EBCDIC function to add SI/SO brackets to the DBCS string.
DBCENTER	Centralize DBCS string.
DBLEFT	Left-justify DBCS string.
DBRIGHT	Right-justify DBCS string.
DBRLEFT	Return remainder from DBLEFT-processed DBCS string.
DBRRIGHT	Return remainder from DBRIGHT-processed DBCS string.
DBTODBCS	Convert SBCS (single-byte character set) string to the equivalent DBCS string.
DBTOSBCS	Convert valid DBCS-characters to the equivalent SBCS-characters (other characters remain unchanged).
DBUNBRACKET	EBCDIC function to remove SI/SO brackets to the DBCS string.
DBVALIDATE	Validate DBCS string.
DBWIDTH	Return byte-length of DBCS string.

10.2 FUNCTION DEFINITIONS

10.2.1 ABBREV – Test Whether String Is an Abbreviation

The ABBREV function tests whether a substring is the abbreviation of a string; i.e., whether **substring** corresponds to the first characters of **string**.
The function returns the **value**:

- 1   **substring** corresponds to **string**
- 0   **substring** does not correspond to **string**

Syntax:
```
►►──value=ABBREV(string,substring──┬────────┬─)──►◄
                                   └─,length─┘
```

string

The string to be tested.

substring
>   The argument.

length
>   The minimum length of the argument. Default: The length of **substring**.

Example:
```
x = ABBREV("translate","trans"); /* 1 */
y = ABBREV("translate","trans",4); /* 1 */
z = ABBREV("translate","transform"); /* 0 */
```

10.2.2 ABS – Return Absolute Value
The ABS function returns the absolute (unsigned) **value**.

Syntax:
```
▸▸──value=ABS(number)───◂
```

number
>   The data to be converted.

Example:
```
x = ABS(-123); /* 123 */
y = ABS(4567); /* 4567 */
```

10.2.3 ADDRESS – Return the Name of the Current Environment
The ADDRESS function returns the name of the current environment (**envname**). The environment is either the default environment or that set with the ADDRESS instruction.

Syntax:
```
▸▸──envname=ADDRESS()───◂
```

Example:
```
x = ADDRESS();
```
This code sets x to be the name of the current environment; e.g., CMD.

10.2.4 ARG – Return Argument

The ARG function returns the **value** of the argument passed to the invoking routine.
Depending on the specified option, one of four values is returned:

- the number of arguments
- the specific argument
- the presence of the specified argument
- the absence of the specified argument

Syntax:

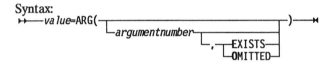

argumentnumber
> The number of the argument to be returned. Default: The total number of
> arguments.

EXISTS

> Return 1 (true) if the specified argument exists.
> Return 0 (false) if the specified argument does not exist.

OMITTED

> Return 1 (true) if the specified argument does not exist.
> Return 0 (false) if the specified argument exists.

Example:
```
CALL alpha beta, gamma;
...
alpha:
x = ARG(); /* 2 */
y = ARG(1) /* beta */
z = ARG(3,'E') /* 0, the third argument is not present */
```

10.2.5 BITAND – Logical And

The BITAND function returns the **value** of the Logical And with the content of the second string on the content of the first string. The operation is performed bit by bit
from left to right. The & operation (see Section 2.5.4) performs a Logical And on
complete fields, which must have either 0 or 1 as content.

The following list describes the Logical AND processing:

```
0 AND 0 -> 0
0 AND 1 -> 0
1 AND 0 -> 0
1 AND 1 -> 1
```

Syntax:

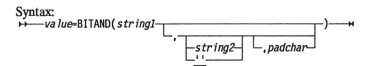

string1

    First string.

string2

    Second string. Default: A null string ('' or "").

padchar

    Padding-character **padchar**, if specified, is added to **string2**, if **string2** is shorter than **string1**.

Example:

```
x = BITAND("123","22","4"); /* 020 */
```

10.2.6 BITOR – Logical Or

The BITOR function returns the **value** of the Logical Or with the content of the second string on the content of the first string. The operation is performed bit by bit from left to right. The | operation (see Section 2.5.4) performs a Logical Or on complete fields, which must have either 0 or 1 as content.

The following list describes the Logical OR processing:

```
0 OR 0 -> 0
0 OR 1 -> 1
1 OR 0 -> 1
1 OR 1 -> 1
```

Syntax:

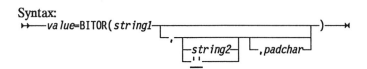

string1

>   First string.

string2

>   Second string. Default: A null string.

padchar

>   Padding-character **padchar**, if specified, is added to **string2**, if **string2** is shorter than **string1**.

Example:

```
x = BITOR("123","22","4"); /* 327 /
```

10.2.7 BITXOR – Logical Exclusive-Or (XOR)

The BITXOR function returns the **value** of the Logical XOR (bit reversal) with the content of the second string on the content of the first string. The operation is performed bit by bit from left to right. The && operation (see Section 2.5.4) performs a Logical Exclusive-Or on complete fields, which must have either 0 or 1 as content.

The following list describes the Logical XOR processing:

```
0 XOR 0 -> 0
0 XOR 1 -> 1
1 XOR 0 -> 1
1 XOR 1 -> 0
```

Syntax:

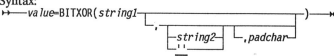

string1

>   First string.

string2

>   Second string. Default: A null string ('' or "").

padchar

>   Padding-character **padchar**, if specified, is added to **string2**, if **string2** is shorter than **string1**.

Example:

```
x = BITXOR("123","0202"x,"04"x); /* 307 */
```

10.2.8 B2X – Convert Binary Data to Hexadecimal

The B2X (binary-to-hexadecimal) function converts a binary-coded data string (0's and 1's) to its hexadecimal equivalent. The hexadecimal code (one hexadecimal digit) for each group of four binary digits in the data string is assigned to the result field. The binary string may contain embedded blanks at four-digit boundaries. Binary strings whose length is not a multiple of four will be left-padded with 0's.

Syntax:
>>──*value*=B2X(*string*)──><

string

     The data to be processed.

Example:

```
x = B2X("11110000"); /* F0 */
x = B2X("0101 0000 1010"); /* 50A */
x = B2X("101"); /* 5 */
```

10.2.9 CENTRE (CENTER) – Centralize Data

The CENTRE function centralizes the specified data. The centralization is made by filling the data to the specified length with equal numbers of padding-characters on each side of the data.

Note: This function has two alternative spellings, CENTRE and CENTER, to cater to the British and American ways of spelling. The two functions are identical.

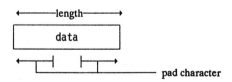

Syntax:

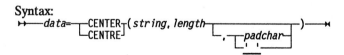

string1

     Data to be centralized.

length

     Length of the centralized data.

padchar

     Padding-character. Default: ' ' (blank).

Example:
```
x = CENTER("alpha",9);
```
This code assigns ' alpha ' to x.

10.2.10 – Read a String of Characters
The CHARIN function returns a string of characters read from the specified input stream. The characters are read byte by byte, and include any control characters such as carriage-returns present.

Syntax:

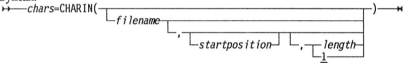

chars
> The read characters. A null string is returned if no characters can be read (e.g., end of file).

filename
> The file (fully-qualified file name) from which the characters are to be read. Default: The default input stream.

startposition
> The position in the input stream from which the characters are to be read. Position 1 is first in the input stream. Default: The characters are read from the current position in the input stream.

length
> The number of characters to be read. If **length** is 0, then the current pointer will be positioned according to the value specified by **startposition**, and no data will be returned. Default: 1

Example:
```
x = CHARIN("b:datafile.txt",,10);
```
This code reads 10 characters from the file B:DATAFILE.TXT starting at the current position.

10.2.11 CHAROUT – Write a String of Characters
The CHAROUT function writes a string of characters onto the specified output stream. The characters are written byte by byte, and include any control characters such as carriage-returns present. A nonzero value will be returned if not all the characters

can be written. If neither data nor a line number are specified, the file is closed after the write position has been set to the end of the file.

Syntax:

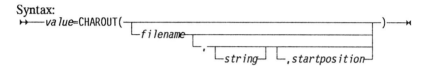

filename
> The file (fully-qualified file name) on which the characters are to be written. Default: The default output stream.

string
> The data to be written. This may be the null-string, in which case no data are written.

startposition
> The position in the output stream where the characters are to be written. The current contents will be overwritten. Position 1 is first in the output stream. Default: The characters are written at the current position in the output stream.

Note: If neither **string** nor **startposition** is specified, then the current position pointer will be set to the current end of the data stream.

Examples:
> x = CHAROUT("b:datafile.txt",alpha,10);

writes the contents of the variable alpha at position 10 in the file B:DATAFILE.TXT.

> x = CHAROUT("b:datafile.txt");

This code sets the current position pointer to the end of the file B:DATAFILE.TXT.

10.2.12 CHARS – Interrogate the Status of the Input Stream (Character Mode)
The CHARS function returns the status of the specified input stream:
- 1   Data remain in the input stream.
- 0   The input stream is empty.

Note: Certain implementations return the actual number of characters remaining.

Syntax:

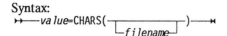

filename
> The file from which the status is to be obtained. Default: The default input stream.

Example:
```
x = CHARS("b:datafile.txt");
```
This code assigns a nonzero value to x if data in the file B:DATAFILE.TXT remain to be read.

10.2.13 COMPARE – Compare

The COMPARE function compares two data fields. The two fields are compared character by character from left to right. A shorter field is padded on the right with the pad character. The position of the first nonequal character is returned: 0 indicates that the two data fields (padded, if necessary) are equal.

A character comparison is also made for numeric fields. For example, COMPARE returns the not equal condition for the two numeric fields 1.2E+1 and 12, although these two fields are numerically equal.

Syntax:
```
►►──value=COMPARE(string1,string2────────────)──►◄
                            └,─┬─padchar─┬──┘
                              └' '┘
```

string1
> First data field.

string2
> Second data field.

padchar
> Padding-character. Default: ' ' (blank).

Example:
```
x = COMPARE("translate","translation"); /* x = 9 */
```

10.2.14 CONDITION – Return Condition

The CONDITION function returns the specified condition. This function is usually used in an error exit to determine the cause of error.

Syntax:

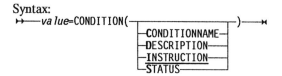

CONDITIONNAME

Return the current condition from the list:

ERROR
FAILURE
HALT
NOVALUE
SYNTAX

DESCRIPTION

Return the descriptive text associated with the condition. There may not necessarily be any descriptive text available.

An example of descriptive text is the name of the symbol causing the condition.

INSTRUCTION

Return the name of the invoking instruction, either CALL or SIGNAL. INSTRUCTION is the default.

STATUS

Return the status of the trapped condition from the list:

DELAY   any new occurrence is delayed
OFF   the condition is disabled
ON   the condition is enabled

Note: The status may change during the course of execution.

Chapter 7 (Debugging) contains an example of the use of the CONDITION function.

10.2.15 COPIES – Duplicate Data

The COPIES function duplicates a data field the specified number of times.

Syntax:

↦——*data*=COPIES(*string, number*)——↦

string

The source data field.

number

The number of copies to be created.

Example:

```
x = COPIES("beta",2); /* betabeta */
```

10.2.16 C2D – Convert Character Data to Decimal

The C2D (character-to-decimal) function converts data to its decimal equivalent. The internal code for the data field is converted to a signed decimal number. The sign of the converted data is taken from the leftmost bit of the data field.

Note: The C2D function is code-dependent; that is, different results are returned in the mainframe (EBCDIC) and personal computer (ASCII) environments. For example, the uppercase character 'A' has the ASCII code X'41' and the EBCDIC code X'C1'.

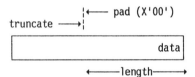

Syntax:

$$\blacktriangleright\!\blacktriangleright\!\!-\!value\!=\!C2D(\,string\!\underset{\llcorner\,,\ length\lrcorner}{}\!)\!-\!\blacktriangleright\!\blacktriangleleft$$

string

        The data field.

length

        The length of the data field. If necessary **string** will be padded on the left with hexadecimal zeros to achieve the required length. If **length** is less than the field length, **string** will be truncated from the left.

Example (ASCII):

```
x = C2D('F0'x);
y = C2D('F0'x,2);
```

assigns the value -240 to x (the leftmost bit of '0' (= 'F0'x) is set) and 240 to y (the leftmost bit of '0' padded to length 2 (= '00F0'x) is not set).

10.2.17 C2X – Convert Character Data to Hexadecimal

The C2X (character-to-hexadecimal) function converts data to its hexadecimal equivalent. The hexadecimal code (two hexadecimal digits) for each character of the data field is assigned to the result field.

Note: the C2X function is code-dependent; that is, different results are returned in the mainframe (EBCDIC) and personal computer (ASCII) environments.

Syntax:
    ⊢⊢──*va lue*=C2X(*str ing*)────⊣

string
        The data to be processed.

Example (ASCII):
        x = C2X("0"); /* 30 */

10.2.18 DATATYPE – Determine Data Type

The DATATYPE function can be used in two ways:

- Return the form of the data (numeric or character, character is nonnumeric).
- Confirm (or otherwise) that the data has a particular form.

Syntax:
    ⊢⊢──*va lue*=DATATYPE(*str ing*

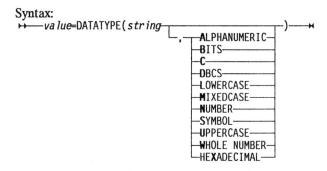

string
        The data field to be tested. The optional keyword specifies the class of data to
        be tested. If the data field being tested contains valid data for the specified
        class, 1 (true) is returned; otherwise the result is 0 (false). If no class keyword
        is specified then the value NUM or CHAR is returned, depending on whether the
        field contains numeric data or not. Table 10.1 defines the data content for each
        class.

Class	Content	Comment
Alphanumeric	a-z A-Z 0-9	
Bits	0 1	
C		SBCS/DBCS data
Dbcs		DBCS data
Lowercase	a-z	
Mixedcase	a-z A-Z	
Number		valid REXX number
Symbol		valid REXX symbol
Uppercase	A-Z	
Whole number		nonexponential number
heXadecimal	a-f A-F 0-9	

Table 10.1. Class content.

Example:
```
x = DATATYPE("ag",'X')s
y = DATATYPE(1.2E4);
z = DATATYPE(1.2F4);
```
This code assigns 0 (false) to x ("g" is not a valid hexadecimal character), NUM to y, and CHAR to z (1.2F4 is not a valid number).

10.2.19 DATE – Return Current Date
The DATE function returns the current date in the specified format. Table 10.2 summarizes the date formats.

Syntax:

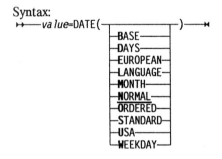

Class	Content	Comment
Basedate		Days Since January 1, 0001
Days		Days Since January 1, Xxxx
European	Dd/mm/yy	
Language	Dd Month Yyyy	
Month	Month	Month Name
Normal	Dd Mon Yyyy	
Ordered	Yy/mm/dd	
Standard	Yyyymmdd	
Usa	Mm/dd/yy	
Weekday		Day Name

Table 10.2. Date formats.

BASEDATE

The number of days (including the current day) since January 1, 0001.

DAYS

The number of days (including the current day) since January 1 of the current year.

EUROPEAN

The date in the European form dd/mm/yy.

LANGUAGE

Language-specific date format – dd month yyyy. The month name is according to the national language.

MONTH

The English name of the current month; e.g.: January.

NORMAL

The date in default format: dd mon yyyy ("mon" is the 3-character English abbreviation for month; e.g.: Jan for January.

ORDERED

The date in the sortable format: yy/mm/dd.

STANDARD
>   The date in the sortable format: yyyymmdd.

USA
>   The date in the American form: mm/dd/yy.

WEEKDAY
>   The name (in English) of the current day of the week; e.g.: Sunday.

Example (assuming the current date is February 2, 1993):
```
x = DATE(); /* 2 Feb 1993' */
y = DATE('J'); /* 93033 */
z = DATE('W'); /* Tuesday */
```

10.2.20 DELSTR – Delete Substring
The DELSTR function deletes a substring starting at the specified position from a data field.

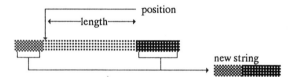

Syntax:
```
▸▸──data=DELSTR(string,position─┬─────────┬─)──◂
                                └─, length─┘
```

string
>   The data field from which the substring is to be deleted.

position
>   The starting position in the data field of the substring to be deleted. The first character in the field is at position 1.

length
>   The length of the substring to be deleted. Default: The complete data remaining in the string.

Example:
```
x = DELSTR("alpha",3,2); /* ala */
```

10.2.21 DELWORD – Delete Words
The DELWORD function deletes one or more words from a string of words.

Syntax:

```
►►──data=DELWORD( string, wordnumber─┬─────────────┬─)──►◄
                                     └─, wordcount─┘
```

string
> The data field from which the words are to be deleted.

wordnumber
> The starting position (word number) of the first word to be deleted. The first word has word number 1.

wordcount
> The number of words to be deleted. Default: All the remaining words in the string.

Example:
```
x = DELWORD("a bb ccc",2,1); /* a ccc */
```

10.2.22 DIGITS – Return the NUMERIC DIGITS Setting
The DIGITS function returns the current precision for numeric values, which is set using the NUMERIC DIGITS instruction.

Syntax:

```
►►──value=DIGITS()──►◄
```

Example:
```
NUMERIC DIGITS 4;
x = DIGITS(); /* 4 */
```

10.2.23 D2C – Convert Decimal Data to Character
The D2C (decimal-to-character) function converts a decimal value to character (internal code). This is equivalent to converting a decimal number to signed binary. The sign of the binary number is propagated to the specified length.

Note: The D2C function is code-dependent; that is, different results are returned in the mainframe (EBCDIC) and personal computer (ASCII) environments.

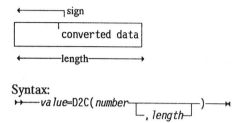

Syntax:
```
►►──value=D2C( number─┬──────────┬─)──►◄
                      └─, length─┘
```

number
> The data field.

length
> The length (in characters) of the result. The sign of the input **number** will be propagated if necessary. An error results if no **length** is specified for a negative **number**. Default: If no **length** is specified, then the length of the result is such that no '00'x characters are present at the start of the result field.

Example (ASCII):
```
x = D2C(48); /* '0' */
```

10.2.24 D2X – Convert Decimal Data to Hexadecimal

The D2X (decimal-to-hexadecimal) function converts a decimal value to the hexadecimal digits representing its internal code (binary value). The sign of the binary number is propagated to the specified length.

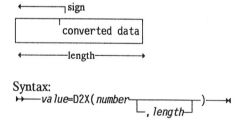

Syntax:
```
►►──value=D2X( number─┬───────────┬─)──►◄
                      └─, length─┘
```

number
> The data field.

length
> The length (in characters) of the result. The sign of the input **number** will be propagated if necessary. An error results if no **length** is specified for a negative **number**. Default: If no **length** is specified, then the length of the result is such that no '00'x characters are present at the start of the result field.

Example:
```
x = D2X(240); /* F0 */
```

10.2.25 ERRORTEXT – Return Message Text

The ERRORTEXT function returns the message text that applies to the specified message number. No text is returned for a nonexistent message.

Syntax:
```
⊢⊢──messagetext=ERRORTEXT(errornumber)──⊣
```

errornumber

> The message number for which the message text is to be retrieved.

Example:
```
SAY ERRORTEXT(40);
```
This example displays the message: Incorrect call to routine.

10.2.26 FORM – Determine NUMERIC FORM Setting

The FORM function returns the current display form for numeric values, which is set using the NUMERIC FORM instruction.

Syntax:
```
⊢⊢──value=FORM()──⊣
```

Example:
```
NUMERIC FORM SCIENTIFIC;
x = FORM(); /* SCIENTIFIC */
```

10.2.27 FORMAT – Format Numeric Value

The FORMAT function formats a numeric value for display. Default formatting is made when the FORMAT function is not used.

Syntax:

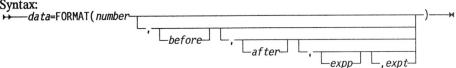

before

> The number of digits to be formatted before the decimal point; leading zeros (except for a single zero before the decimal point) are suppressed.

after

> The number of digits to be formatted after the decimal point.

expp

> The number of digits (places) to be used for the exponential. If omitted, the number of digits necessary to represent the exponent is used.

expt

> The number of digits to trigger the exponential representation.

Example:

```
x = FORMAT("12.3",3,2) /* ' 12.30' */
y = FORMAT("1234",,,2,2) /* 1.234E+03 */
```

10.2.28 FUZZ – Determine NUMERIC FUZZ Setting

The FUZZ function returns the current number of digits to be ignored for numeric comparisons. The NUMERIC FUZZ instruction sets this value.

Syntax:
```
►►──value=FUZZ()──►◄
```

Example:

```
NUMERIC FUZZ 2;
x = FUZZ(); /* 2 */
```

10.2.29 INSERT – Insert Substring

The INSERT function inserts a substring into the specified position of a data field.

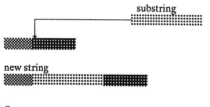

new string

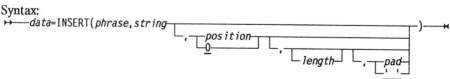

Syntax:
```
►►──data=INSERT(phrase,string─┬──────────────────────────────────────┬──)──►◄
                               └─,─┬─position─┬──┬─────────────────────┘
                                   └─0─┘      └─,─┬─length─┘ └─,─┬─pad─┘
```

phrase

> The data field that is to be inserted into the specified **string**.

string

> The data field into which the **phrase** is to be inserted.

position

> The position in **string** after which **phrase** is to be inserted. Default: 0 (i.e., **phrase** is inserted before the start of **string**).

length

> The length of the **phrase** to be inserted.

pad

> The padding-character to be used if the specified **length** is greater than the implicit length of phrase. Default: ' ' (blank)

Example:

```
x = INSERT("alpha","beta",3); /* betalphaa */
```

10.2.30 LASTPOS – Determine Last Position of Phrase

The LASTPOS function determines the last position of a phrase in a string. This is done by searching backwards starting from the specified position. The value 0 is returned if the phrase is not found.

Syntax:

phrase

> The data field that is to be used as search argument.

string

> The data field to be searched.

startposition

> The position from which the search is to start. Default: The last position in **string**.

Example:

```
x = LASTPOS("lt","deltaepsilon"); /* 3 */
```

10.2.31 LEFT – Left-align String

The LEFT function left-aligns a string, padded if necessary.

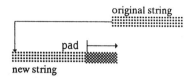

Syntax:
```
▸▸───data=LEFT(string, length────────)───▸
                       └─,─┬─pad─┬─┘
                          └─' '─┘
```

string

> The data field containing the words to be aligned.

length

> The final length of the aligned **string**.

pad

> The padding-character to be used if the specified **length** is greater than the implicit length of **string**. Default: ' ' (blank)

Example:
```
x = LEFT("alpha",8); /* 'alpha   ' */
```

10.2.32 LENGTH – Determine Length of String
The LENGTH function returns the length of a string. The length includes any blanks at the start or end of the string.

Syntax:
```
▸▸───value=LENGTH(string)───▸
```

string

> The data field whose length is to be returned.

Example:
```
x = LENGTH(" alpha  ");
```
This example returns 8 (includes one leading blank and two trailing blanks).

10.2.33 LINEIN – Read a Line (Record)
The LINEIN function either returns a line (record) of character data read from the specified input stream or sets the current position pointer to the specified line (record). The line (record) is delimited according to the conventions of the host environment. Any delimiting characters such as carriage-return or line-feed are not returned.

Syntax:

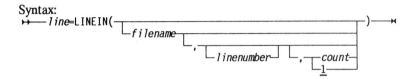

line

> The read record. A null string is returned for a zero count or at end of file.

filename

> The file (fully-qualified file name) from which the line is to be read. Default:
> The default input stream.

linenumber

> The position in the input stream from which the line (record) is to be read.
> Position 1 is the first line (record) in the input stream. Default: The line
> (record) is read from the current position in the input stream.

count

> Either 0 or 1:
> 1   A line (record) is to be read.
> 0   The current position pointer is to be positioned to the start of the line
> identified by **linenumber**. Default: 1

Example:

```
x = LINEIN("b:datafile.txt",10,0);
```

This example sets the current position pointer of the file B:DATAFILE.TXT to the start of
line 10.

10.2.34 LINEOUT – Write a Line (Record)

The LINEOUT function either writes a line (record) of character data onto the specified
output stream or sets the current position pointer to the end of the specified output
stream. A nonzero value will be returned if the line cannot be written. The line
(record) will be delimited according to the conventions of the host environment; any
necessary delimiting characters such as carriage-return or line-feed will be generated.
If neither data nor a line number are specified, the file is closed after the write position has been set to the end of the file.

Syntax:

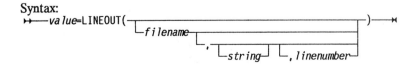

filename
> The file (fully qualified file name) on which the line is to be written. Default: The default output stream.

string
> The data to be written. This may be the null-string, in which case no data are written.

linenumber
> The position in the output stream at which the line (record) is to be written. Position 1 is the first line (record) in the output stream. Default: The line (record) is written at the current position in the output stream.

Example:
```
x = LINEOUT("b:datafile.txt",,1);
```
This example sets the current position pointer of the file B:DATAFILE.TXT to the start of the file.

10.2.35 L I NES – Interrogate the Status of the Input Stream (Line Mode)

The LINES function returns the status of the specified input stream. The status is either:

0   The input stream is empty.

>0   There are still lines (records) in the input stream. The actual number of lines are returned for QUEUE:.

Syntax:

```
►►──status=LINES(─┬──────────┬─)──►◄
                  └─filename─┘
```

filename
> The file from which the status is to be obtained. Default: The default input stream.

Example:
```
x = LINES("b:datafile.txt");
```
This example assigns a nonzero value to x if lines in the file B:DATAFILE.TXT remain to be read.

10.2.36 MAX – Determine the Maximum of a Series of Numeric Values

The MAX function returns the largest numeric (signed) value from a series of numbers. The maximum count of the numbers that can be processed is implementation dependent (the maximum number of values in OS/2 is 20). More values can be processed either by cascading or with a loop.

Cascading the MAX function:
```
x = MAX(.,.,...);
x = MAX(x,...);
```
etc.

Using the MAX function for an array of values:
```
x = -999999999; /* set minimum value */
DO i = 1 TO n;
   x = MAX(x,a.i);
END;
```
This example assumes that the data values are in the array a. with n values.

Syntax:

number
> A numeric value.

Example:
```
x = MAX(1,-4,2); /* 2 */
```


10.2.37 MIN – Determine the Minimum of a Series of Numeric Values
The MIN function returns the smallest numeric (signed) value from a series of numbers. The maximum count of the numbers that can be processed is implementation dependent (the maximum number of values for OS/2 is 20). More values can be processed either by cascading or with a loop.

Cascading the MIN function:
```
x = MIN(.,.,...);
x = MIN(x,...);
```
etc.

Using the MIN function for an array of values:
```
x = 999999999; /* set maximum value */
DO i = 1 TO n;
   x = MIN(x,a.i);
END;
```
This example assumes that the data values are in the array a. with n values.

Syntax:

number
>   A numeric value.

Example:
```
x = MIN(1,-4,2); /* -4 */
```

10.2.38 OVERLAY – Overlay Part of a String With a Phrase
The OVERLAY function overlays part of a string with a phrase (substring).

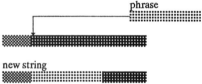

Syntax:

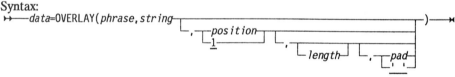

phrase
>   The data field that is to overlay the specified **string**.

string
>   The data field into which the **phrase** is to be overlaid.

position
>   The position in **string** after which **phrase** is to be overlaid. Default. 1 (i.e., **phrase** is overlaid at the start of **string**).

length
>   The length of the **phrase** to be overlaid. Default: The implicit length of **phrase**.

pad
>   The padding-character to be used if the specified **length** is greater than the implicit length of phrase. Default: ' ' (blank).

Example:
```
x = OVERLAY("beta","epsilon",3); /* 'epbetan' */
```

10.2.39 POS – Search for Substring
The POS function searches for the first occurrence of a substring in a string. POS returns the first position of the substring in the searched string; 0 = substring not found.

Syntax:
```
►►──value=POS(phrase,string──┬──────────────────────┬──)──►◄
                             └─,─┬─startposition─┘
                                 └─1─────────────┘
```

phrase
>   The data field being searched for.

string
>   The data field being searched.

startposition
>   The starting position in **string**. Default: 1.

Example:
```
x = POS("ps","epsilonpsi",5); /* 8 */
```

10.2.40 QUEUED – Determine the Number of Entries in the Queue (Stack)
The QUEUED function returns the number of entries in the current queue.

Note: The LINES('QUEUE:') function performs equivalent processing.

Syntax:
```
►►──value=QUEUED()──►◄
```

Example:
```
RXQUEUE('Create'); /* create new queue */
PUSH "alpha";
PUSH "beta";
x = QUEUED(); /* 2 */
```

10.2.41 RANDOM – Generate a (Pseudo-)Random Number
The RANDOM function generates a pseudo-random number (positive integer). The bounds of the generated number may be specified. A **seed** value may be specified for

the initialization of the random number generation process; if the same seed value is specified, then the same random number will be generated.

Tip: Even if no seed is specified, the same pseudo-random number may, depending on the implementation, always be generated. If this is undesirable, then a seed value should be generated using some variable source; e.g., from the time-of-day clock.

Syntax:

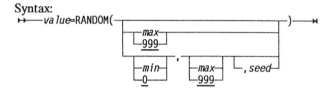

max

A positive integer that specifies the upper limit for the generated value. Default: 999.

min

A positive integer that specifies the lower limit for the generated value. Default: 0.

seed

A positive integer used to initialize the random number generation process. However, this is not the random number returned. The same random number is always generated if the same seed and bounds are specified.

Example:
```
x = RANDOM();
y = RANDOM(,,40);
```
This example returns two random numbers for x, and y. The random number generated for y is repeatable; that is, the same number will always be generated.

10.2.42 REVERSE – Reverse the Sequence of Data

The REVERSE function reverses the sequence of data in a string; i.e., the first byte is returned as the last byte, etc.

original string

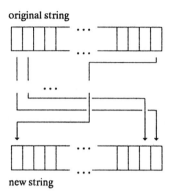

new string

Syntax:
▸▸──*data*=REVERSE(*string*)──▸◂

string

>The data being processed.

Example 1:

```
x = REVERSE("beta"); /* ateb */
```

Example 2:

```
str = "alpha beta   gamma    "
x = REVERSE(str)
PARSE VAR x lastword .
SAY REVERSE(lastword) /* 'gamma' */
```

This example displays the last word in a string (where the number of words in the string is unknown).

10.2.43 RIGHT – Right-Align String

The RIGHT function right-aligns a string, padded if necessary.

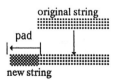

Syntax:
▸▸──*data*=RIGHT(*string, length*─┬───────┬─)──▸◂
                                 └─,─┬─*pad*─┬─┘

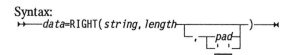

string

> The data field containing the words to be aligned.

length

> The final length of the aligned **string**.

pad

> The padding-character to be used if the specified **length** is greater than the implicit length of **string**. Default: ' ' (blank)

Example:
```
x = RIGHT("alpha",8); /* '    alpha' */
```

10.2.44 SIGN – Determine Numeric Sign

The SIGN function returns the sign of a number:

-1 The number is less than 0.
 0 The number equals 0.
+1 The number is greater than 0.

Syntax:
```
►►──value=SIGN(number)──►◄
```

number

> The data field to be processed.

Example:
```
x = SIGN(-2); /* -1 */
y = SIGN(0); /* 0 */
z = SIGN(2); /* 1 */
```

10.2.45 SOURCELINE – Return "Program Line"

The SOURCELINE function can be used in one of two ways:

- Return the program (source file) line corresponding to the specified line number.
- Return the last program line if no line number is specified.

Note: The SIGL special variable contains the source file number of the line from which a CALL or SIGNAL was invoked.

Syntax:
```
►►──data=SOURCELINE(──────────────────)──►◄
                      └─linenumber─┘
```

linenumber
> The line number to be retrieved from the source exec.

Chapter 7 (Debugging) includes an example of the use of the SOURCELINE function.

10.2.46 SPACE – Insert Fill-Character Between Words

The SPACE function inserts the specified fill-character between words. The word-string is normalized (the string is delimited into its individual words) before the SPACE operation is performed.

Syntax:

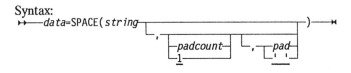

string
> The data field to be processed.

padcount
> The number of padding-characters (**pad**) to be placed between each word in the returned string. Default: 1.

pad
> The padding-characters to be placed between each word in the returned string. Default: ' ' (blank).

Example:
```
x = SPACE("a bb  c",3 ,'*'); /* 'a***bb***c' */
```

10.2.47 STREAM – Perform Stream-Level Processing

The STREAM function performs stream-level processing on the specified character stream.

Syntax:
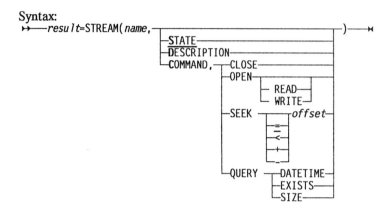

name
>   The name of the stream to be processed.

STATE
>   Return the current stream status. **result** returned with:
>
>   ERROR   an error has occurred on the stream
>   NOTREADY   the stream is not ready
>   READY   the stream is ready for processing (normal status)
>   UNKNOWN   the stream is in an unknown (not open) status
>
>   STATE is the default operation.

DESCRIPTION
>   Return the current stream status. **result** returned with the same keyword as for
>   STATE, a colon (:), and any further status information that is available.

COMMAND
>   Pass the specified command to the stream:
>
>   OPEN   Open the stream. The processing mode may be specified (READ,
>   WRITE) – by default the stream is opened for reading and writing.
>   **result** is returned with the subsequent open status: 'READY' (the
>   stream was successfully opened) or an appropriate error
>   message.
>
>   CLOSE   Close the stream. **result** is returned with the subsequent status:
>   'READY' (the stream was successfully closed), an appropriate error
>   message, or a null string (if the stream was not open).

SEEK	Position the stream. The stream must be in the open state. **offset** specifies the number of characters for the positioning, and may be prefixed by a mode character:

=	offset from the start of the stream (default)
<	offset from the end of the stream
+	offset forward from the current position
-	offset backward from the current position.

If the positioning was successful, STREAM returns the new position in **result**.

QUERY	Return the stream status in **result**. A null result string indicates that no information can be returned (e.g., stream cannot be found). The suboperand specifies the information required:
DATETIME	return the stream's date and time stamps (mm-dd-yy hh:mm:ss)
EXISTS	return the stream's full path specification (e.g., c:\alpha\beta.txt)
SIZE	return the byte size for a persistent stream.

Example 1:
```
    x = STREAM("c:alpha.txt",'C','CLOSE')
```
This statement closes the file c:alpha.txt.

Example 2:
```
    result = STREAM('a0.cmd','C','QUERY SIZE')
    IF result = ''
      THEN SAY 'file error'
      ELSE SAY 'size:' result
```
This exec displays the byte size of the file a0.cmd.

10.2.48 STRIP – Remove Padding-characters at the Start or End of a String
The STRIP function removes the specified fill-character at the start or end (or start and end) of a string.

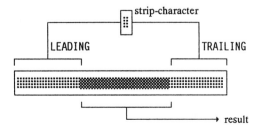

Syntax:

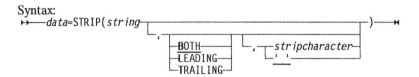

string

> The data field to be processed.

BOTH

> The specified strip-character is removed from both the start and end of the **string**. Default.

LEADING

> The specified strip-character is removed from the start of the **string**.

TRAILING

> The specified strip-character is removed from the end of the **string**.

stripcharacter

> The character to be removed from the **string**. Default: ' ' (blank).

Example:

```
x = STRIP(" alpha ",'L');
y = STRIP(" alpha ",'T');
z = STRIP("(alpha)",,'(');
```

This example returns 'alpha ', ' alpha' and 'alpha)', respectively.

Tip: If parentheses (or similar paired but nonequal delimiters) are to be removed from string, then the STRIP function must be used twice; once on the original string to remove the leading delimiter, and once on the intermediate result to remove the trailing delimiter. For example

```
x = STRIP(alpha,'L',"(");
x = STRIP(x,'T',")");
```

removes delimiting parentheses from the contents of alpha.

10.2.49 SUBSTR – **Extract Substring**

The SUBSTR function extracts a substring from the specified position of a data field.

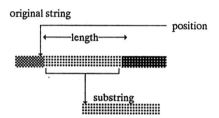

original string

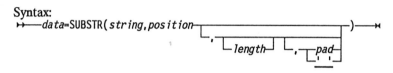

position

length

substring

Syntax:

$\rightarrowtail$—*data*=SUBSTR(*string,position*————————)—→

length   *,*—*pad*

string

The source data field from which the substring is to be extracted.

position

The position in **string** after which the substring is to be extracted.

length

The length of the substring to be extracted. If omitted, the remaining string is extracted.

pad

The padding-character to be used if the specified **length** is not entirely contained in **string**. Default: ' ' (blank)

Example:
```
w = SUBSTR("alpha",3); /* pha */
x = SUBSTR("alpha",3,2); /* ph */
y = SUBSTR("alpha",3,4); /* pha */
z = SUBSTR("alpha",3,4,'*'); /* pha* */
```

10.2.50 SUBWORD – Extract Series of Words from Word-String

The SUBWORD function extracts the specified number of words from a word-string starting at the specified word number.

Syntax:

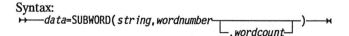

$\rightarrowtail$—*data*=SUBWORD(*string,wordnumber*————)—→

,wordcount

string

The data field to be processed.

wordnumber
> The number of the starting word in **string** from which the words are to be extracted.

wordcount
> The number of words to be extracted. Default: All remaining words in **string**.

Example:
```
x = SUBWORD("a bb cc ddd e",2,3); /* 'bb cc ddd' */
```

10.2.51 SYMBOL – Determine the Status of a Symbol
The SYMBOL function returns the status of a symbol. This status is:

VAR   The symbol has been assigned a value, and has not been dropped with the DROP function.

LIT   The symbol has not been assigned a value, or has been dropped with the DROP function, or is a literal (numeric or character).

BAD   The symbol is not a valid name – however, in many cases a REXX error (invalid expression) will be raised.

Syntax:
```
►►——value=SYMBOL(name)——►◄
```

name
> The symbol to be tested.

Example:
```
alpha = "beta";
x = SYMBOL("alpha"); /* VAR */
y = SYMBOL(alpha); /* LIT */
```

10.2.52 TIME – Return the Current Time-of-Day
The TIME function returns the current time-of-day. The time is returned in one of the specified formats. Table 10.3 summarizes the time formats.

Syntax:

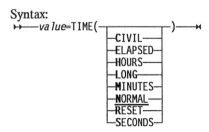

The time fields have the form:

- hh is the hour (00 through 23), except for 'Civil'
- mm is the minute (00 through 59)
- ss is the number of seconds (00 through 59)
- uuuuuu is the number of microseconds

Class	Format	Comment
Civil	hh:mmxx	xx = AM or PM
Elapsed	sssssss.uuuuuu	elapsed-clock
Hours	hh	
Long	hh:mm:ss.uuuuuu	
Minutes	mmmm	since midnight
Normal	hh:mm:ss	
Reset	sssssss.uuuuuu	since elapsed-clock reset
Seconds	sssss	since midnight

hh = hours mm = minutes ss = seconds uu = microseconds

Table 10.3. Time formats.

CIVIL

The time of day in the form: hh:mmxx
hh is the hour (1 through 12, leading zeros are suppressed); xx is either am or pm, depending on whether the time is before midday (am) or after midday (pm). The minute is truncated; e.g.: 10 minutes 59 seconds is returned as 10.

ELAPSED

The time elapsed since the elapsed-clock was set. This time is returned in the form: sssssss.uuuuuu
The elapsed-clock is set by either the **Elapsed** or **Reset** operand.

HOURS

The hours since midnight in the form: hh

LONG

The time of day in the long form: hh:mm:ss.uuuuuu

MINUTES

The minutes since midnight in the form: mmmm

NORMAL
>   The time of day in the default form: hh:mm:ss

RESET
>   The time that has elapsed since the elapsed-clock was set or reset. This time is
>   returned in the form: sssssss.uuuuuu. The elapsed-clock is reset to zero.
>   The elapsed-clock is set by either the **Elapsed** or **Reset** operand.

SECONDS
>   The seconds since midnight in the form: sssss

Example:
```
x = TIME('E');
y = TIME('E');
SAY y-x;
```
displays the elapsed time since the two invocations of the TIME function; i.e., the processing time required for this function. This is equivalent to the following code
(assuming the processing times for Elapsed and Reset are identical, which is probably
not the case):
```
x = TIME('R');
x = TIME('E');
SAY x;
```

10.2.53 TRACE – Return (and Set) the Current Trace Mode
The TRACE function returns the current trace mode and sets the trace mode to the
specified option. Chapter 7 (Debugging) contains a detailed description of the use of
the TRACE function.

Syntax:

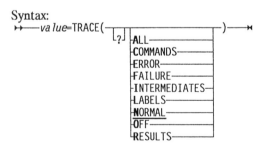

ALL
>   All expressions are displayed before being executed.

COMMANDS
>   Host commands are displayed before being executed.

ERROR
Host commands that return a nonzero code are displayed after being executed.

FAILURE
Host commands that return a negative code are displayed after being executed. This is the same as the **Normal** setting.

INTERMEDIATE
All expressions are displayed before being executed. Intermediate results are also displayed.

LABELS
Labels are displayed as they are reached.
Tip: This setting is useful for following the program paths.

NORMAL
Host commands that return a negative code are displayed after being executed.

OFF
Stop trace.

RESULTS
All expressions are displayed before being executed. End results are also displayed.
Tip: This setting is recommended for general debugging.

?
Turn on interactive debugging.

Note: ? is a binary switch (toggle) that reverses the current setting of the option.

Example:
```
x = TRACE();
y = TRACE('0');
```
This example returns the current trace mode in x and y, respectively. The first invocation does not alter the trace mode; the second invocation disables tracing (option 'OFF').

10.2.54 TRANSLATE – **Translate**

The TRANSLATE function transforms the contents of the input data based on translation tables. The TRANSLATE function has two forms:

- translation tables present
- translation tables not present

The translation is performed character by character from left to right. When translation tables are present, the entries in the input table (**input-table**) are replaced by the corresponding entries in the output table (**output-table**); entries that are not present remain unchanged. When translation tables are not present, the input is translated from lowercase to uppercase.

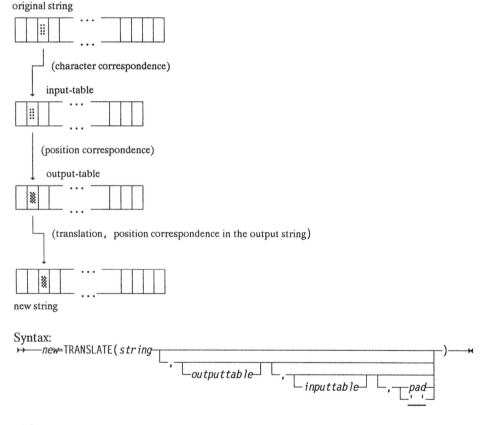

Syntax:

string
  The data to be processed.

outputtable
  The character to be substituted for the character in the same position of **input-table**.

inputtable
> The characters to be translated. The position of the entries (characters) in this table is used as the index to the entries in the **outputtable**; e.g., the first entry in **inputtable** indexes to the first entry in **outputtable**. The first occurrence is used if the same character appears more than once.
>
> If a character from **string** is not present in the **inputtable**, it is passed unchanged to the function result field.

pad
> The character to be used for padding, if **outputtable** is shorter than **inputtable**. Default: ' ' (blank).

Example:
```
x = TRANSLATE("alpha"); /* ALPHA */
y = TRANSLATE("beta","34","ab"); /* 4et3 */
```

Tip: TRANSLATE is a powerful function that can often simplify processing by normalising data. For example, the TRANSLATE function is used in the following example to convert alphabetic data to uppercase and replace nonalphabetic characters by an asterisk. The TRANSLATE function could be similarly used to normalize data strings to word-strings; i.e., separate words with blanks, which can then be processed using standard word-parsing functions.

```
fld = "abcIJK 123  QRS";
UpperCase = "ABCDEFGHIJKLMNOPQRSTUVWXYZ";
AllChars = UpperCase||XRANGE();   /* uppercase + '00'x - 'FF'x */
fld = TRANSLATE(fld);             /* convert to uppercase */
fld = TRANSLATE(fld,UpperCase,AllChars,"*");
SAY fld;
```
This code displays 'ABCIJK******QRS'.

10.2.55 TRUNC – Truncate Numeric Value
The TRUNCATE function is used to format a number with a specified number of decimal places. The NUMERIC DIGITS setting limits the size of the formatted number.

Syntax:

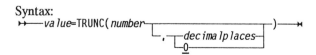

number
> The value to be processed.

decimalplaces
>   The number of decimal places (digits to the right of the decimal point) to be
>   returned. Default: 0.

Example:
```
x = TRUNC("123.45"); /* 123 */
y = TRUNC("123.45",3); /* 123.450 */
```

10.2.56 VALUE – Return the Content of a Symbol
The VALUE function returns the content of the specified symbol. This approximates
indirect addressing. The VALUE function can be used in compound variable names
where the index is an arithmetic expression (see Example 2). The VALUE keyword is
also used in certain instructions, where it has the same meaning as this function.
>   The VALUE function can also be used to access environment variables.

Syntax:

name
>   The symbol whose content is to be returned.

newvalue
>   The new value to be assigned to **name**.

selector
>   The variable pool to be accessed. OS2ENVIRONMENT accesses the OS/2 environment
>   variables. *Note*: the SETLOCAL and ENDLOCAL functions can be used to save and
>   restore, respectively, current environment variables.

oldvalue
>   The current value of the variable **name**.

Example 1:
```
alpha = "beta";
beta = "gamma";
x = VALUE(alpha); /* gamma */
y = VALUE("alpha"); /* beta */
```

Example 2:
```
SAY value(a.value(i+1));
```

This example displays the content of the stem variable a. indexed by i+1; e.g., if i is 2, the content of a.3 is displayed.

Example 3:
```
oldpath = VALUE('path','c:os2\os2lib','OS2ENVIRONMENT');
```
This example sets the PATH OS/2 environment variable to C:OS2\OS2LIB.

10.2.57 VERIFY – Test Whether only Characters in a Phrase Are Present in String
The VERIFY function returns either:

- the first position of a character in the string that is present in the specified phrase (Match option), or
- the first position of a character in the string that is not present in the specified phrase (Nomatch option).

The processing is performed character by character from left to right.

Syntax:

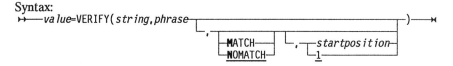

string
> The source data to be processed.

phrase
> The data field that contains the characters to be tested.

startposition
> The starting position. Default: 1.

MATCH
> The test is to be performed for the first matching character from **string** that also occurs in **phrase**.

NOMATCH
> The test is to be performed for the first character from **string** that does not occur in **phrase**. Default.

Example:
```
x = VERIFY("beta","ab",'M'); /* 1 */
y = VERIFY("beta","ab",'N'); /* 2 */
z = VERIFY("abcabc","abcd",'N'); /* 0 */
```

10.2.58 WORD – Fetch Word

The WORD function fetches the specified word from a word-string. The value 0 is returned if the specified word number is not present in the word-string.

Syntax:

```
►►──data=WORD(string,wordnumber)──►◄
```

string

>   The data field to be processed.

wordnumber

>   The number of the word in **string** to be fetched. Position 1 is the first word in **string**.

Example:

```
x = WORD("a bb ccc dddd",3); /* ccc */
```

10.2.59 WORDINDEX – Determine the Character Position of a Word in a Word-String

The WORDINDEX function returns the character position of the start of the specified word number in a word-string. The value 0 is returned if the specified word number is not present in the word-string.

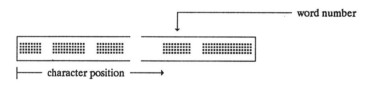

Syntax:

```
►►──charpos=WORDINDEX(string,wordnumber)──►◄
```

string

>   The word-string to be processed.

wordnumber

>   The number of the word in **string** whose position is to be determined.

Example:

```
x = WORDINDEX("a bb ccc dddd",3); /* 6 */
```

10.2.60 WORDLENGTH – Determine Word Length

The WORDLENGTH function returns the length of the specified word number in a word-string. The value 0 is returned if the specified word number is not present in the word-string.

Syntax:

```
►►── length=WORDLENGTH(string,wordnumber)──►◄
```

string

      The data field to be processed.

wordnumber

      The number of the word in **string** whose length is to be determined.

Example:

```
x = WORDLENGTH("alpha beta gamma",2); /* 4 */
```

10.2.61 WORDPOS – Determine Word-Number of Word in Word-String

The WORDPOS function searches the word-string for the specified phrase and returns the corresponding word number. The value 0 is returned if the specified phrase is not present in the word-string.

Syntax:

```
►►──value=WORDPOS(phrase,string─┬──────────────────────┬─)──►◄
                                └─,─┬─startwordnumber─┬─┘
                                    └─1───────────────┘
```

string

      The data field to be processed.

phrase

      The phrase to be used to search word-string.

startwordnumber

      The number of the word in **string** at which the search is start. Default: 1

Example:

```
x = WORDPOS("ccc","a bb ccc dddd"); /* 3 */
```

10.2.62 WORDS – Determine Number of Words in Word-String

The WORDS function returns the number of words in a word-string.

Syntax:
```
►►──value=WORDS(string)──►◄
```

string

> The data field to be processed.

Example:
```
x = WORDS("alpha beta gamma  delta"); /* 4 */
```

10.2.63 XRANGE – Define a Range of Hexadecimal Values
The XRANGE function creates a string of character-codes lying in the range of values (including the bounds).

Syntax:
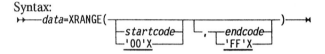

startcode

> The lower bound of the range (inclusive). Default: '00'x.

endcode

> The upper bound of the range (inclusive). Default: 'FF'x.

Note: If **endcode** is less than **startcode**, wrap-around will occur.

Warning: Care should be taken with the definition of code tables, especially if the application is going to be ported to other hardware environments.
For example, the table of uppercase characters must be defined by specifying each character:
```
"ABCDEFGHIJKLMNOPQRSTUVWXYZ".
```
The shorter definition using the XRANGE function XRANGE('A','Z') is only valid for ASCII codes; the statement
```
XRANGE('A','I')XRANGE('J','R')XRANGE('S','Z')
```
would be required to yield the equivalent results in both ASCII and EBCDIC environments.

Example:
```
x = XRANGE('0','9');
```
defines '30313233343536373839'x (ASCII).

```
x = XRANGE('9','0');
```
defines '393A3B3C3D3E3E3F'x through '292A2B2C2D2E2F30'x (ASCII).

10.2.64 X2B – Convert Hexadecimal Data to Binary

The X2B (hexadecimal-to-binary) function converts a string of hexadecimal digits (0 through 9, and A through F) to the equivalent binary data. The data is converted from left to right, with four binary-coded digits being used for each hexadecimal digit. The input hexadecimal string may contain embedded blanks on byte boundaries. A 0 will be added to the start of the input string if its length is not even.

Syntax:
```
►►──value=X2B(hexstring)──►◄
```

hexstring
> The string of hexadecimal digits to be processed.

Example:
```
x = X2B("C1"); /* 11000001 */
x = X2B("C");  /* 1100 */
x = X2B("1 C2"); /* 000111000010 */
```

10.2.65 X2C – Convert Hexadecimal Data to Character

The X2C (hexadecimal-to-character) function converts a string of hexadecimal digits (0 through 9, and A through F) to the equivalent character (internal machine format) data. The input hexadecimal string may contain embedded blanks on byte boundaries. The data is converted from left to right, with two hexadecimal digits being used for each character. A 0 will be added to the start of the input string if its length is not even.

Note: The X2C function is code-dependent; that is, different results are returned in the mainframe (EBCDIC) and personal computer (ASCII) environments.

Syntax:
```
►►──value=X2C(hexstring)──►◄
```

hexstring
> The string of hexadecimal digits to be processed.

Example (ASCII):
```
x = X2C("4142"); /* AB */
```

10.2.66 X2D – Convert Hexadecimal Data to Decimal

The X2D (hexadecimal-to-decimal) function converts the binary representation of a string of hexadecimal digits (0 through 9 and A through F) to its equivalent decimal (numeric) value. If a length is specified, the input hexadecimal string is truncated or padded with 0's to this length, and processed as a signed number. If no length is specified, the input hexadecimal string is processed as an unsigned number.

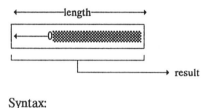

Syntax:
```
►►──value=X2D( hexstring─┬──────────┬─)──►◄
                         └─, length─┘
```

hexstring

   The string of hexadecimal digits to be processed.

length

   The length (in hexadecimal digits) of the input data. The input **hex-string** is padded on the left with 0's or truncated to the specified **length**.

Example:
```
x = X2D("F0") /* 240 */
x = X2D("F0",2) /* -16 */
x = X2D("F0",4) /* 240 */
```

10.3 WORKED EXAMPLE

The sample EDIT exec illustrates the use of several built-in REXX functions. The EDIT function returns a numeric value in the usual (comma-delimited) notation; e.g., 1234567 as 1,234,567. To simplify the processing, only an integer result with a maximum length of 21 digits is returned.

```
Edit: PROCEDURE
  PARSE ARG x . /* get argument */
  IF DATATYPE(x,'NUMBER') = 0 THEN RETURN '' /* test for numeric */
  x = FORMAT(x,21,0,,21) /* convert to nonexponential nondecimal */
  x = STRIP(x,'L') /* remove leading blanks */
  gct = LENGTH(x)/3 /* get number of blocks-of-three */
  IF gct = 0 THEN RETURN 0 /* empty field */
  wk = '' /* clear workarea */
  DO i = 1 TO gct
    l = LENGTH(x)
    y = SUBSTR(x,l-2) /* get right-hand block (max. 3 characters) */
    wk = y','wk /* prefix to previous result */
    x = DELSTR(x,l-2) /* delete block */
```

```
END
wk = x','wk /* prefix remainder */
wk = STRIP(wk,'L',',') /* remove leading commas */
RETURN wk
```

11

REXX Built-In Functions (Non-SAA)

11.1 INTRODUCTION

The REXX language, as defined in the SAA specification, contains a wide range of general functions. However, most implementations have a number of useful environment-specific functions. This chapter describes those specific to Procedures Language 2. Chapter 14 describes the REXXUTIL utility function package, which contains many additional environment-specific functions. The main difference between the two groups of functions is that the REXXUTIL functions must first be registered before they can be used, whereas the functions described in this chapter can be used as built-in functions.

Appendix E summarizes the functions available in each implementation.

11.2. FUNCTION DEFINITIONS

The environment-specific, built-in functions specific to Procedures Language 2 are:

BEEP	sound the audible signal
DIRECTORY	get/set directory
ENDLOCAL	restore environment information
FILESPEC	return file specification information
SETLOCAL	save environment information

11.2.1 BEEP – Sound the Audible Signal
The BEEP function sounds the audible signal at a specified frequency for a stated duration.

Syntax:
```
┣━━━CALL BEEP frequency,duration ━━━┫
```

frequency

> The frequency (hertz) in the range 37 through 32767 Hz.

duration

> The duration (milliseconds) in the range 1 through 60000 milliseconds (= 1 minute).

Example:
```
CALL BEEP 1000, 200;
```
issues a 1000 Hz tone for 0.2 seconds.

11.2.2 DIRECTORY – Get/Set Directory

The DIRECTORY function returns the current directory, and, optionally, changes it to the specified new directory.

Syntax:
```
┣━━━currentdir=DIRECTORY(━━━━━━━━━━━━)━━━┫
                        └─newdirectory─┘
```

currentdir

> The current directory. If **newdirectory** is specified, **currentdir** is the new directory name (a null string ('') indicates that an error has occurred).

newdirectory

> The new directory name. If **newdirectory** is not specified, the current directory name is returned.

Example:
```
curdir = DIRECTORY(); /* return the current directory */
newdir = DIRECTORY("c:\alpha\beta"); /* set new directory */
```


11.2.3 ENDLOCAL – Restore Environment Information

The ENDLOCAL function restores the environment information (environment variables, current path) in effect before it was saved with a previous SETLOCAL function call. ENDLOCAL is invoked implicitly at the end of the exec, if SETLOCAL without a subsequent ENDLOCAL has been called.

Note: The ENDLOCAL and SETLOCAL functions can be nested.

Syntax:
```
┣━━━rc=ENDLOCAL()━━━┫
```

rc

> The return code:
>
> 1   The initial environment has been successfully restored.
>
> 0   An error occurred or no SETLOCAL call has been made.

Example:

```
CALL SETLOCAL; /* save current environment */
DIRECTORY("c:\alpha\beta"); /* set new directory */
...
CALL ENDLOCAL; /* restore original environment */
```

11.2.4 FILESPEC − Return File Specification Information

The FILESPEC function returns the selected item (drive, directory, or path) from the specified file specification.

Syntax:

```
▸▸──result=FILESPEC(──┬─DRIVE─┬─,filespec)──▸◂
                      ├─NAME──┤
                      └─PATH──┘
```

option

> The required item (only the initial letter is necessary):
>
> DRIVE   the drive identifier for the **filespec** (e.g., C:)
>
> NAME   the filename from the **filespec** (e.g., alpha.txt)
>
> PATH   the directory path from the **filespec** (e.g., \beta\gamma\).

filespec

> The file specification. *Note*: **filespec** need not physically exist.

result

> The result. A null string ('') indicates that the requested item could not be found.

Example:

```
filespec = "c:\alpha\beta\gamma.txt
drive = FILESPEC('D',filespec); /* c: */
path = FILESPEC('P',filespec); /* \alpha\beta\ */
file = FILESPEC('N',filespec); /* gamma.txt */
```

11.2.5 SETLOCAL − Save Environment Information

The SETLOCAL function saves the current environment information (environment variables, current path). The ENDLOCAL function can be used to restore this information.

Note: The ENDLOCAL and SETLOCAL functions can be nested.

Syntax:

►►——*rc*=SETLOCAL()——►◄

rc

The return code:

1   The current environment has been successfully saved.
0   An error occurred.

Example:
```
CALL SETLOCAL; /* save current environment */
CALL DIRECTORY "c:\alpha\beta"; /* set new directory */
 ...
CALL ENDLOCAL; /* restore original environment */
```

12

Utility Commands

12.1 INTRODUCTION

OS/2 REXX supplies four standard utility routines:

PMREXX	Invoke a REXX exec as a PM application (command).
REXXTRY	Run a REXX instruction (command).
RXQUEUE	Process external data queues (function).
RXQUEUE	Redirect program terminal output onto a REXX queue (filter).

12.2 PMREXX – Invoke a REXX Exec as a PM Application

The PMREXX command can be used to run a REXX exec as a Presentation Manager (PM) application. PMREXX opens a window for terminal input and output. All terminal input and output is saved in this scrollable window. This means that SAY output, etc. can be reviewed at the end of the session.

12.2.1 Invocation

Syntax:

/T

        Activate interactive trace.

CommandName

> The name of the command to be invoked. The **CommandName** can include path information. If no path information is supplied, the standard search sequence is used. The default extension is CMD.

Arguments

> The arguments to be passed to the command.

Example:

The command

```
PMREXX alpha 3 4
```

invokes the PMREXX processor to execute the alpha.cmd exec with argument "3 4".

alpha.cmd:

```
/* rexx */
PARSE ARG p1 p2
SAY 'enter multiplicand:'
PARSE PULL m
x = p1 * m + p2
SAY 'result:' x
```

Figure 12.1 shows the form of the PMREXX window as displayed for the alpha command.

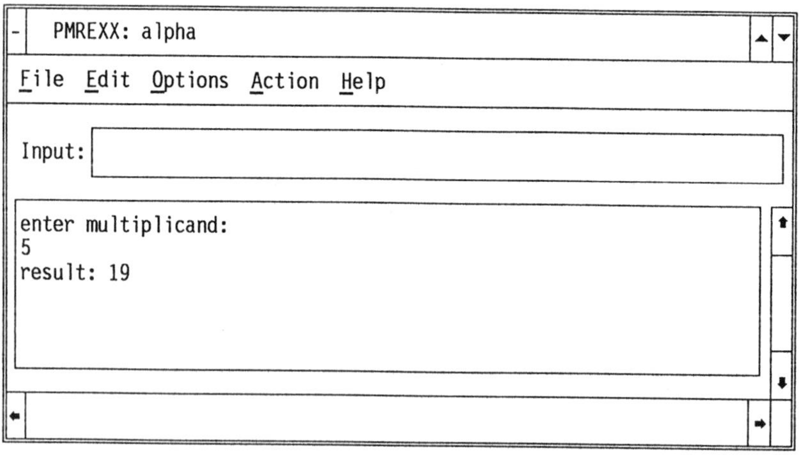

Figure 12.1. Form of the PMREXX window.

When 5 is input, the result 19 is calculated $(3 \cdot 5 + 4)$ and displayed.

The output window contains:

- SAY instruction output
- STDOUT and STDERR output for secondary processes started from the REXX exec
- REXX trace output

The input window contains:

- PULL instruction data
- STDIN input for secondary processes started from the REXX exec

PMREXX menu options:

Action	Stop the exec, trace the next clause (= single-step), repeat the last clause, deactivate trace mode, etc.
Edit	Cut, paste, etc.
File	Save screen output, etc.
Options	Restart the exec, activate trace, etc.

The REXX or PMREXX on-line help can be used to obtain further information on the PMREXX command. PMREXX displays the message: procedure not found, if the exec does start with a comment line.

12.3 REXXTRY – Run a REXX Instruction

The REXXTRY command interprets the specified REXX instruction, and so used to simulate the instruction processing. The instruction being run can accept terminal input; e.g., with the PULL instruction.

Syntax:

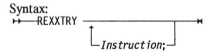

Instruction
    The instruction to be processed. If omitted, the user will be prompted.

Examples:

    REXXTRY SAY 1+2

displays 3

    REXXTRY i = 5; SAY i+3

displays 8

```
REXXTRY PARSE PULL i; SAY i+3
```
will wait for keyboard input, and use the input value in the second instruction. For example, if 6 were input, 9 would be displayed.

12.4 QUEUE INTERFACE

There are two services for the processing of REXX queues:

RXQUEUE function processes external data queues
RXQUEUE filter redirects program terminal output onto a REXX queue

12.4.1 RXQUEUE function

The RXQUEUE function processes external data queues. The first parameter specifies the subfunction:

Create	Create a new queue.
Delete	Delete a named queue.
Get	Return the name of the current queue.
Set	Set the name of the current queue.

One use of named queues is to pass data among execs, which may be in different sessions.

12.4.1.1 CREATE – **Create a Queue.** Create a queue with the specified **queuename**. If **queuename** is omitted, a queue name is generated. If a queue with the specified **queuename** already exists, a new queue with a generated queue name is created. In all cases the subfunction returns the name of queue created.

Syntax:
```
►►──nQueueName = RXQUEUE(CREATE─────────────)──►◄
                               └─, QueueName─┘
```

QueueName
      The name of the queue to be created.

nQueueName
      The name of the created queue.

Example:
```
qname = "ALPHA"
nqname = RXQUEUE("create",qname);
if (nqname <> qname) THEN SAY "queue exists already"
```
Create a queue with the name alpha. Issue a message if the alpha queue exists already.

12.4.1.2 DELETE – **Delete a Named Queue.** Delete the named queue **queuename.** The function returns the queue status.

Syntax:
$\rightarrow\!\!\!\rightarrow\!\!-retcode$ = RXQUEUE(DELETE, *QueueName*)$\longrightarrow\!\!\!\rightarrow$

QueueName
    The name of the queue to be deleted.

retcode
    Return code:

0	Successful processing.
5	Invalid queue name.
9	Named queue does not exist.
10	Queue is being used.
12	Insufficient memory.
1000	Initialization error.

Example:
```
frc = RXQUEUE("delete","alpha");
IF frc <> 0 THEN SAY "RXQUEUE DELETE error:" frc;
```

Delete the queue with the name alpha.

12.4.1.3 GET – **Get the Name of the Currently Active Queue.** Return the name of the current queue.

Syntax:
$\rightarrow\!\!\!\rightarrow\!\!-QueueName$ = RXQUEUE(GET)$\longrightarrow\!\!\!\rightarrow$

queuename
    The name of the currently active queue.

Example:
```
qname = RXQUEUE("get");
SAY "QNAME:" qname;
```

Display the name of the currently active queue.

12.4.1.4 SET – **Set Queue Name.** Set the current queue to the specified name. The previous name of the queue is returned.

Syntax:
$\rightarrow\!\!\!\rightarrow\!\!-OldQueueName$ = RXQUEUE(SET, *NewQueueName*)$\longrightarrow\!\!\!\rightarrow$

NewQueueName
>   The new name of the queue.

OldQueueName
>   The previous name of the queue.

Example:
```
oqname = RXQUEUE("set","beta");
SAY "QNAME:" oqname;
```

Set the queue name to "beta" and display the previous name of the queue.

12.4.1.5 Example. This example uses the USER named queue to pass data between execs (global data).

RX1.CMD
```
/* rexx - RX1 */
CALL RXQUEUE 'Create','user' /* create USER queue */
CALL RXQUEUE 'Set','user' /* set current queue */
PUSH 4 /* set value into queue */
CALL rx2 /* invoke RX2 exec */
PARSE PULL va /* get value from queue */
SAY va /* 2 - from RX2 */
```

RX2.CMD
```
/* rexx - RX2 */
CALL RXQUEUE 'Set','user' /* set queue name */
PARSE PULL va /* get value from queue */
SAY va /* 4 - from RX1 */
PUSH 2 /* set new value */
RETURN
```

12.4.2 RXQUEUE Filter

The RXQUEUE filter redirects program terminal output to a REXX queue.

Syntax:

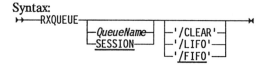

QueueName
>   The name of the queue where the output is to be placed. If omitted, the content of the RXQUEUE environment variable is used as queue name. If RXQUEUE contains no value, the default name SESSION is used.

/CLEAR
All entries are removed from the queue.
/FIFO
Entries are stored FIFO (first-in, first-out). Default.
/LIFO
Entries are stored LIFO (last-in, first-out).

Example:

The sample exec performs the processing:
- Create a new queue q1 (qn contains the actual queue name).
- Filter the DIR command output backwards (LIFO) into this queue.
- Set this queue to be the current queue.
- Extract and display the free space from the last entry.
- Delete the queue.

```
qn = RXQUEUE('Create','q1'); /* create new queue */
"DIR a: | RXQUEUE" qn "/LIFO" /* filter output into queue */
CALL RXQUEUE 'Set', qn; /* set queue to be active */
PARSE PULL line . . freespace .
SAY "free space:" freespace
rc = RXQUEUE('Delete', qn); /* delete queue */
```

13

Worked Example

13.1 INTRODUCTION

One feature missing from OS/2 REXX is a high-level, file-oriented, input/output routine, rather than the line-mode input/output functions (LINEIN, LINEOUT, etc.). REXX provides EXECIO as such a host command in the MVS and VM/CMS environments. Whereas a single call to EXECIO can process a complete file, a loop is required for the standard line-mode input/output functions to achieve the same result.

This chapter uses the following implementation of EXECIO as an example of how REXX facilities can be used in a practical way.

To avoid overloading the sample implementation with unnecessary details, the EXECIO command as shown here has the simplified syntax:

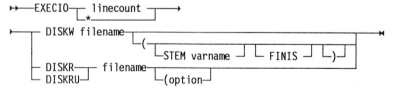

Furthermore, to reduce the coding size, only the DISKW (disk write) operation is implemented in the worked example – the coding for the DISKR (disk read) and DISKRU (disk read and update) operations are similar.

The worked example in this chapter implements EXECIO as an exec. The worked example in Chapter 18 shows the programmed implementation (as a subcommand programmed in C). Such programmed implementations can be necessary when performance is critical.

The explanation of the DISKW parameters follows:

- **linecount**   The number of lines to be written. * – the complete file. Records are written until either this count is reached or a null line is fetched.

- **filename**   The name of the file to be written. This name conforms to the usual rules with regard to path information.

- **varname**   The name of the stem variable that contains the records to be written (**varname**.1, **varname**.2, etc.). If the STEM keyword is omitted, the records will be fetched from the current queue.

- FINIS   The output file is to be closed at the end of the processing.

The EXECIO return code (RC variable) indicates the processing status:

0   successful processing
otherwise error (e.g., syntax error).

13.2 EXEC IMPLEMENTATION

Because an exec can only be invoked as an external function or subroutine, its calling sequence has been slightly changed. The SUBCOM function receives the command string as parameter (for example, CALL SUBCOM "EXECIO * DISKW data.txt (stem b. finis"). If the SUBCOM function detects any syntactical error, it exits with a nonzero return code. The processing exec main routine (SUBCOM) decomposes the input statement into its component items, and calls the ProcessIO internal function with this information to perform the file processing. This sample exec uses the queue to pass information between these two routines; each queue item is prefixed by an identifier.

13.2.1 Exec Code

```
1       SUBCOM:
2       PARSE UPPER ARG cmd lines op filename linenum '(' parm ')';
3       IF cmd <> 'EXECIO' THEN RETURN 1;
4       nq = RXQUEUE('Create');
5       oq = RXQUEUE('Set',nq);
6       IF lines = '' THEN RETURN 3;
7       IF filename = '' THEN RETURN 3;
8       SELECT
9         WHEN op = 'DISKW' THEN DO;
10          PARSE VAR parm kywd parm;
11          SELECT
12            WHEN kywd = 'STEM' THEN DO;
13              PARSE VAR parm varname finisparm .;
14              IF varname = '' THEN RETURN 5;
                PUSH '_VARNAME' varname;
```

```
15                    PUSH '_FINIS' finisparm;
16                  END;
17                  WHEN kywd = 'FINIS' THEN
                      PUSH '_FINIS' kywd;
18                  WHEN kywd = '' THEN NOP;
19                  OTHERWISE
                      RETURN 4;
20              END;
21            END;
22            OTHERWISE
                RETURN 2;
23          END;
24          PUSH '_FILENAME' filename;
25          PUSH '_OP' op;
26          PUSH '_LINES' lines;

27          prc = PerformIO();
28        RETURN prc;

29        PerformIO:
30          DO i = 1 TO queued();
              PARSE PULL cmd parm;
31            x.cmd = parm;
            END;
32          CALL RXQUEUE 'Set',oq;
33          IF x._lines = '*';
              THEN ct = 999999; /* set high-value */
              ELSE ct = x._LINES;
34          SELECT
35          WHEN x._op = 'DISKW' THEN DO;
36            CALL LINEOUT x._filename,,1; /* position at file start */
37            IF SYMBOL('X._VARNAME') = 'LIT' THEN DO;
                DO i = 1 TO ct;
38                IF queued() = 0 THEN LEAVE;
39                PULL line;
                  CALL LINEOUT x._filename, line;
40              END;
41            END;
42            ELSE DO i = 1 TO ct;
43              IF SYMBOL(VALUE(x._varname)i) = 'LIT' THEN LEAVE;
43              line = VALUE(VALUE(x._varname)i);
                CALL LINEOUT x._filename, line;
44            END;
45            IF x._finis = 'FINIS' THEN
```

```
                       CALL STREAM x._filename,'Command','Close';
46              END;
47              OTHERWISE
                       RETURN -1; /* unsupported operation */
48              END;
49         RETURN 0; /* successful processing */
```

13.2.2 Exec Code Explanation

1   Entry point for the SUBCOM routine.

2   Convert the passed arguments to uppercase. Parse these arguments into **cmd**, **lines**, **op**, **filename** and **linenum**. **parm** (if present) is enclosed within parentheses – the terminal right-parenthesis is optional.

3   Exit if **cmd** is not EXECIO (error code 1).

4   Create a new queue. The allocated name is set in **nq**.

5   Set this queue to be the current queue. The name of the previous queue is set into **oq**.

6   Exit if **lines** is null.

7   Exit if **filename** is null.

8   Open SELECT block.

9   Process if **op** contains DISKW.

10   Parse **parm** into **kywd parm**; that is, extract the first word from **parm**.

11   Open inner-SELECT block

12   Process if **kywd** contains STEM.

13   Parse **parm** into the two words **varname** and **finisparm** (any further operands are ignored).

14   Exit if **varname** is not specified. Push **varname** (prefixed by _VARNAME) into the queue.

15   Push **finisparm** (prefixed by _FINIS) into the queue.

16   End STEM processing.

17   Process FINIS keyword processing.

18   Perform no processing if **kywd** is empty. This statement is required for syntax reasons.

19   Any other **kywd** value is invalid. Exit with error code 4.

20   End of the inner-SELECT block.

21   End of DISKW processing.

22   Any other **op** value is invalid. Exit with error code 2.

23   End of the outer-SELECT block.

24   Push **filename** (prefixed by _FILENAME) into the queue.

25   Push **op** (prefixed by _OP) into the queue.

26   Push **lines** (prefixed by _LINES) into the queue.

27   Invoke the internal PerformIO function.

28   Terminate the SUBCOM routine.

29   Entry-point for PerformIO internal function.

30   Retrieve each queued entry.

31   Place the value into the stem variable x. . The keyword is the second part of the stem variable; for example, X._OP. When all the queued entries have been retrieved, each keyword can be directly retrieved from the variable pool using its name (associative storage).

32   Reset the previous queue to be the current queue.

33   If an asterisk denotes the number of lines, **ct** is set to a high-value, otherwise the explicit count is used.

34   Open a SELECT-block.

35   Perform DISKW processing.

36   Position to write at the start of the output file.

37   If the symbol X._VARNAME does not contain a value (i.e., is a literal), process the next block.

38   Terminate the block if there are no entries remaining in the queue.

39   Otherwise get the next entry from the queue, and write it to the output file.

40   End of the block from statement 37.

41   Process the stem variables – i is the stem variable number.

42   If the compound variable does not exist (i.e., its name is a literal), terminate the loop.

43   Write the value of the compound variable to the file.

44   End of the block from statement 41.

45   Close the output file if the FINIS keyword has been specified.

46   End of the DISKW processing.

47   Otherwise, exit with error code -1 (unsupported operation).

48   End of the SELECT-block.

49   Normal function return.

13.2.3 Sample Exec Invocation

```
/* REXX */
/* set data */
B.1 = 'delta'
B.2 = 'epsilon'
B.3 = 'beta'
CALL SUBCOM "EXECIO * DISKW data.txt (stem b. finis"
IF RC = 0 THEN SAY "write ok"
```

Part 2

Advanced REXX

14

REXXUTIL Utility Functions

14.1 INTRODUCTION

Most REXX implementations have a number of extensions that do not belong to the SAA definition of the REXX language. In OS/2 these extensions are contained in the REXXUTIL **utility function package**. REXXUTIL functions are typically used for: software installation procedures, profile editors, initialization settings backup routines, etc.

REXXUTIL is a DLL package that contains OS/2-specific functions. These functions can be grouped into the categories:

- access profile variables (SysIni)
- perform message processing (RxMessageBox, SysGetMessage)
- perform miscellaneous processing (SysDropFuncs, SysOS2Ver, SysSetIcon, SysSleep, SysWaitNamedPipe)
- perform text-mode terminal input and output (SysCls, SysCurPos, SysCurState, SysGetKey)
- process Workplace Shell (WPS) classes and objects (SysCreateObject, SysDeregisterObjectClass, SysDestroyObject, SysSetObjectData, SysQueryClassList, SysRegisterObjectClass)
- process extended attributes (SysGetEA, SysPutEA, SysTextScreenRead, SysTextScreenSize)
- process files and directories (SysDriveInfo, SysDriveMap, SysFileDelete, SysFileTree, SysFileSearch, SysMkDir, SysRmDir, SysSearchPath, SysTempFileName),

and give REXX execs access to many useful OS/2 control program services.

Note: The options for REXXUTIL functions cannot be abbreviated. For example, the option FREE for the SysDriveMap function must be written as such.

14.1.1 Registration of REXX Utility Functions

REXXUTIL functions must first be registered before they can be used. The registration applies to the complete OS/2 environment. This registration can be made in two ways:

- The required functions are registered individually.
- The complete library of utility functions is registered.

RexxUtil is the library name. The external function name and the handler name are identical for REXXUTIL functions. The STARTUP.CMD procedure can contain the registration code for frequently used function.

For example, the SysCls function is registered as follows:

```
CALL RxFuncAdd 'SysCls', 'RexxUtil', 'SysCls'
```

The SysLoadFuncs function registers the complete REXXUTIL library:

```
CALL RxFuncAdd 'SysLoadFuncs', 'RexxUtil', 'SysLoadFuncs'
CALL SysLoadFuncs
```

Chapter 17 contains a detailed description of the RXFUNCADD function.

14.1.2 Access Profile Variables

OS/2 makes wide use of profile files to contain nontemporary information for programs, the Workplace Shell, etc. The information in these profile files is retained between OS/2 startups. The programmer can also use his own (nonsystem) profile files; for example, to pass data between execs in different sessions (a form of global variables).

SysIni	Access profile variables.

14.1.3 Perform Message Processing

OS/2 REXX has two functions to access OS/2 message files; the MKMSGF (make message file) utility is used to create message file entries. The RxMessageBox function can only be invoked in the a Presentation Manager (PM) environment; e.g., PMREXX.

RxMessageBox	Display a message box.
SysGetMessage	Retrieve message from a message file.

14.1.4 Perform Text-Mode Terminal Input and Output

The REXXUTIL library contains functions that provide limited full-screen support:

SysCls	Clear screen.
SysCurPos	Move cursor.
SysCurState	Set cursor status.
SysGetKey	Read keyboard input.

SysTextScreenRead	Read characters from screen.
SysTextScreenSize	Get screen size.

14.1.5 Process Workplace Shell (WPS) Classes and Objects

WPS is the user's interface to the OS/2 paradigm. REXXUTIL provides functions to automate the WPS processing; e.g., for program installation routines.

SysCreateObject	Create an object.
SysDeregisterObjectClass	Deregister an object class.
SysDestroyObject*	Delete an object.
SysQueryClassList	Retrieve object class list.
SysRegisterObjectClass	Register object class.
SysSetObjectData*	Alter settings of an object.

* OS/2 2.1.

14.1.6 Process Extended Attributes

OS/2 makes extensive use of extended attributes to contain file-specific data. For example, REXX stores tokenized (preprocessed) execs as extended attributes. The programmer can also use application-specific extended attribute variables to store file-specific information.

SysGetEA	Read file extended attribute.
SysPutEA	Write file extended attribute.

14.1.7 Process Files and Directories

Some of these functions duplicate standard OS/2 commands, but provide information that can be more easily processed in REXX execs. Other functions provide searching facilities, at both file name and content level.

SysDriveInfo	Return drive information.
SysDriveMap	Return accessible drives.
SysFileDelete	Delete a file.
SysFileTree	Find file.
SysFileSearch	Find text string.
SysMkDir	Create a file directory.
SysRmDir	Remove (delete) a file directory.
SysSearchPath	Search path for file.
SysTempFileName	Generate a unique file name.

14.1.8 Miscellaneous Functions
The remaining functions do not fit into any of the previous categories:

SysDropFuncs	Drop (deregister) all REXXUTIL functions.
SysOS2Ver	Return OS/2 version.
SysSetIcon	Associate an icon with a file.
SysSleep	Set interval wait.
SysWaitNamedPipe	Perform wait on named pipe.

14.2 REXX UTILITY FUNCTION DEFINITIONS

This section contains a detailed description of the REXXUTIL functions. Extended descriptions (and sample uses) are provided for those functions whose usefulness may not be immediately apparent.

Most functions return a value that is either the function result or the processing status. For functions that process files, 3 indicates that the file (path) was not found.

14.2.1 RxMessageBox – Display a PM Message Box
Display a PM message box. RxMessageBox can only be used by a PM application or from an exec invoked with the PMREXX command.

Syntax:

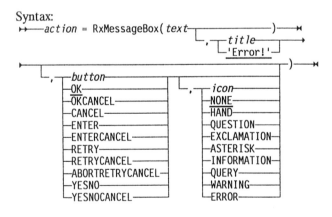

text

        Message box text.

title

        Message box title. Default: Error!.

button

The message box button style:

OK	a single OK button (the default)
OKCANCEL	an OK button and a CANCEL button
CANCEL	a single CANCEL button
ENTER	a single ENTER button
ENTERCANCEL	an ENTER button and a CANCEL button
RETRYCANCEL	a RETRY button and a CANCEL button
ABORTRETRYCANCEL	an ABORT button, a RETRY button, and a CANCEL button (described in the documentation, but not currently implemented)
YESNO	a YES button and a NO button
YESNOCANCEL	a YES button, a NO button, and a CANCEL button

icon

The message box icon style:

NONE	no icon (the default)
HAND*	a hand (the error icon is displayed)
QUESTION*	a question mark (?)
EXCLAMATION*	an exclamation mark (!)
ASTERISK	an asterisk (*)
INFORMATION	the information icon
QUERY*	the query icon (same as QUESTION)
WARNING*	the warning icon (same as EXCLAMATION)
ERROR*	the error icon

*The acoustical signal sounds.

action

Code for the selected message box button:

1	the OK button was pressed
2	the CANCEL button was pressed
3	the ABORT button was pressed
4	the RETRY button was pressed
5	the IGNORE button was pressed
6	the YES button was pressed
7	the NO button was pressed
9	the ENTER button was pressed

Example:
```
action = RxMessageBox('alpha','hand','OKCANCEL','HAND')
```

14.2.2 SysCls – Clear Screen
Clear the screen. The SysCls function has no parameters.

Example:
```
CALL SysCls
```

14.2.3 SysCreateObject – Create an Object
Create a new class instance. This function corresponds to the OS/2 WinCreateObject function.

Note: The SysCreateObject function can be used to execute a DOS program, etc. (see Example 2).

Syntax:

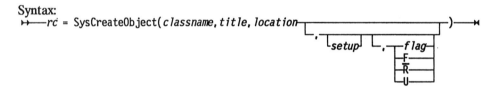

classname
>   The registered object class name.

title
>   The object title. The line-feed character ('0a'x) can be used to split the title onto the next line (see Example 1).

location
>   The object location. The location may be a descriptive path (e.g., C:\OS|2 2.0 Desktop\Toolkit), file path, or folder name.
>
>   Location ids of predefined system folders:
>
> | | |
> |---|---|
> | <WP_CONFIG> | the System Setup folder |
> | <WP_DESKTOP> | the Desktop |
> | <WP_DRIVES> | the Drives folder |
> | <WP_INFO> | the Information folder |
> | <WP_NOWHERE> | the hidden folder |
> | <WP_OS2SYS> | the System folder |
> | <WP_START> | the Setup folder |
> | <WP_TEMPS> | the Templates folder |

setup
>   Setup argument list. Each item in the list is terminated with a semicolon. The list may not contain blanks between the entries.

flag

> The creation flag (only the first character is significant):
>
> F (FailIfExists)   the object creation will fail if the object already exists (default)
>
> R (ReplaceIfExists)the object information will be replaced if the object already exists
>
> U (UpdateIfExists) the object information will be updated if the object already exists.

rc

> The WinCreateObject return code:
>
> 0 (FALSE) Object has not been created.
>
> 1 (TRUE) Object has been created.

14.2.3.1 Class Arguments. The most frequently used application classes (workplace objects) are:

WPFolder	Folder object class.
WPProgram	Program object class. Program class objects are executable programs that can be run by double-clicking the program object. System-defined program objects include: DOS Full Screen, DOS Window, OS/2 Full Screen, OS/2 Window (all in the Command Prompts folder), all objects in the Productivity folder, some objects in the Information folder, and so on.
WPShadow	Shadow object class. A shadow class object is linked to another object class. There are no system-created instances of this class.

The **setup**-string consists of keyname = value pairs supported by the appropriate class. With the exception of the OBJECTID parameter, all parameters have safe defaults.

These three classes are derived from the WPObject class. The classes have setup parameters that are common to the WPObject class, and those specific to the class.

WPObject setup parameters

OBJECTID	*<objectid>*	**objectid** is the unique identifier to be assigned to the object.
ICONFILE	*filename*	**filename** (path) contains the object's icon.
HELPPANEL	*id*	**id** is the object's default help panel.
TEMPLATE	YES	Create the object as a template.
	NO	Do not create the object as a template.
ICONRESOURCE	*id,module*	The object's icon – **id** identifies an icon resource in the **module** (DLL) library.
ICONPOS	*x,y*	The initial icon position – **x** and **y** are expressed as percentages.

VIEWBUTTON	HIDE	Object has hide button.
	MINIMIZE	Object has minimize button.
MINWIN		Object's action on minimization:
	HIDE	Object will hide.
	VIEWER	Object will minimize to the minimized object viewer.
	DESKTOP	Object will minimize to the Desktop viewer.
CONCURRENTVIEW	YES	Open views of the object will be created on open.
	NO	Open views of the object will reappear on open.
OPEN		Object's open action on creation:
	DEFAULT	Open default view.
	SETTINGS	Open settings view.

The following parameters can take the value YES or NO, where NO implies a double negative (e.g., NODELETE=NO means delete):

NODELETE	Do not allow object to be deleted.
NOCOPY	Do not allow object to be copied.
NOMOVE	Do not allow object to be moved to another folder.
NOSHADOW	Do not allow shadow to be created.
NOTVISIBLE	Do not display object.
NOPRINT	Do not allow object to be printed.
NORENAME	Do not allow object to be renamed.
NODRAG	Do not allow object to be dragged.
NOLINK	Do not allow a object to be linked.

WPFolder setup parameters

ICONVIEW	FLOWED	Icon view flowed.
	NONFLOWED	Icon view nonflowed.
	NOLINES	No grid lines.
WORKAREA	YES	Folder is a Workarea.

WPProgram setup parameters

EXENAME	*filename*	**filename** is the fully qualified executable program name (with extension).
PARAMETERS	*args*	**args** specifies the individual arguments to be passed to the program. **args** may include substitution characters that are prompted for in a window: ? prompts for input, [ ] displays prompt text.
STARTUPDIR	*pathname*	**pathname** is the fully qualified name of the working directory.

PROGTYPE		the session type:
	FULLSCREEN	OS/2 full screen
	PM	Presentation Manager
	SEPARATEWIN	WIN-OS2 window running in a separate VDM (virtual DOS machine)
	VDM	DOS full screen
	WIN	WIN-OS2 full screen
	WINDOWABLEVIO	OS/2 window
	WINDOWEDVDM	DOS window
	WINDOWEDWIN	WIN-OS2 window.
MINIMIZED	YES	Start program minimized.
MAXIMIZED	YES	Start program maximized.
NOAUTOCLOSE		Window processing on program termination:
	YES	Do not close.
	NO	Close.
ASSOCFILTER	*filters*	The filename filters for the files associated with this program – multiple filters are separated by commas.
ASSOCTYPE	*type*	The type of files associated with this program – multiple items are separated by commas.
HELPLIBRARY	*filename*	**filename** is the object's help library.

DOS session settings are made using the SET keyword with the required setting specified as keyname = parameter. The parameter is either a value (e.g., SET DOS_FILES=20) or a binary setting: 1 (ON), 0 (OFF) (e.g., SET DOS_BACKGROUND_EXECUTION=1). DOS_DEVICE entries are separated with the line-feed ('0a'x) character.

WPShadow setup parameters

SHADOWID	*<objectname>*	The object for which this object is a shadow. **objectname** is the base object's id (OBJECTID).
	filename	**filename** is the fully qualified file name.

Example 1 (create a folder, and place objects in it):
```
/* create a folder */
LF = '0a'x /* line-feed */
classname = 'WPFolder'
title = '"C"'LF'Folder' /* split heading over two lines */
location = '<WP_DESKTOP>'
setup = 'OBJECTID=<C_FOLDER>;ICONFILE=c:\c.ico;'
CALL BuildObject
```

```
/* place program objects in the folder */
classname = 'WPProgram'
title = 'C Set/2 Help'
location = '<C_FOLDER>'
setup = 'EXENAME=c:\os2\view.exe;'||,
        'PARAMETERS=dde4help.inf;'||,
        'OBJECTID=<C_HELP>;'||,
        'STARTUPDIR=c:\ibmc\help;'
CALL BuildObject

classname = 'WPProgram'
title = 'C Compile'
location = '<C_FOLDER>'
setup = 'PROGTYPE=WINDOWABLEVIO;'||,
        'EXENAME=icc.exe;'||,
        'PARAMETERS=/c [Enter program name];'||,
        'STARTUPDIR=c:\pgm;'||,
        'NOAUTOCLOSE=YES;'
CALL BuildObject
EXIT

BuildObject:
  CALL SysCreateObject classname,title,location,setup,'R'
  RETURN
```

This example creates a folder with title C Folder (spread over two lines) and C.ICO
icon. Two program class entries (class WPProgram) for help and compilation are placed
in this folder (location <C_FOLDER>).

Example 2 (execute a DOS program):

```
classname = 'WPProgram'
title = 'DOS program'
location = '<WP_NOWHERE>' /* hidden folder */
setup = 'EXENAME=C:\PGM\C2.EXE;'||, /* DOS program name */
        'PROGTYPE=WINDOWEDVDM;'||, /* DOS session type (windowed) */
        'STARTUPDIR=C:\;'||, /* startup directory */
        'SET DOS_FILES=20;'||, /* DOS settings */
        'OPEN=DEFAULT;' /* open instance; i.e., execute DOS program */
CALL SysCreateObject classname,title,location,setup,'R'
"EXIT" /* return to desktop */
```

This example creates a program class entry in the hidden folder (<WP_NOWHERE>). This
entry (the DOS program C:\PGM\C2.EXE) is to be executed on its creation
(OPEN=DEFAULT).

14.2.4 SysCurPos – Move Cursor

Return the current cursor position after moving the cursor to the specified row and column (optional).

Syntax:

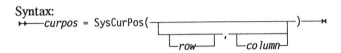

row

The new row number; 0 is the top line on the screen.

column

The new column number; 0 is the leftmost screen column.

curpos

The current (new) column position; in the form "row column".

Example:
```
pos = SysCurPos() /* return current cursor position */
pos = SysCurPos(0,0) /* place cursor at the first screen position */
```

14.2.5 SysCurState – Set Cursor Status

Set the cursor status to visible or hidden.

Syntax:
```
⊢⊢——CALL SysCurState ——ON——————⊢
                      └─OFF─┘
```

ON

Make the cursor visible (display mode).

OFF

Hide the cursor.

Example:
```
CALL SysCurState 'OFF' /* hide cursor */
```

14.2.6 SysDeregisterObjectClass – Deregister an Object Class

Deregister an object class.

Syntax:
```
⊢⊢——rc = SysDeregisterObjectClass(classname)——⊢
```

classname

> The object class name.

rc

> The `WinDeregisterObjectClass` return code:
> 0 (FALSE) Object has not been deregistered.
> 1 (TRUE) Object has been deregistered.

Example:

    CALL SysDeregisterObjectClass 'UserREXX'

14.2.7 SysDestroyObject – Delete an Object (OS/2 2.1)
Delete an object.

Syntax:
►►──*rc* = SysDestroyObject(*objectid*)──►◄

objectid

> The object identifier (<OBJECTID> parameter).

rc

> The return code:
> 0 (FALSE) Object has not been destroyed (e.g., object does not exist).
> 1 (TRUE) Object has been destroyed.

Example:

    CALL SysDestroyObject '<USER_FOLDER>'
The <USER_FOLDER> object is deleted.

14.2.8 SysDriveInfo – Return Drive Information
Return drive information.

Syntax:
►►──*result* = SysDriveInfo(*drive*)──►◄

drive

> The drive whose information is required. For example, c:.

result

> The drive information in the form:
>
> drive: free total label

drive: the drive identifier
free   the unused space (bytes) on the drive
total   the total drive size
label   the drive label

A null string (") is returned if the drive is not accessible.

Example:
```
info = SysDriveInfo('d:')
```

returns information of the form
```
D:  15108096      33454080      DELTA
```

14.2.9 SysDriveMap – Return Accessible Drives
Return a list of the accessible drives.

Syntax:

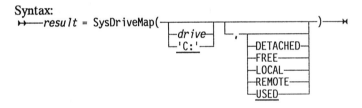

drive
> The last drive to be accessed. Default: C:.

option
> The drive-map option:

> DETACHED   the detached LAN resources
> FREE   the drives that are free
> LOCAL   the local drives
> REMOTE   the remote drives
> USED   the accessible or in-use drives

result
> A string of the drive letters (each separated by a blank).

Example:
```
map1 = SysDriveMap('d:')
map2 = SysDriveMap(,'free')
```

This example returns information of the form:
```
D: E: F: G:,
H: I: J: K: L: M: N: O: P: Q: R: S: T: U: V: W: X: Y: Z:, respectively
```

14.2.10 SysDropFuncs – **Drop (Deregister) All REXXUTIL Functions**

Drop all REXXUTIL functions; that is, make the REXXUTIL uncallable. The SysDropFuncs function has no parameters.

Example:

```
CALL SysDropFuncs
```

14.2.11 SysFileDelete – **Delete a File**

Delete a file with fully qualified filename. The SysFileDelete function performs equivalent processing to the DEL command, except no message is issued if an error occurs.

Syntax:

```
►►──rc = SysFileDelete(filename)──►◄
```

filename

> The fully-qualified filename of the file to be deleted.

rc

> The SysFileDelete return code:
> 0   ok, file deleted
> nonzero   file not deleted (not found, invalid parameter, etc.)

Example:

```
rc = SysFileDelete('c:test.dat')
```

14.2.12 SysFileTree – **Find File**

Return a list of all files that match the file specification.

Syntax:

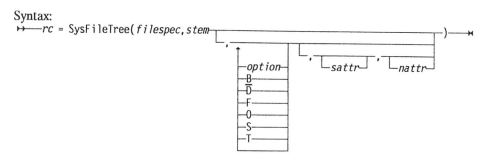

filespec

> The generic file search specification. The search specification can include meta-characters.
> For example, c:*.cmd – search the C disk for cmd files.

stem

The stem variable into which the information for the matching files is to be stored. **stem**.0 is returned with the number of matching files found.

option

The search criteria (one or more from the list):

B	Search for both directories and files (default).
D	Search only for directories.
F	Search only for files.
0	Return only the file specifications. Default: date, time, size attributes, and file specification.
S	Search subdirectories.
T	Return date and time (in the form: yy/mm/dd/hh/mm).

For example, 'FT' – search only for files, and return date and time.

sattr

The selection mask attributes. Only those files with matching attributes will be returned. The position in the mask corresponds to the attributes: archive, directory, hidden, read-only, and system, respectively. The mask may contain the characters:

*	Setting not tested.
+	Attribute must be set.
–	Attribute must not be set.

***** is the default mask.

Examples

--+-+	Select only those files with hidden or system attributes set.
***+*	Select the read-only files.

nattr

The new mask attributes. The matching files will receive these attributes. The position in the mask corresponds to the attributes: archive, directory, hidden, read-only, and system, respectively. The mask may contain the characters:

*	Setting remains unchanged.
+	Attribute will be set.
–	Attribute will be cleared.

***** is the default mask.

Example

***+*	Set all selected files to read-only.

rc

Return code:

0   successful processing

2   insufficient storage

Example:

```
rc = SysFileTree('c:\pgm\*.c',s.,'FT')
IF rc = 0 THEN DO I = 1 TO s.0
  SAY i s.i
END
```

returns information of the form:

```
1 91/10/28/19/35      1167  A----  C:\pgm\CALLREXX.C
2 92/06/19/17/02       304  A----  C:\pgm\CPULL.C
3 92/10/05/18/31       952  A----  C:\pgm\fconcat.c
```

14.2.13. SysF i leSearch – Find Text String

Return a list of all lines in a file that contain the specified text string.

Syntax:

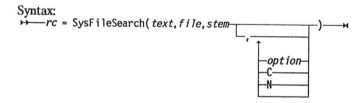

text

The text string argument.

file

The file to be searched.

stem

The stem variable into which the matching lines are to be stored. **stem.0** is returned with the number of matching lines found.

option

One or more options from the list:

C   Perform a case-sensitive search (default is case-insensitive).

N   Also return line number.

rc

> Return code:
> 0   successful processing
> 2   insufficient storage
> 3   file open error

Example:

```
rc = SysFileSearch('exit','c:\pgm\fexit.c',s.,'NC')
IF rc = 0 THEN DO I = 1 TO s.0
  SAY i s.i
END
```

displays information of the form:

```
1 1 /* fexit.c - register system exit and invoke command */
2 7 #define INCL_RXSYSEXIT /* system exit definitions */
3 12 char exitname[] = "CMD";
4 13 char exitmodname[] = "URX";
5 21 RXSYSEXIT sysexit[2];
```

14.2.14 SysGetEA – Read File Extended Attribute
Return the extended attribute for the specified file.

Syntax:
>>──rc = SysGetEA(*file, eaname, varname*)──><

file

> The file to be processed.

eaname

> The extended attribute name.
> The standard extended attribute (SEA) names are: .ASSOCTABLE, .CODEPAGE, .COMMENTS, .HISTORY, .ICON, .KEYPHRASES, .LONGNAME, .SUBJECT, .TYPE, .VERSION. The SysPutEA function contains a more extensive description of standard extended attributes. User extended attribute names should not start with a period.

varname

> The REXX variable into which the extended attribute value is to be placed.

rc

> Return code:
> 0   successful processing
> nonzero error (the OS/2 return code)

Example 1:
```
rc = SysGetEA('c:test.fil','.TYPE','var')
```

This example returns the standard extended attribute type for the file C:TEST.FIL in the variable VAR.

Example 2:
```
rc = SysGetEA('c:test.fil','author','var')
```

This example returns the value of the user extended attribute AUTHOR in the variable VAR.

14.2.15 SysGetKey – Read Keyboard Input
Read the next character from the keyboard buffer. If the keyboard buffer is empty, SysGetKey will wait for input.

Syntax:

ECHO
Echo (display) the pressed key.
NOECHO
Do not echo the pressed key.

key

The pressed key. The value '00'x or 'e0'x indicates that one of the extended keys was pressed (e.g., Alt-1) – a further call to SysGetKey is necessary to get the extended data (see Example 2).

Example 1:
```
key = SysGetKey('NOECHO')
```

This example returns the input character in the variable KEY (without display).

Example 2:
```
key = SysGetKey('NOECHO')
IF key = '00'x /* extended character */
  THEN key = SysGetKey('NOECHO')
IF key = 'e0'x /* extended character */
  THEN key = SysGetKey('NOECHO')
```

This example also returns the extended character.

14.2.16 SysGetMessage – Retrieve Message from System Message File

Retrieve a message from an OS/2 message file. The OS/2 2.0 Toolkit MKMSGF utility is used to create message files.

Syntax:

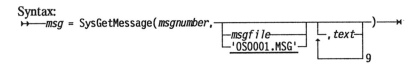

msgnumber
>   The number of the message whose text is to be retrieved.

msgfile
>   The name of the message file that contains the message. Default: 0S0001.MSG.

text

>   A text variable that is to be inserted into the message. Up to nine text variables can be inserted into the message text.

msg

>   The retrieved message with the inserted text.

Example:
```
msg1 = SysGetMessage(200,'c:\pgm\msgfile.msg')
msg2 = SysGetMessage(201,'c:\pgm\msgfile.msg','alpha','beta')
msg3 = SysGetMessage(201,'c:\pgm\msgfile.msg')
msg4 = SysGetMessage(100)
```
returns (200 and 201 are assumed to be user-written messages)
```
test message
MSG0201: abort alpha beta program
MSG0201: abort %1 %2 program
SYS0100: Cannot create another system semaphore,
```
respectively.

14.2.17 SysIni – Access Profile Variables

The OS/2 profile variables are stored as binary files. These files are retained between OS/2 startups, but also can be used between sessions. The SysIni function provides similar access to the profile variables as the PrfOpenProfile, PrfCloseProfile, PrfQueryProfile..., and PrfWriteProfile... system APIs.

Syntax:

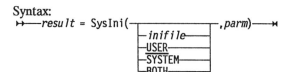

parm:

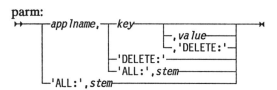

Note: All **parm** entries are case-sensitive.

inifile

The profile file to be accessed; **inifile** may be a file specification or one of the parameters:

USER	The user profile file (OS2\OS2.INI). Default.
SYSTEM	The system profile file (OS2\OS2SYS.INI).
BOTH	Both the user and system profile files are searched.

Warning: Because the system profile files (SYSTEM, USER) contain important operational information, the user should not change their contents; the user should use application-specific files (see Example 1 and 2).

parm

The processing option. The keyword (DELETE:, ALL:), or its absence, and the presence of the **value** operand specifies the processing to be performed:

key and **value**	Set **key** to **value**.
key and no **value**	Retrieve **key** (as function **result**).
ALL: and **applname**	Retrieve all values for application **applname** as stem variable **stem**.
ALL: and no **applname**	Retrieve all application values as stem variable **stem**.
DELETE: and **key**	Delete the value for **key** in application **applname**.
DELETE: and no **key**	Delete all values for application **applname**.

applname

The application name used to store the profile information. Application names beginning with PM_ are reserved for system use.

key

The keyword name for the profile item.

value

The keyword value for the profile item.

stem

The name of the REXX stem variable that is to receive the profile information. **stem.**0 is returned with the number of items found.

result

One of the values:

" (null string)   profile variable set or deleted
ERROR: an error occurred
value   for single value retrieval

Example 1:
```
result1 = SysIni('c:\pgm\user.ini','test','alpha','beta')
result2 = SysIni('c:\pgm\user.ini','test','alpha')
result3 = SysIni('c:\pgm\user.ini','test','alpha','DELETE:')
result4 = SysIni('c:\pgm\user.ini','test','alpha')
```

return

(null string)
beta
(null string)
ERROR:,

respectively.

This example uses an application-specific profile (C:\PGM\USER.INI).

Example 2:
```
/* rexx – rx1.cmd */
va = 1
CALL SysIni 'c:\user.ini','appl','va',va /* set value */
CALL rx2
va = SysIni('c:\user.ini','appl','va') /* get value */
SAY va /* 2 */

/* rexx – rx2.cmd */
va = SysIni('c:\user.ini','appl','va') /* get value */
SAY va /* 1 */
va = 2
CALL SysIni 'c:\user.ini','appl','va',va /* set value */
RETURN
```

This example illustrates the use of an application profile to pass data between execs. The variable VA is passed between the two execs (global variable). Although in this example the first exec directly invokes the second exec, the same method can be used to pass data between execs (or programs) in other sessions.

Example 3:
```
result = SysIni('USER','ALL:',s.)
IF result = '' THEN DO i = 1 TO s.0
  SAY i s.i
END
```
This example lists all applications for a specific profile (OS2\OS2.INI).

Example 4:
```
result = SysIni('USER','PM_National','ALL:',s.)
IF result = '' THEN DO i = 1 TO s.0
  SAY i s.i
END
```
This example lists all entries for a specific application (PM_National).

Example 5:
```
key = 'iCountry'
result = SysIni('USER','PM_National',key)
SAY key result
```
This example lists the value for a specific application key (PM_National, iCountry). For example, 1 = USA, 49 = Germany.

Example 6:
```
result = SysIni('USER','PM_National','iMeasurement',2)
```
This example sets the value for a specific application key. Here the measurement system is set to 2 (metric).

Note: Many USER and SYSTEM application variables require special values; e.g., '3000'x and '3100'x to disable or enable the print screen function, respectively.
```
result = SysIni('USER','PM_ControlPanel','PrintScreen','3000'x)
```
Furthermore, many settings are active only after the computer has been rebooted.

14.2.18 SysMkDir – Create a File Directory
Create directory. SysMkDir performs equivalent processing to the MD command, except no message is issued if an error occurs.

Syntax:
↦──*rc* = SysMkDir(*dirspec*)──⊣

dirspec

The directory specification.

rc

The function return code:

0	directory created
5	access denied
26	not a DOS (OS/2) disk
87	invalid parameter
108	drive locked
206	file name exceeds range (e.g., more than 8 characters for FAT disk)

Example:

```
rc = SysMkDir("c:\xx")
```

14.2.19 SysOS2Ver – Return OS/2 Version

Return information pertaining to the current OS/2 version. The SysOS2Ver function has no parameters.

Syntax:

$\rightarrowtail\!\!-result = \text{SysOS2Ver()}\!-\!\!\!\rightarrowtail$

result

The OS/2 version: 'vv.r' (vv = version, r = release).

Example:

```
ver = SysOS2Ver()
```

returns, for example, 2.00 in the variable VER.

14.2.20 SysPutEA – Write File Extended Attribute

Write the extended attribute for the specified file.

Syntax:

$\rightarrowtail\!\!-rc = \text{SysPutEA}(file, eaname, value)\!-\!\!\!\rightarrowtail$

file

The file to be processed.

eaname

The extended attribute name. Standard extended attribute names (see Section 14.2.20.1) commence with a period. User-specific extended attribute names should be chosen in accordance with some scheme.

value

The extended attribute value.

rc

Return code:
0   successful processing
nonzero   error (the OS/2 return code)

Example:

```
rc = SysPutEA('c:test.fil','author','asr')
```

sets the AUTHOR user extended attribute for the file C:TEST.FIL to asr.

14.2.20.1 Standard Extended Attributes. The OS/2 operating system has ten standard extended attributes (SEAs):

.ASSOCTABLE	information (type, extension (optional), icon data (optional)) for applications with the associated data files – one or more multivalued, multityped information blocks (each information block is itself a multivalued, multityped entry)
.CODEPAGE	the code page for the file
.COMMENTS	general notes for the file
.HISTORY	modification history
.ICON	icon data for the file
.KEYPHRASES	keytext phrases (multivalues)
.LONGNAME	long file name
.SUBJECT	file description
.TYPE	file type (user-defined or one of the predefined types: Plain Text, OS/2 Command File, DOS Command File, Executable, Metafile, Bitmap, Icon, Binary Data, Dynamic Link Library, C Code, Pascal Code, COBOL Code, FORTRAN Code, Assembler Code, Library, Resource File, Object Code)
.VERSION	file version number (ASCII or binary)

These attributes can be associated with an application (program, file, etc.). The .ASSOCTABLE and .TYPE are of most interest to the application developer, and only these SEAs will be discussed in more detail, although the general considerations apply to all SEAs.

Depending on their type, SEAs may contain either ASCII, binary data, or both. There are three types of SEA data fields:

- multivalued, multityped
  (EAT_MVMT, code-page, number of entries, data type, data, data type, data, ...)
- multivalued, single type
  (EAT_MVST, code-page, number of entries, data type, data, data, ...)
- ASN.1 data type
  (ISO ASN.1 multivalued data stream)

With the exception of the data entries, all entries are a binary word (2 bytes). The data type has one of the values:

- EAT_MVMT   'DFFF'x   multivalued, multityped
- EAT_MVST   'DEFF'x   multivalued, single type
- EAT_BINARY   'FEFF'x   binary data
- EAT_ASCII   'FDFF'x   ASCII data.

The other data types are not discussed here.

Each data field starts with a binary word that contains the length of the following data. Binary data fields must be specified in the format appropriate for the Intel hardware architecture (byte reversed); e.g., the binary word 4 is specified as '0400'x.

Example 1:

```
EAT_MVMT = 'dfff'x
EAT_ASCII = 'fdff'x
EAT_BINARY = 'feff'x
EAF_DEFAULTOWNER = '0100'x /* flag */
Type = 'WORD'
FileExt = 'DOC'
info = EAT_MVMT||,
       '0000 0100'x||, /* 0 code page, 1 block */
       EAT_MVMT||,
       '0000 0300'x||, /* 0 code page, 3 entries */
       EAT_ASCII||,
       D2C(LENGTH(Type))||'00'x||, /* length */
       Type||, /* type */
       EAT_ASCII||,
       D2C(LENGTH(FileExt))||'00'x||, /* length */
       FileExt||, /* extension */
       EAT_BINARY||,
       '0200'x||, /* length */
       EAF_DEFAULTOWNER /* flags */
rc = SysPutEA("c:\word5\word.exe",".ASSOCTABLE",info)
```

This exec associates both the application type WORD and the extension DOC with the program WORD.EXE.

Example 2:

```
EAT_ASCII = 'fdff'x
EAT_MVMT = 'dfff'x
type = 'WORD'
info = EAT_MVMT||,
       '0000 0100'x||, /* 0 code page, 1 entry */
       EAT_ASCII||,
       D2C(LENGTH(type))||'00'x||, /* length */
       type
rc = SysPutEA("c:a.txt",".TYPE",info)
```

This exec sets the file C:A.TXT to be a WORD file.

14.2.21 SysQueryClassList – Retrieve Object Class List
Retrieve the list of the registered object classes.

Syntax:
```
►►──CALL SysQueryClassList stem──►◄
```

stem

> The stem variable into which the retrieved object classes (class name and module name) are to be placed. **stem**.0 is set to contain the number of returned items.

Example:

```
CALL SysQueryClassList s.
DO i = 1 TO s.0
  SAY i s.i
END
```

returns information of the form:

```
1 Mindex MINXOBJ
2 WPTouch TCP
3 WPPrinter WPPRINT
4 WPSpool WPPRINT
```

14.2.22 SysRegisterObjectClass – Register Object Class
Create a new object class.

Syntax:
```
►►──rc = SysRegisterObjectClass(classname,modulename)──►◄
```

classname

> The object class name.

modulename
> The module file that contains the object definition. The object definition must have been created with SOM (System Object Model).

rc
> The WinRegisterObjectClass return code:
> 0 (FALSE) Object has not been registered.
> 1 (TRUE) Object has been registered.

Example:
> rc = SysRegisterObjectClass('UserREXX','c:\urexx\urexx.dll')

14.2.23 SysRmDir – Remove (Delete) a File Directory
Delete directory. SysRmDir performs equivalent processing to the RD command, except that no message is issued if an error occurs.

Syntax:
> ⊢⊢──*rc* = SysMkDir(*dirspec*)──⊣

dirspec
> The directory specification.

rc
> The function return code:
> 0   directory created
> 5   access denied
> 26   not a DOS (OS/2) disk
> 87   invalid parameter
> 108   drive locked
> 206   file name exceeds range

Example:
> rc = SysRmDir("c:\xx")

14.2.24 SysSearchPath – Search Path for File
Search file path for file.

Syntax:
> ⊢⊢──*filespec* = SysSearchPath(*pathname, filename*)──⊣

pathname
> The environment variable that contains the list of file directories to be searched (each file directory is separated by a semicolon).

filename
> The file that is to be searched for.

filespec
> The file specification for the found file. A null value (") indicates that the file was not found.

Example:
```
filespec = SysSearchPath('LIB','rexx.lib')
```

returns, for example, in the variable FILESPEC
```
C:\TOOLKT20\OS2LIB\rexx.lib
```

14.2.25 SysSetIcon – Associate an Icon with a File
Associate an icon with a file.

Syntax:
```
►►──rc = SysSetIcon( filename, iconfilename)───►◄
```

filename
> The file for which the icon is to be associated.

iconfilename
> The file that contains the icon definition.

rc
> The return code:
> 0 (FALSE) error
> 1 (TRUE) icon has been associated.

Example:
```
rc = SysSetIcon('c:\pgm\xx1.cmd','c:\pgm\user.ico')
```

14.2.26 SysSetObjectData – Alter Settings of an Object (OS/2 2.1)
Change an object's characteristics. This function can also be used to open an object instance.

Syntax:
```
►►──rc = SysSetObjectData( objectid, setup)───►◄
```

objectid
> The object identifier (<OBJECTID> parameter).

setup

>   Setup argument list. Section 14.2.3 (SysCreateObject) contains a description of
>   the arguments.

rc

>   The return code:
>   0 (FALSE) Object data have not been changed (e.g., object does not exist).
>   1 (TRUE) Object data have been changed.

Example:
```
      CALL SysSetObjectData '<USER_FOLDER>','OPEN=DEFAULT'
```
The <USER_FOLDER> object is opened.

14.2.27 SysSleep – Set Interval Wait
Pause execution of the REXX exec for the specified interval.

Syntax:
```
 ⊢──CALL SysSleep seconds───⊣
```

seconds

>   The number of seconds in the interval.

Example:
```
      CALL SysSleep 5
```
The exec execution is paused for five seconds.

14.2.28 SysTempFileName – Generate a Unique File Name
Create a unique file or directory name.

Syntax:
```
 ⊢──filename = SysTempFileName(template┬──────────┬)──⊣
                                        └,┬─filter─┘
                                          └'?'─────┘
```

template

>   The template for the form of name to be generated. The template specifies
>   between one and five filter characters (default ?) that are replaced with a
>   numeric value to produce a unique name.

filter

>   The filter character used in **template**. SysTempFileName replaces each filter
>   character with a numeric value.

filename
>   The generated file name. A null string (") is returned if a file name cannot be
>   generated.

Example:
```
fn1 = SysTempFileName('c:\pgm\temp?.???')
fn2 = SysTempFileName('c:\pgm\temp@.@@@','@')
```
returns, for example
```
c:\pgm\temp3.494
c:\pgm\temp7.069
```

14.2.29 SysTextScreenRead – Read Characters from Screen
Read text characters from the specified screen location.

Syntax:
```
►►──string = SysTextScreenRead( row, column──────────)──►◄
                                         └─, length─┘
```

row
>   The screen row; 0 is the top row.

column
>   The screen column; 0 is the leftmost column.

length
>   The number of characters to read. Default: all characters up to the end of the
>   screen.

Example:
```
string = SysTextScreenRead(2,0,25)
```
This example reads into the STRING variable the 25 characters starting at row 2 column
0.

14.2.30 SysTextScreenSize – Get Screen Size
Return the screen size (in character coordinates).

Syntax:
```
►►──size = SysTextScreenSize()──►◄
```

size
>   The screen size returned as row column.

Example:
```
size = SysTextScreenSize()
```

returns, for example, "25 80" in the variable SIZE.

14.2.31 SysWaitNamedPipe – Perform Wait on Named Pipe

Perform a timed wait on the named pipe.

Syntax:

name

The pipe name. Named pipes have names of the form '\PIPE\pipename'.

timeout

The wait interval in microseconds. Special values:

0   The default timeout value.

-1   Wait until the named pipe is not busy.

rc

The DosWaitNPipe return code:

0   The named pipe is no longer busy.

230   Invalid pipe name.

231   Timeout occurred before the named pipe became free.

Example:
```
rc = SysWaitNamedPipe("\PIPE\USERPIPE",0)
IF rc = 0
  THEN "cpgm" /* invoke client program */
  ELSE SAY 'pipe error' rc
```

This example initiates a wait (with default timeout interval) on the specified named pipe (here, \PIPE\USERPIPE). The CPGM client program is invoked when the pipe becomes free; otherwise, an error message is displayed.

14.3 EXAMPLE

The following exec shows how REXXUTIL functions can be used to perform rudimentary full-screen input/output.

Two text fields are displayed on the screen: City: (10,5), and Zip: (11,5). The parenthesized values are the row and column, respectively. The corresponding input data start at column 10 of the appropriate line. The input data entries are displayed on completion of the exec.

Two cursor control keys: Left (←) and Right (→) are fully supported. Three other control keys: Up (↑), Down (↓), and Del are not handled (to avoid introducing unnecessary complexity into the code).

```
/* REXX - rudimentary full-screen support */
CALL RxFuncAdd 'SysLoadFuncs','RexxUtil','SysLoadFuncs'
CALL SysLoadFuncs /* register RexxUtil function package */

CALL SysCls /* clear screen */
CALL SysCurPos 10,5
SAY  "City:"
CALL SysCurPos 11,5
SAY  " Zip:"

CALL GetData 10,10,24 /* city */
CALL GetData 11,10,5 /* zip */
/* get screen data */
city = GetFld(10,10)
zip = GetFld(11,10)
/* display */
CALL SysCurPos 20,1
SAY 'city' city 'zip' zip
EXIT

GetData:
  PARSE ARG line, col, len
  mincol = col /* left bound */
  maxcol = col+len-1 /* right bound */
  CALL SysCurPos line,col
  DO FOREVER
    key = SysGetKey('NOECHO')
    IF key = '0d'x THEN RETURN /* enter */
    IF key = '00'x THEN key = SysGetKey('NOECHO')
    IF key = 'e0'x THEN key = SysGetKey('NOECHO')
    SELECT
      WHEN key = '4b'x /* left */
        THEN DO
          col = col-1
          col = MAX(col,mincol) /* left bound */
          CALL SysCurPos line,col
        END
```

```
     WHEN key = '4d'x /* right */
       THEN DO
         col = col+1
         col = MIN(col,maxcol) /* right bound */
         CALL SysCurPos line,col
       END
     WHEN key = '48'x /* up */
       THEN NOP
     WHEN key = '50'x /* down */
       THEN NOP
     WHEN key = '53'x /* del */
       THEN NOP /* not supported */
     OTHERWISE
       SAY key /* echo */
       col = col+1
       col = MIN(col,maxcol) /* right bound */
       CALL SysCurPos line,col
   END
 END

GetFld:
  str = SysTextScreenRead(ARG(1),ARG(2),80-ARG(2))
  str = STRIP(str,'T',' ')
  RETURN str
```

15

Host Commands

15.1 INTRODUCTION

One of the most important features of REXX is its integration of host environments. The OS/2 commands are the default host environment, but application-specific command handlers can also be used. Chapter 16 describes the requirements for user-written command handlers.

The host command environment processes all statements that are not recognized as REXX instructions. The ADDRESS instruction sets the name of the current host command environment. CMD, the OS/2 command handler, is the initial command environment. The ADDRESS function returns the name of the current host command environment.

15.2 USE OF HOST COMMANDS

The ADDRESS instruction can be used in two ways:

- With a command – the host command environment applies only for the specific instruction.
- Without a command – the host command environment is set globally, and remains until changed.

Example:

```
ADDRESS USER "DEL *" /* USER handler processes the DEL command */
ADDRESS USER /* set USER as global command handler */
"DEL *" /* process by USER handler */
ADDRESS CMD "DEL *" /* process by OS/2 CMD handler */
```

15.2.1 Command Output

Many commands issue terminal output; e.g., the DIR command displays the names of the found files. If this output is to be processed, it can be redirected to a file (> or >> operator) or piped with the RXQUEUE filter to a REXX queue (see Section 12.4).

Some commands have more than one terminal output; normal output on STDOUT, and error messages on STDERR, with the RC variable being set to 0 or 1, respectively. Multiple output can only be redirected to files (see Example 2). OS/2 has three standard file IDs: STDOUT (0), STDIN (1), STDERR (2).

Example 1:
```
ADDRESS CMD
"DIR a: > c:\dirfile"
"DIR a: | RXQUEUE"
```

In both cases the directory output is saved in a REXX-processable form: the C:\DIRFILE file or the current REXX queue, respectively.

Example 2:
```
ADDRESS CMD
"@DIR g: > cout 2>&1" /* redirect STDERR to file */
IF RC <> 0 THEN SAY ' CMD error'
DO WHILE LINES('cout') > 0
  SAY LINEIN('cout')
END
```

The output (both normal and error messages) of the DIR command is written the COUT file, which is subsequently listed with the SAY instruction. The @ preceding the command name causes the display of the command execution to be suppressed.

15.2.2 Distinguishing Between Commands and REXX Instructions

Several REXX instructions have the same names as OS/2 commands; e.g., CALL, EXIT. Such OS/2 commands must be written within quotes or apostrophes in order to be passed to the OS/2 command processor.

Example:
```
CALL time /* invoke REXX routine TIME */
"CALL time" /* invoke the OS/2 procedure TIME */
```

15.2.3 Equivalent REXX Functions

Several OS/2 commands are available as equivalent REXX functions or as REXXUTIL functions. Such functions issue a function return value rather than displaying an error message should an error occur.

Equivalent functions:

DIRECTORY	CD
SysCls	CLS
SysFileDelete	DEL
SysFileTree	DIR
SysFind	FIND
SysMkDir	MD
SysOS2Ver	VER
SysRmDir	RD

15.3 STARTING SESSIONS

There are two program-initiated ways to start sessions:

- the OS/2 Workplace Shell (described in Section 14.2.4)
- the OS/2 START command.

The OS/2 START command is simpler to use, but the Workplace Shell offers additional flexibility to set session parameters.

15.3.1 START Command

The OS/2 START command starts a program in another session. The START command determines the application type and runs it in the appropriate session; however, these defaults can be overridden. The program may be started either directly or through the command processor.

START syntax:

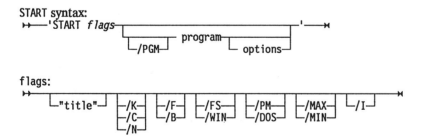

flags:

title

    The window title bar.

/K   Start the session with the command processor, and keep the new session on completion. Default for non-PM application.

/C   Start the session with the command processor, and close the new session on completion.

/N   Start the new session directly. Close the new session on completion. Default for PM application.

/F   Start the session in foreground. Default for /FS, /WIN and /PM.
/B   Start the session in background.

/FS   Full-screen session
/WIN Windowed session

/PM   PM session
/DOS DOS session

/MAX Maximize a windowed session
/MIN Minimize session

/I   The new session inherits the current environment

program
>   The file specification that defines executable program.

options
>   Options to be passed to the application.

15.4 DOS COMMANDS

DOS commands (in the form of a batch file) can be invoked using the START command or the OS/2 Workplace Shell.

Note: When the Workplace Shell is used, the combined size of the EXENAME parameter list and the PARAMETERS list cannot exceed 102 bytes, otherwise the batch file cannot be started (the message erroneously states that insufficient memory is available).

Example 1 (using the START command):
```
'START "DOS program" /B /K /DOS /WIN c:\dosdir.bat C D'
```

Example 2 (using the Workplace Shell):
```
classname = 'WPProgram'
title = 'DOS program'
location = '<WP_NOWHERE>' /* hidden folder */d
setup = 'EXENAME=c:\dosdir.bat;'||,
        'PROGTYPE=WINDOWEDVDM;'||,
        'OPEN=DEFAULT;'||,
        'NOAUTOCLOSE=YES;'||,
        'PARAMETERS=C D;'
CALL SysCreateObject classname,title,location,setup,'R'
```

Both these examples invoke the C:\DOSDIR.BAT batch file with parameter C D as a windowed DOS application (PROGTYPE=WINDOWEDVDM); the PROGTYPE=VDM parameter could be used to invoke a full-screen DOS application.

16

Application Programming Interface (API)

16.1 INTRODUCTION

One of the strengths of REXX is its extensibility. REXX is extendible by allowing programmers to make use of REXX services in their applications. In OS/2, Application Programming Interfaces (APIs) provide these services. APIs are standard functions provided with the product, in this case OS/2 REXX. This book describes the 32-bit APIs provided with OS/2 2.x. The 16-bit APIs provided with OS/2 1.x are still available, but should only be used for old programs that have not been converted (the 32-bit APIs have the advantages of flat addressing, improved performance, and so on). Other than when used in Application Programming Interface, the term *application* in this book refers to programs written in a conventional (non-REXX) programming language. Although the C language is used for the examples in this book, other 32-bit programming languages (such as PL/I) Assembler, can be used.

This book writes the API function names in mixedcase (e.g., RexxRegisterExitExe). The C compiler (C Set/2, see Appendix J) maps mixedcase external names to the required uppercase function names.

The examples shown in this book illustrate the invocation and passing of parameters; the program functionality and error checking are not necessarily representative of practical applications. To enable the standard C functions to be used (e.g., strcpy()), the examples also assume that RXSTRINGs do not contain embedded null-characters. If this is not the case, memory functions (memcmp(), memcpy(), etc.) must be used.

There are two general uses of REXX APIs:

- for an application (*user program*) that makes use of REXX services (e.g., invoke a REXX exec);
- to make an application accessible from a REXX exec (an *external routine*).

The following API classes are available:

- invocation of the REXX interpreter
- subcommand (environment) handlers
- external function handlers
- system exit handlers
- variable pool interface
- macrospace interface
- halt and trace functions

RexxStart, the REXX interpreter API, enables a program to invoke a REXX exec or macrospace exec. The REXX exec code may be contained within the program (an **in-store exec**) to enable a conventional program to make use of REXX services.

External functions are extensions to the standard set of functions, and may be written in REXX or a conventional programming language.

Subcommand handlers process the command passed to them – a command being any non-REXX statement. The ADDRESS instruction specifies the name of the current subcommand (and by implication, the name of the processing handler).

Whether external routines are implemented as subcommands or functions is largely a personal preference. Functions must be used when orthogonality is required; that is, when results are to be used in expressions. Functions are normally chosen when a result is to be returned. Subcommand environments have two advantages over external functions: possible duplicate function names (name-space pollution) are avoided (only one subcommand environment can be active at any one time, even though more than one handler may be concurrently registered); and subcommands are more flexible for the specification of complex argument strings.

System exits are programmed functions that replace the standard routines for certain instructions and exec processing. Named system exits are activated when the REXX interpreter is invoked with the RexxStart function.

The variable pool interface allows programs to access the variables of the currently active REXX exec.

A macrospace is one or more execs preloaded into main-storage. Such macrospaces can be stored as an external file. Macrospaces can significantly improve performance by avoiding disk access when execs are called; for example, as macros for an editor.

The halt and trace functions are used to raise the HALT condition or to change the interactive debugging mode of a running exec.

The OS/2 2.x Toolkit <rexxsaa.h> header file contains the required definitions for REXX-related function prototypes, structures, and so forth. Subsets for particular interface groups can be selected by defining one or more of the following macros:

INCL_REXXSAA	complete REXX support
INCL_RXSUBCOM	REXX subcommand handler support
INCL_RXSHV	REXX shared variable pool support
INCL_RXFUNC	REXX external function support
INCL_RXSYSEXIT	REXX system exit support
INCL_RXMACRO	REXX macrospace support
INCL_RXARI	REXX asynchronous trace/halt support

Example 1:

```
#define INCL_RXFUNC
#define INCL_RXSHV
#include <rexxsaa.h>
```

Include the standard REXX definitions (e.g., RXSTRINGs), and the definitions for external functions and shared variable pool support.

Example 2:

```
#define INCL_REXXSAA
#include <rexxsaa.h>
```

Include the complete REXX definitions.

16.1.1 SAA Application Programming Interfaces

The SAA Procedures Language Level 2 specifies two application programming interfaces:

- the variable pool interface
- the system exits interface

The SAA specification states the services to be provided, but not their implementation. The OS/2 REXX implementation is SAA-conform.

16.1.2 Function Return Value

The API functions return a *function return value*, which indicates the processing status of the function. This return value does not necessarily indicate whether the requested service has been successfully performed – an additional parameter contains this information (where required).

16.2 EXTERNAL PROGRAM ROUTINES

An external program routine can have two forms:

- An EXE-program (routine) contained in the using program (local routine).
- A DLL (dynamic link library) program contained in a DLL (global routine). Such global routines can be used by any REXX program or exec.

External program routines must be *registered* with REXX before they can be used.

16.2.1 Schematic EXE-Program Processing

Figure 16.1 shows the schematic processing for the registration and use of an EXE external function (the "REXX control" entry refers to internal REXX control tables).

16.2.1.1 Registration of an EXE-Program. An EXE program is local to the application using it.

There are registration functions for the three types of EXE external programs (the program type is shown in parentheses):

- RexxRegisterExitExe (system exit)
- RexxRegisterFunctionExe (function)
- RexxRegisterSubcomExe (subcommand environment)

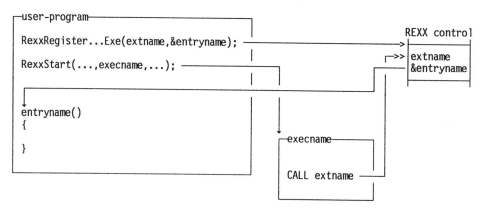

Figure 16.1. Schematic processing for an EXE external function.

Example:

```
#define INCL_RXFUNC /* function definitions */
#include <rexxsaa.h>
#include <stdio.h> /* printf, etc. */
#include <stdlib.h> /* exit */
RexxFunctionHandler fintname; /* function prototype */

int main(void)
```

```
{
  ULONG rc;
  rc = RexxRegisterFunctionExe("fextname",(PFN)fintname);
  if (rc != 0) /* registration error */
  {
    printf("RexxRegisterFunction:%ld\n",rc);
    exit();
  }
}

ULONG APIENTRY fintname(
  PUCHAR     FunctionName,
  ULONG      argc,
  PRXSTRING argv,
  PSZ        QueueName,
  PRXSTRING retval)
{
  static int count = 1;
  static char str[6];

  sprintf(str,"%d\0", (int)count++); /* convert updated count to display
format */
  MAKERXSTRING(*retval,str,strlen(str)); /* return result */
  return 0; /* function RC */
}
```

16.2.2 Schematic DLL-Program Processing

Figure 16.2 shows the schematic processing for the registration and use of a DLL external function.

16.2.2.1 DLL Access. The user DLL is located through the LIBPATH entry in the CONFIG.SYS file. Figure 16.3 shows how the definitions are used to access a DLL module.

16.2.2.2 Registration of a DLL-Program. A DLL program is global for all applications.

There are registration functions for the three types of external DLL programs:

- RexxRegisterExitDll (system exit)
- RexxRegisterFunctionDll (function)
- RexxRegisterSubcomDll (subcommand environment)

The program type is shown in parentheses.

Equivalent REXX service functions (see Chapter 17) are also available for registration processing of functions and subcommand environments:

- RXFUNCADD, RXFUNCDROP, RXFUNQUERY (function)
- RXSUBCOM (subcommand environment)

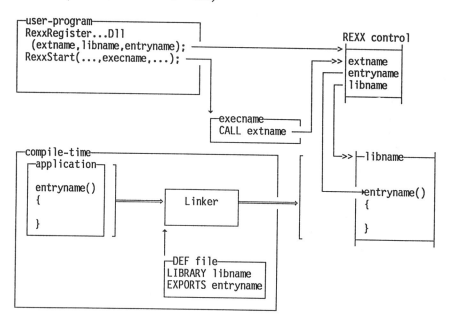

Figure 16.2. Schematic processing for a DLL external function.

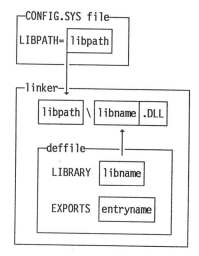

Figure 16.3. Access to a DLL module.

Example 1. C language DLL registration code:
```
char fextname[] = "alpha";
char libname[] = "beta"; /* beta.dll */
char fintname[] = "gamma";
RexxRegisterFunctionDll(fextname,libname,fintname);
```

Example 2. The equivalent REXX exec DLL registration function:
```
rc = rxfuncadd('alpha','beta','gamma');
```

These two examples register for the external function alpha the handler gamma in library beta.

16.3 RXSTRINGS

REXX processing routines make extensive use of RXSTRING structures to describe REXX variables explicitly. A RXSTRING contains a pointer to the data (strptr) and the explicit length of the data (strlength). Other than for RXSTRINGs passed to handlers, the data do not have a terminal null-character; the data may contain embedded null-characters. For RXSTRINGs passed to handlers (null-terminated RXSTRINGs) strlength does not include the terminating null-character. Figure 16.4 shows the RXSTRING format.

A RXSTRING has the structure:
```
typedef struct {
    ULONG strlength; /* length of string */
    PCH   strptr;    /* pointer to string */
} RXSTRING;
```

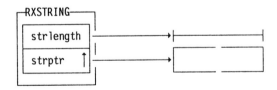

Figure 16.4. RXSTRING format.

There are three forms of RXSTRING:

- RXSTRING contains a zero string – strptr non-NULL, strlength 0 (the RXZEROSTRING macro returns true).
- RXSTRING contains a null string (an **empty RXSTRING**) – strptr NULL (the RXNULLSTRING macro returns true).
- RXSTRING contains a value – strptr non-NULL and strlength nonzero (the RXVALIDSTRING macro returns true).

The REXX interpreter provides a default RXSTRING for handler's returned data (strlength 256). DosAllocMem can be used to allocate a new RXSTRING.

Appendix H contains descriptions of useful macros and functions for the manipulation of RXSTRINGs.

16.4 RexxStart – INVOKE REXX INTERPRETER

The RexxStart function invokes the REXX interpreter to execute the specified REXX exec. This exec may be either an external file or in-storage statements.

Prototype:
```
LONG APIENTRY RexxStart(
  LONG Argc,
  PRXSTRING Argv,
  PSZ ProcName,
  PRXSTRING Instore,
  PSZ EnvName,
  LONG CallType,
  PRXSYSEXIT SysExits,
  PSHORT ReturnCode,
  PRXSTRING Result);
```

A NULL entry indicates that the entry is not used.

The RexxStart function return value indicates its processing status:

<0	interpreter error
0	ok
>0	an OS/2 error

Argc (LONG)

> The number of elements in the **Argv** array. This count includes any omitted arguments.

Argv (PRXSTRING)

> A pointer to an array of RXSTRING elements that are to be passed to the exec. Omitted arguments are represented as null RXSTRINGs.

ProcName (PSZ)

> The interpretation of **ProcName** depends on the **Instore** value.
>
> **Instore** NULL   **ProcName** is a pointer to a zero-terminated string that contains the file name of the exec to be executed (.CMD is the default extension). If drive and path are omitted, the

normal file OS/2 search logic is used (current directory, environment path).

Instore not NULL   **ProcName** is a pointer to the name returned by the PARSE SOURCE instruction, unless both **Instore** RXSTRINGs are null, in which case **ProcName** is the name of a macrospace exec.

Instore (PRXSTRING)

An array of two RXSTRINGs that describe the in-storage REXX exec to be executed:

instore[0]   REXX exec source
instore[1]   tokenized REXX exec

The tokenized REXX exec is intermediate code returned by the REXX interpreter after processing the exec source. If this intermediate code is available, it will be used as the REXX exec. To deactivate the tokenized REXX exec (e.g., for the first call) its entry must be invalidated (e.g., strlength set to 0).

Each line of the in-store REXX exec must be terminated with the carriage-return (\r) and, optionally, new-line (\n) characters.

If both **Instore** RXSTRINGs are null, the REXX interpreter searches the macrospace for **ProcName**.

EnvName (PSZ)

The name of the initial ADDRESS environment. An environment is registered with RexxRegisterSubcomExe or RexxRegisterSubcomDll.

CallType (LONG)

The type of REXX exec to be executed:

RXCOMMAND (0)   command
RXSUBROUTINE (1)   subroutine
RXFUNCTION (2)   function

SysExits (PRXSYSEXIT)

An array of system exit entries. The exit handler must have been registered with RexxRegisterExitExe or RexxRegisterExitDll.

A RXSYSEXIT entry has the format:

```
typedef struct {
  PSZ    sysexit_name;
  LONG   sysexit_code;
} RXSYSEXIT;
```

sysexit_name   name of exit handler

sysexit_code	system exit type code:
RXFNC (2)	external function call
RXCMD (3)	subcommand call
RXMSQ (4)	external data queue
RXSIO (5)	standard input and output
RXHLT (7)	halt processing
RXTRC (8)	trace processing
RXINI (9)	initialization processing
RXTER (10)	termination processing
RXENDLST (0)	final entry in list

ReturnCode (PSHORT)

The integer form of **Result**. 0 if **Result** is nonnumeric.

Result (PRXSTRING)

The value returned by the RETURN or EXIT instruction. If **Result** is too small (including zero length), the REXX interpreter will allocate storage to contain the result. If **Result** is NULL, no result will be returned. The user application is responsible for freeing this storage with the DosFreeMem function (see Section 16.4.1).

According to the OS/2 REXX specifications, the REXX interpreter does not set a null-character at the end of the **Result** data value. Even though the current REXX interpreter does actually set this null-character, programs should be programmed in accordance with the specification; that is, explicitly set the terminal null-character where required.

Example 1 (internal exec):

```
#define INCL_RXSUBCOM /* Subcommand interface definitions */
#include <rexxsaa.h>
#include <stdio.h>
#include <string.h>

int main(void)
{
  RXSTRING Instore[2];
  char exec[] = "PARSE ARG p1 p2\r"\
                "SAY p1\r"\
                "SAY p2\r"\
                "PARSE SOURCE info\r"\
                "SAY 'source' info\r"\
                "return 'delta'\r";
  char arg1[] = "alpha beta";

  SHORT rc;
```

```
        LONG Argc;
        RXSTRING Argv;
        RXSTRING Result;

        char str[1000];
        char buf[100];
        MAKERXSTRING(Result,buf,sizeof(buf)); /* pre-assign result buffer */
        Argc = 1; /* no. of arguments */
        Argv.strptr = arg1;
        Argv.strlength = strlen(arg1);
        Instore[0].strlength = strlen(exec);
        Instore[0].strptr = exec;
        Instore[1].strlength = 0; /* invalidate */
        Instore[1].strptr = NULL;

        /* first call */
        RexxStart(Argc, &Argv, "gamma", Instore, NULL, RXCOMMAND,
                NULL, &rc, &Result);
        /* create processable result */
        str[RXSTRLEN(Result)] = 0x00; /* set string-end */
        printf("result:%s\n",str);
        /* second call - use tokenized list */
        RexxStart(Argc, Argv, "gamma", Instore, NULL, RXCOMMAND,
                NULL, &rc, &Result);
        /* release buffer if system-allocated */
        if (RXSTRPTR(Result) != buf)
          DosFreeMem(RXSTRPTR(Result));
        }
```

SAY output:
```
        alpha
        beta
        source OS/2 COMMAND gamma
        alpha
        beta
        source OS/2 COMMAND gamma
```

Example 2 (external exec):
```
        #define INCL_RXSUBCOM /* subcommand interface definitions */
        #include <rexxsaa.h>
        #include <stdio.h>
        #include <string.h>

        int main(void)
        {
```

```
    char arg1[] = "alpha beta";
    SHORT rc;
    LONG Argc;
    RXSTRING Argv;
    RXSTRING Result;
    char str[1000];
    char buf[100];

    /* pre-assign result buffer */
    MAKERXSTRING(Result,buf,sizeof(buf));
    Argc = 1; /* no. of arguments */
    Argv.strptr = arg1;
    Argv.strlength = strlen(arg1);
    /* invoke external exec */
    RexxStart(Argc, &Argv, "a:\\x1.xxx", NULL, NULL, RXCOMMAND,
              NULL, &rc, &Result);
    /* create processable result */
    str[RXSTRLEN(Result)] = 0x00; /* set string-end */
    printf("result:%s\n",str);
    /* release buffer if system-allocated */
    if (RXSTRPTR(Result) != buf)
      DosFreeMem(RXSTRPTR(Result));
  }
```

Example 3 (use of a macrospace function):

```
    #include <rexxsaa.h>
    int main(void)
    {
      char arg[] = "alpha beta";
      char msf[] = "a1"; /* macrospace function name */
      RXSTRING Instore[2];
      SHORT rc;
      LONG Argc;
      RXSTRING Argv;
      RXSTRING Result;
      char str[256];
      Argc = 1; /* no. of arguments */
      MAKERXSTRING(Argv,arg,strlen(arg));
      Instore[0].strptr = NULL;
      Instore[1].strptr = NULL;
      MAKERXSTRING(Result,str,sizeof(str));
      RexxStart(Argc, &Argv, msf, Instore, NULL, RXCOMMAND,
                NULL, &rc, &Result);
    }
```

16.4.1 Release of Interpreter-Allocated Storage

The RexxStart interpreter will allocate a storage area if the specified buffer is too small to contain the returned result. The user is responsible for the release of this allocated area with the DosFreeMem control program service. The result RXSTRING entry contains the address and length of the current buffer. If the address differs from that of the preassigned buffer, then a new buffer has been allocated, as shown in the following example.

Example (fragment):

```
RXSTRING Result;
char buf[100];

MAKERXSTRING(Result,buf,sizeof(buf)); /* pre-assign result buffer */
RexxStart(Argc, &Argv, "gamma", Instore, NULL, RXCOMMAND,
          NULL, &rc, NULL); /* call REXX interpreter */
/* test whether new buffer has been allocated */
if (RXSTRPTR(Result) != buf) /* compare address */
  DosFreeMem(RXSTRPTR(Result)); /* different - free */
```

16.5 EXTERNAL FUNCTION

An external function is a function that is not contained in the exec. There are three forms of such functions:

- built-in REXX functions
- routines written in REXX
- routines programmed in a REXX-supported language (e.g., C, Assembler), called *external programmed functions*

Built-in functions (see Chapter 10) are standard functions described in the REXX language specifications (e.g., ABBREV). External REXX routines are named files (the function name) with the .CMD extension contained in the library search sequence. Whereas these two types of external functions can be used directly, external programmed functions must be registered with REXX before they can be used and must conform with the REXX calling sequence.

Figure 16.5 shows the schematic processing for an external programmed function. Figure 16.6 shows the parameter transfer in an external function.

16.5.1 Function Package

External program functions are grouped as a **function package**. There are two forms of function package:

- global (DLL file)
- local (EXE file)

In both cases the required functions must be registered with REXX before they can be used. Registration involves making the function's location known to the REXX interpreter. The location is either the memory address (for an EXE file) or the library name and module name (for a DLL function).

16.5.1.1 Function Registration Program. To save the user from having to register the individual functions, the function package should contain a special function, the *global registration function* that registers all other functions in the package. The standard IBM function packages use this technique – for example, the SysLoadFuncs function registers the complete REXXUTIL package. The system startup procedure STARTUP.CMD, which is executed during the OS/2 system initiation, can be used to contain registration code for frequently-used function packages.

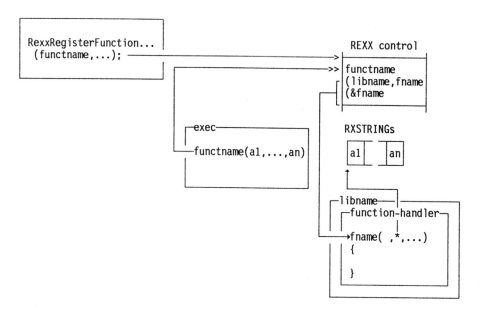

Figure 16.5 External programmed function (schematic processing).

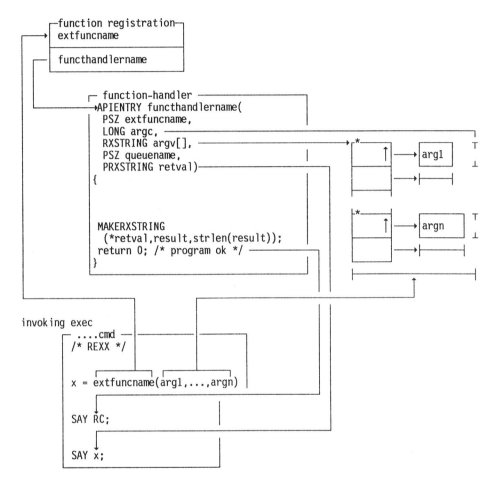

Figure 16.6. Parameter transfer in an external function.

Example:

```
#define INCL_RXFUNC /* function definitions */
#include <rexxsaa.h>
#include <stdio.h>

int main(void)
{
#define NF 2 /* number of functions */
#define MODULENAME "URXFUNCT" /* DLL module name */
USHORT urc, i;
char *apfn[NF] = {"F1", "F2"}; /* function names */
```

```
for (i=0; i < NF; i++)
{
  urc = RexxRegisterFunctionDll(apfn[i],MODULENAME,apfn[i]);
  if (urc != 0)
  {
    printf("Registration error %s rc:%hd\n",apfn[i],urc);
    return 4; /* terminate */
  }
}
return 0;
}
```

This sample program registers the list of function names specified in the array apfn.

16.5.1.2 Selective Function Registration. Selective function registration is an alternative to global registration, and can be implemented by having a single DLL module that contains the programmed REXX functions. The DLL module has a common router function that passes control to the specified internal function. This method avoids the requirement of exporting the complete library of function names.

The following exec illustrates this technique of selective function registration, as implemented in the subsequent program:

```
CALL RxFuncAdd 'F2','URXFUNCT','ROUTER'
CALL F2 'alpha','beta'
```

F2 is the name of the function to be registered, which is used as alias for the router function (ROUTER). The invocation of F2 actually passes control to the router function, which uses the passed function name (here F2) to access the linkage table (which has two entries: F1 and F2) to obtain the internal address of the corresponding function.

The sample program (DLL module) contains two simple functions: F1 and F2, and the ROUTER control function.

```
#define INCL_RXFUNC /* function definitions */
#include <rexxsaa.h>
#include <stdio.h>
RexxFunctionHandler ROUTER; /* control function prototype */
RexxFunctionHandler f1; /* application function prototype */
RexxFunctionHandler f2; /* application function prototype */

typedef struct {
  PFN afptr; /* function internal address */
  char *pfn; /* pointer to function name */
} FDEF;
#define N 2 /* number of functions */
FDEF fdef[2] = { (PFN)f1, "F1",
```

```
                     (PFN)f2, "F2"};

ULONG APIENTRY ROUTER(
  PUCHAR    FunctionName,  /* function invocation name */
  ULONG     Argc,          /* argument count */
  PRXSTRING Argv,          /* function arguments */
  PSZ       QueueName,     /* current queue name */
  PRXSTRING RetVal)        /* function return value */
{
  INT i;
  ULONG rc;
  for (i=0; i<N; i++) /* search transfer-table for function */
  {
    if (strcmp(FunctionName,fdef[i].pfn) == 0) /* function found */
    {
      rc = (fdef[i].afptr)(FunctionName,Argc,Argv,QueueName,RetVal));
      return rc;
    }
  }
  printf("function %s not found\n",FunctionName);
  return 43; /* routine not found */
}

ULONG APIENTRY f1(
  PUCHAR    FunctionName,
  ULONG     Argc,
  PRXSTRING Argv,
  PSZ       QueueName,
  PRXSTRING RetVal)
{
  static char result[] = "1";
  MAKERXSTRING(*RetVal,result,strlen(result)); /* function result */
  return 0; /* function RC */
}

ULONG APIENTRY f2(
  PUCHAR    FunctionName,
  ULONG     Argc,
  PRXSTRING Argv,
  PSZ       QueueName,
  PRXSTRING RetVal)
{
  static char result[] = "2";
  /* display parameters */
```

```
{
  int i;
  for (i=0; i < Argc; i++)
    printf("Argv %d %s\n",i,RXSTRPTR(Argv[i]));
}
MAKERXSTRING(*RetVal,result,strlen(result)); /* function result */
return 0; /* function RC */
}
```

16.5.2 Invocation Parameters

An external program function has a function prototype of the form:

```
typedef ULONG RexxFunctionHandler(
  PUCHAR FunctionName,
  ULONG Argc,
  PRXSTRING Argv,
  PSZ QueueName,
  PRXSTRING RetVal);
```

Example:

```
RexxFunctionHandler fclock;
```

defines the function prototype for the external program function fclock.

An external program function receives the following parameters:

FunctionName (PUCHAR)
> The function external name – the name with which the function was invoked.

Argc (ULONG)
> The number of arguments passed.

Argv (PRXSTRING)
> The function arguments (null-terminated RXSTRINGs).

QueueName (PSZ)
> The current queue name.

RetVal (PRXSTRING)
> The function return value.

The function return value indicates the function execution status (RC in the invoking exec):

   0   ok
   nonzero error

The standard REXX error code 40 (Incorrect call to routine) can be returned to indicate an invocation error.

16.5.3 Function Registration

REXX has four functions for registering and using external functions:

RexxRegisterFunctionDll	Register DLL function.
RexxRegisterFunctionExe	Register EXE function.
RexxDeregisterFunction	Deregister function.
RexxQueryFunction	Test function status.

Note: The external function name (the name used to invoke the function) can generally be chosen arbitrarily; that is, it can be used to define a *function alias* – exceptions are those functions that validate the invocation name. Despite this flexibility, the external function name will normally be the same as the entry point.

The function return value indicates the function registration status:

RXFUNC_OK (0)	successful processing
RXFUNC_DEFINED (10)	ok, function already registered
RXFUNC_NOMEM (20)	insufficient memory to process function
RXFUNC_NOREG (30)	function not registered
RXFUNC_MODNOTFND (40)	DLL module name not found
RXFUNC_ENTNOTFND (50)	entry point not found in DLL module

16.5.3.1 RexxRegisterFunctionDll – **Register DLL Function.** The RexxRegisterFunctionDll function registers an external function that resides in a DLL module.

Prototype:
```
APIRET APIENTRY RexxRegisterFunctionDll(
    PSZ FunctionName,
    PSZ ModuleName,
    PSZ EntryPoint);
```

FunctionName (PSZ)
    External function name – the name used to invoke the function.

ModuleName (PSZ)
> The name of the DLL file that contains the function handler. **ModuleName** does not include the .DLL extension.

EntryPoint (PSZ)
> The name of the function handler in the DLL.

Example:
```
#define INCL_RXFUNC /* function definitions */
#include <rexxsaa.h>
char fextname[] = "alpha";
char libname[] = "beta"; /* beta.dll */
char fintname[] = "gamma";
RexxRegisterFunctionDll(fextname,libname,fintname);
```

Note: This example uses distinct names for the external function name (alpha) and the entry point name (gamma) – this creates, in effect, an alias name for the function. Usually the two names will be the same.

16.5.3.2 `RexxRegisterFunctionExe` – **Register EXE Function.** The `RexxRegisterFunctionExe` function registers an external function that resides within the application code.

Prototype:
```
APIRET APIENTRY RexxRegisterFunctionExe(
   PSZ FunctionName,
   PFN EntryPoint);
```

FunctionName (PSZ)
> External function name – the name used to invoke the function.

EntryPoint (PFN)
> The address of the function handler EXE-code.

Example:
```
#define INCL_RXFUNC /* function definitions */
#include <rexxsaa.h>
#include <stdio.h>
RexxFunctionHandler fintname; /* function prototype */

int main(void)
{
  RXSTRING Result;
  char buf[256];
  short rc;
```

```
    RexxRegisterFunctionExe("fextname",(PFN)fintname); /* register function */
    MAKERXSTRING(Result,buf,sizeof(buf)); /* create result buffer */
    RexxStart(0, NULL, "c:\\y1.cmd", NULL, NULL, RXCOMMAND, NULL, &rc,
             &Result); /* invoke REXX exec that uses this function */
}

ULONG APIENTRY fintname(
  PUCHAR    FunctionName,
  ULONG     Argc,
  PRXSTRING Argv,
  PSZ       QueueName,
  PRXSTRING RetVal)
{
  static int count = 1;
  static char str[6];
  sprintf(str,"%d\0", count++); /* convert count to display format */
  MAKERXSTRING(*RetVal,str,strlen(str)); /* return result */
  return 0; /* function ok */
}
```

16.5.3.3   RexxDeregisterFunction   –   **Deregister**   **Function.**   The RexxDeregisterFunction function deregisters an external function.

Prototype:
```
    APIRET APIENTRY RexxDeregisterFunction(PSZ FunctionName);
```

FunctionName (PSZ)
     External function name.

16.5.3.4 RexxQueryFunction – **Test Function Status.** The RexxQueryFunction function returns the status of an external function.

Prototype:
```
    APIRET APIENTRY RexxQueryFunction(PSZ FunctionName);
```

FunctionName (PSZ)
     The external function name whose status is required.

Example:
```
    #define INCL_RXFUNC /* function definitions */
    #include <rexxsaa.h>
    #define FN "FO"
    USHORT urc;
```

```
urc = RexxQueryFunction(FN);
if (urc != 0) /* function not registered */
  printf("Query %s rc:%hd\n",FN,urc);
```

16.5.4 Sample Program Function

The FCONCAT function concatenates the specified parameters, and returns the resulting string as the function result. *Note*: To avoid overloading the example, the result is not checked for overflow.

```
#define INCL_RXFUNC
#include <rexxsaa.h>
#include <stdio.h>
#define MAXSIZE 250

ULONG APIENTRY fconcat(
  PSZ        FunctionName, /* function invocation name */
  ULONG      Argc,         /* argument count */
  RXSTRING   Argv[],       /* function arguments */
  PSZ        QueueName,    /* current queue name */
  PRXSTRING  RetVal)       /* function return value */
{
  int i;
  static char result[MAXSIZE];

  if (Argc < 1)
    return -1; /* nok - invalid number of arguments */

  result[0] = 0x00; /* clear result */
  for (i=0; i < Argc; i++)
    strcat(result,Argv[i].strptr);
  MAKERXSTRING(*RetVal,result,strlen(result)); /* return result */
  return 0; /* function ok */
}
```

Sample invocation (FCONCAT is in URXFUNC.DLL):

```
/* REXX - test fconcat */
CALL RxFuncAdd 'fconcat','urxfunc', 'fconcat'
x = fconcat("alpha","beta","gamma")
SAY x /* result - alphabetagamma */
```

16.6 SUBCOMMAND

A subcommand environment processes REXX commands passed to that environment. The environment is specified with either the ADDRESS instruction or the RexxStart function. Figure 16.7 shows the schematic processing for a subcommand. Figure 16.8 shows the parameter transfer in a subcommand environment

16.6.1 Invocation Parameters

A subcommand has a function prototype of the form:

```
typedef ULONG RexxSubcomHandler(
    PRXSTRING Command,
    PUSHORT Flags,
    PRXSTRING RetVal);
```

Example:

```
RexxSubcomHandler fuser;
```

defines the function prototype for the subcommand program fuser.

A subcommand handler receives the following parameters:

Command (PRXSTRING)

The (null-terminated RXSTRING) command passed to the subcommand program.

Flags (PUSHORT)

The subcommand program execution status:

RXSUBCOM_OK (0)	Ok.
RXSUBCOM_ERROR (1)	A subcommand error occurred.
RXSUBCOM_FAILURE (2)	A subcommand failure occurred.

RetVal (PRXSTRING)

The subcommand return value (REXX RC variable).

The subcommand handler return value should be set to 0 to indicate successful completion – **Flags** contains the execution status.

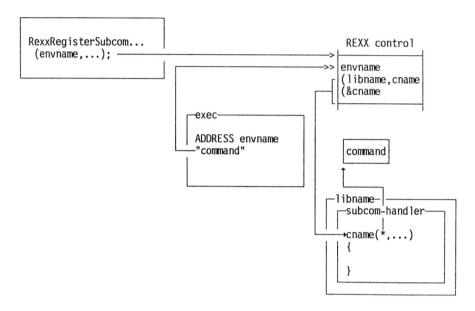

Figure 16.7. Subcommand (schematic processing).

16.6.2 Subcommand Registration
REXX has four functions for registering and using subcommand handlers:

RexxRegisterSubcomDll	Register DLL subcommand handler.
RexxRegisterSubcomExe	Register EXE subcommand handler.
RexxDeregisterSubcom	Deregister subcommand handler.
RexxQuerySubcom	Test subcommand handler status.

Although the subcommand environment name is, in principle, arbitrary, some sub-command handlers may validate it.

The function return value indicates the subcommand registration status:

RXSUBCOM_OK (0)	Successful processing.
RXSUBCOM_DUP (10)	Ok, subcommand handler already registered.
RXSUBCOM_NOTREG (30)	Subcommand handler not registered.
RXSUBCOM_NO_CANDROP (40)	Subcommand handler has been registered as not droppable.
RXSUBCOM_LOADERR (50)	Error while loading a DLL module (e.g., module name not found).
RXSUBCOM_NOPROC (127)	The entry point not found in DLL module.
RXSUBCOM_NOMEM (1002)	Insufficient memory to process function.
RXEXIT_BADTYPE (1003)	Program type not recognized.

RXSUBCOM_ERROR (1)	The subcommand handler raised the ERROR condition.
RXSUBCOM_FAILURE (2)	The subcommand handler raised the FAILURE condition.

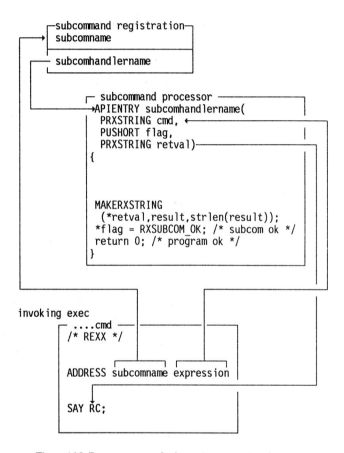

Figure 16.8. Parameter transfer in a subcommand environment.

16.6.2.1 RexxRegisterSubcomDll **– Register DLL Subcommand Handler.** The RexxRegisterSubcomDll function registers a subcommand handler that resides in a DLL module.

Prototype:
```
APIRET APIENTRY RexxRegisterSubcomDll(
    PSZ SubcomName,
    PSZ ModuleName,
    PSZ EntryPoint,
    PUCHAR UserArea,
    ULONG DropAuth);
```

SubcomName (PSZ)
Name of the subcommand environment; i.e., the name used in the ADDRESS instruction.

ModuleName (PSZ)
The name of the DLL file that contains the subcommand handler. **Module-Name** does not include the .DLL extension.

EntryPoint (PSZ)
The name of the subcommand handler in the DLL.

UserArea (PUCHAR)
An 8-byte area for user-defined data. NULL if not used.

DropAuth (ULONG)
Drop authority:

RXSUBCOM_DROPPABLE (0)	Any process can deregister the subcommand.
RXSUBCOM_NONDROP (1)	Only a thread in the same process as that which registered the subcommand can deregister it.

Example:
```
#define INCL_RXSUBCOM /* subcommand definitions */
#include <rexxsaa.h>
char envname[] = "USER";
char modname[] = "URXFUNCT";
char procname[] = "FUNCT";
RexxRegisterSubcomDll(envname,modname,procname,NULL,RXSUBCOM_DROPPABLE);
```

16.6.2.2 RexxRegisterSubcomExe – **Register EXE Subcommand Handler.** The RexxRegisterSubcomExe function registers a subcommand handler that resides within the application code.

Prototype:

```
APIRET APIENTRY RexxRegisterSubcomExe(
  PSZ SubcomName,
  PFN EntryPoint),
  PUCHAR UserArea);
```

SubcomName (PSZ)

Name of the subcommand environment; i.e., the name used in the ADDRESS instruction.

EntryPoint (PFN)

The address of the subcommand handler EXE-code.

UserArea (PUCHAR)

An 8-byte area for user-defined data. NULL if not used.

Example:

The local subcommand (environment: USER, processing program: xuser) displays the passed command and returns its length.

```
#define INCL_RXSUBCOM /* subcommand definitions */
#include <rexxsaa.h>
#include <stdio.h>
#include <string.h>

#define ENVNAME "USER"
RexxSubcomHandler xuser; /* prototype */

main()
{
  SHORT rc;
  RXSTRING Result;
  char buf[256];
  /* register local subcommand handler */
  RexxRegisterSubcomExe(ENVNAME,(PFN)xuser,NULL);
  MAKERXSTRING(Result,buf,sizeof(buf)); /* create result buffer */
  /* invoke REXX exec that uses this function */
  RexxStart(0, NULL, "g:\\pgm\\y2", NULL, NULL, RXCOMMAND,
            NULL, &rc, &Result);
}

ULONG APIENTRY xuser(
  PRXSTRING  cmd,
  PUSHORT    flag,
  PRXSTRING  retval)
```

```
{
  static char result[10];
  printf("CMD:%s\n",RXSTRPTR(*cmd)); /* display input command */
  /* return result */
  sprintf(result,"%d\0",RXSTRLEN(*cmd));
  MAKERXSTRING(*retval,result,strlen(result));
  *flag = RXSUBCOM_OK;
  return 0;
}
```

16.6.2.3 RexxDeregisterSubcom – **Deregister Subcommand Handler.** The
RexxDeregisterSubcom function deregisters a subcommand handler.

Prototype:
```
APIRET APIENTRY RexxDeregisterSubcom(
  PSZ SubcomName,
  PSZ ModuleName);
```

SubcomName (PSZ)
> Name of the subcommand environment; i.e., the name used in the ADDRESS
> instruction.

ModuleName (PSZ)
> The name of the DLL file that contains the subcommand handler. If **Module-
> Name** is NULL, the EXE for the current process will be searched first. If the entry
> is not found, the global subcommand list will be searched.

Example:
```
RexxDeregisterSubcom("USER",NULL);
```

16.6.2.4 RexxQuerySubcom – **Test Subcommand Status.** The RexxQuerySubcom
function returns the status of a subcommand handler.

Prototype:
```
APIRET APIENTRY RexxQuerySubcom(
  PSZ SubcomName,
  PSZ ModuleName,
  PUSHORT Flag,
  PUCHAR UserArea);
```

SubcomName (PSZ)
> Name of the subcommand environment; i.e., the name used in the ADDRESS
> instruction.

ModuleName (PSZ)

The name of the DLL file that contains the subcommand handler. If **Module-Name** is NULL, the EXE for the current process will be searched first. If the entry is not found, the global subcommand list will be searched.

Flag (PUSHORT)

Subcommand registration status:

0   subcommand handler not registered
1   subcommand handler registered

UserArea (PUCHAR)

The address of an 8-byte user area to contain any user information saved with the RexxRegisterSubcomDll or RexxRegisterSubcomExe function. NULL — do not return any information.

Example:

```
USHORT Flag;
RexxQuerySubcom("USER",NULL,&Flag,NULL);
printf("flag:%hd\n",Flag);
```

16.6.3 Sample Subcommand Handler

The sample subcommand handler (FUSER) displays the passed command and sets its length as return value.

```
#include <stdio.h>
#include <string.h>
#define INCL_RXSUBCOM
#include <rexxsaa.h>
RexxSubcomHandler funct; /* prototype */
ULONG APIENTRY funct(
  PRXSTRING   cmd,
  PUSHORT     flag,
  PRXSTRING   retval)
{
  #define MAXSIZE 250
  static char parm[MAXSIZE];
  static char result[10];
  strcpy(parm,cmd->strptr); /* move command to parm */
  printf("CMD:%s\n",parm); /* display input command */
  sprintf(result,"%d\0",strlen(parm)); /* convert result */
  MAKERXSTRING(*retval,result,strlen(result)); /* return result */
  *flag = RXSUBCOM_OK;
  return 0;
}
```

16.7 VARIABLE POOL INTERFACE

The RexxVariablePool function provides the interface with the REXX variable pool. Only the main thread of an application can access the REXX variable pool. Subcommand handlers, external functions, and some system exit handlers, but not EXE modules invoked from a REXX exec, can use the RexxVariablePool function.

The variable pool interface is fully enabled only for the RXCMD, RXFNC, RXINI and RXTER system exits. The RXCMD, RXFNC, RXHLT, RXMSQ, and RXSIO system exits can use only the RXSHV_EXIT operation. The variable pool interface is not available in the other cases. The REXX queue, internal OS/2 facilities (e.g., named pipes, environment variables), etc. can be used to pass data between REXX application programs when the variable pool interface is not available.

RexxVariablePool prototype:
```
APIRET APIENTRY RexxVariablePool(PSHVBLOCK pshvblock);
```

pshvblock (PSHVBLOCK)
> Pointer to a list of SHVBLOCKs.

RexxVariablePool function return values:

    RXSHV_OK (0x00)   execution ok
    RXSHV_NOAVL (0x90)   interface not available

Other values are the ORed shvret return code flags.

The following services are available:

- set variable
- fetch variable
- fetch next (stem) variable
- drop variable
- set exit value
- fetch private information (e.g., the number of arguments passed to the exec)

The RexxVariablePool function uses SHVBLOCKs as its interface. A SHVBLOCK has the format:

```
typedef struct shvnode {
    struct shvnode *shvnext;
    RXSTRING        shvname;
    RXSTRING        shvvalue;
    ULONG           shvnamelen;
    ULONG           shvvaluelen;
    UCHAR           shvcode;
    UCHAR           shvret;
} SHVBLOCK;
```

Multiple SHVBLOCKs may be chained together (shvnext points to the next SHVBLOCK in the chain). The SHVBLOCKs are processed in sequence. To include SHVBLOCK definitions use the preprocessor statement:

```
#define INCL_RXSHV
```

Figure 16.9 shows the SHVBLOCK structure (in the figure,
   * denotes an RXSTRING, and
   ↑ denotes a pointer).

shvnext
Pointer to the next block. NULL indicates the end of chain.

shvname (RXSTRING)
Pointer to the name buffer. shvname.strlength is the length of the name buffer (input name). RexxVariablePool does not append a null-character to returned names.

shvvalue (RXSTRING)
Pointer to the value buffer. shvvalue.strlength is the length of the value buffer (input data value). RexxVariablePool does not append a null character to returned values.

shvnamelen (ULONG)
Length of the returned name (RXSHV_NEXTV).

shvvaluelen (ULONG)
Length of the returned data (RXSHV_NEXTV, RXSHV_FETCH, RXSHV_SYFET, and RXSHV_PRIV).

shvcode (UCHAR)
Function code for this entry:

RXSHV_SET (0)	Set variable from given value.
RXSHV_FETCH (1)	Copy value of variable to buffer.
RXSHV_DROPV (2)	Drop variable.
RXSHV_SYSET (3)	Symbolic name set variable.
RXSHV_SYFET (4)	Symbolic name fetch variable.
RXSHV_SYDRO (5)	Symbolic name drop variable.
RXSHV_NEXTV (6)	Fetch "next" variable.
RXSHV_PRIV (7)	Fetch private information.
RXSHV_EXIT (8)	Set function exit value.

The following section contains a detailed description of each service.

shvret (UCHAR)
> Return code flags:
> RXSHV_OK (0x00)   Execution ok.
> RXSHV_NEWV (0x01)   Variable did not exist.
> RXSHV_LVAR (0x02)   Last variable fetched.
> RXSHV_TRUNC (0x04) Data value truncated.
> RXSHV_BADN (0x08)   Invalid variable name.
> RXSHV_MEMFL (0x10) Out-of-memory failure.
> RXSHV_BADF (0x80)   Invalid shvcode (or shvcode not permitted).

The shvcode field denotes the operation to be performed. There are two modes for variable processing:

- direct
- symbolic

In direct mode (e.g., RXSHV_SET) the variable name field (shvname) contains the name of the variable to be processed – the name entry must be written in uppercase. In symbolic mode (e.g., RXSHV_SYSET) the contents of shvname are treated as being a REXX variable; i.e., the usual REXX substitutions are made.

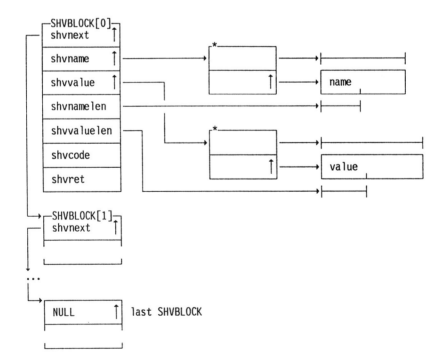

Figure 16.9. SHVBLOCK structure.

If the preassigned buffers are too small for returned data, the REXX interpreter will allocate the appropriate buffers. The user is responsible for the release of such buffers with the DosFreeMem function.

Example 1 (single SHVBLOCK):
Set the REXX variable A to contain 123.

```
char vn[] = "A"; /* variable name */
char vd[] = "123"; /* variable data */
SHVBLOCK shvblk;

shvblk.shvnext = NULL;
shvblk.shvcode = RXSHV_SET;
shvblk.shvname.strptr = vn;
shvblk.shvname.strlength = strlen(vn);
shvblk.shvvalue.strptr = vd;
shvblk.shvvalue.strlength = strlen(vd);
RexxVariablePool(&shvblk);
```

Example 2 (linked SHVBLOCKs):
Set the REXX variables A and BC to contain 123 and 4567, respectively.

```
char vn1[] = "A";
char vd1[] = "123";
char vn2[] = "B";
char vd2[] = "4567";
SHVBLOCK shvblk[2]; /* 2 SHVBLOCKs */

shvblk[0].shvnext = &shvblk[1]; /* pointer to next entry in chain */
shvblk[0].shvcode = RXSHV_SET;
shvblk[0].shvname.strptr = vn1;
shvblk[0].shvname.strlength = strlen(vn1);
shvblk[0].shvvalue.strptr = vd1;
shvblk[0].shvvalue.strlength = strlen(vd1);
shvblk[1].shvnext = NULL; /* end of list */
shvblk[1].shvcode = RXSHV_SET;
shvblk[1].shvname.strptr = vn2;
shvblk[1].shvname.strlength = strlen(vn2);
shvblk[1].shvvalue.strptr = vd2;
shvblk[1].shvvalue.strlength = strlen(vd2);
RexxVariablePool(&shvblk);
```

16.7.1 RXSHV_DROPV (RXSHV_SYDRO) – Drop Variable

The shvname variable is removed from the pool. The following variables must be set:

shvcode	RXSHV_DROPV or RXSHV_SYDRO
shvname.strptr	pointer to name string
shvname.strlength	length of name

Example:

The sample program fragment drops the symbolic REXX variable s.n. For example, if N contains 2, then S.2 will be dropped.

```
char vn[] = "s.n"; /* symbolic variable name */
SHVBLOCK shvblk;

shvblk.shvnext = NULL;
shvblk.shvcode = RXSHV_SYDRO;
shvblk.shvname.strptr = vn;
shvblk.shvname.strlength = strlen(vn);
RexxVariablePool(&shvblk);
```

16.7.2 RXSHV_EXIT – Set Function Exit Value

Set a return value string for an external function or system exit. This service is valid only for external functions, and system exits that return a value (e.g., RXSIO system exit, RXSIOTRD function). The following variables must be set:

shvcode	RXSHV_EXIT
shvvalue.strptr	pointer to value string
shvvalue.strlength	length of value data

Example:

The sample program fragment is a RXSIO (RXSIOTRD) system exit that sets the string 123 as return value.

```
#define INCL_RXSHV /* SHVBLOCK definition */
#define INCL_RXSYSEXIT /* system exit definitions */
#include <rexxsaa.h>

LONG fsysexit(
  LONG  ExitNumber,
  LONG  SubFunction,
  PEXIT ParmBlock)
{
union {
  PEXIT          pexit;
  RXSIOTRD_PARM *ptrd;
} u;
```

```
    SHVBLOCK shvblk;
    char vd[] = "123";

    u.pexit = ParmBlock;
    switch (SubFunction)
    {
      case RXSIOTRD:
        puts("TRD");
        break;
      default:
        return RXEXIT_NOT_HANDLED; /* function RC */
    }
    shvblk.shvnext = NULL;
    shvblk.shvcode = RXSHV_EXIT;
    shvblk.shvvalue.strptr = vd;
    shvblk.shvvalue.strlength = strlen(vd);
    RexxVariablePool(&shvblk);
    return RXEXIT_HANDLED; /* function RC */
}
```

16.7.3 RXSHV_FETCH (RXSHV_SYFET) – Get Variable Value

The contents of the shvname variable are copied into the shvvalue field. The following variables must be set:

shvcode	RXSHV_FETCH or RXSHV_SYFET
shvname.strptr	pointer to name string
shvname.strlength	length of name
shvvalue.strptr	pointer to value string
shvvalue.strlength	length of value buffer
shvvaluelen	returned with length of value

Example:
The sample program fragment gets the REXX variable A and displays its content if the interface does not signal an error condition.

```
    #define INCL_RXSHV /* SHVBLOCK definition */
    #include <rexxsaa.h>
    char vn[] = "A";
    char vd[256];
    SHVBLOCK shvblk;
    int rc;

    shvblk.shvnext = NULL;
    shvblk.shvcode = RXSHV_FETCH;
```

```
shvblk.shvname.strptr = vn;
shvblk.shvname.strlength = strlen(vn);
shvblk.shvvalue.strptr = vd;
shvblk.shvvalue.strlength = sizeof(vd);
rc = RexxVariablePool(&shvblk);
if (rc == 0) printf("vardata: %s\n",vd); /* test function return value */
```

16.7.4 RXSHV_NEXTV – Fetch "Next" Variable

The next variable (name and value) from the pool is returned. Excluded variables are not fetched. The variables are not returned in any specific order. shvret is set to RXSHV_LVAR when the last variable has been fetched. The following variables must be set:

shvcode	RXSHV_NEXTV
shvname.strptr	pointer to name buffer
shvname.strlength	size of name buffer
shvvalue.strptr	pointer to value buffer
shvvalue.strlength	size of value buffer
shvnamelen	returned with length of name
shvvaluelen	returned with length of value

Example:

The sample program fragment retrieves and displays all REXX variables.

```
#define INCL_RXSHV /* SHVBLOCK definition */
#include <rexxsaa.h>
#include <stdio.h> /* printf definition */
char vn[256];
char vd[256];
SHVBLOCK shvblk;
int rc = 0;

shvblk.shvnext = NULL;
shvblk.shvcode = RXSHV_NEXTV;
shvblk.shvname.strptr = vn;
shvblk.shvname.strlength = sizeof(vn);
shvblk.shvvalue.strptr = vd;
shvblk.shvvalue.strlength = sizeof(vd);
while (rc == 0)
{
  rc = RexxVariablePool(&shvblk);
  if (rc == 0)
    printf("varname: %s vardata: %s\n",vn,vd);
}
```

16.7.5 RXSHV_PRIV – Fetch Private Information

Private exec information is returned. The shvname name specifies which item is to be returned:

PARM	the number of arguments passed to the REXX exec
PARM.n	the nth argument passed to the REXX exec
QUEUENAME	the name of the current queue
SOURCE	the REXX source (equivalent to PARSE SOURCE instruction)
VERSION	the REXX version (equivalent to PARSE VERSION instruction)

The following variables must be set:

shvcode	RXSHV_PRIV
shvname.strptr	pointer to name string
shvname.strlength	length of name
shvvalue.strptr	pointer to buffer
shvvalue.strlength	size of buffer
shvvaluelen	returned with length of data

Example:

The sample program fragment fetches and displays the REXX version.

```
#define INCL_RXSHV /* SHVBLOCK definitions */
#include <rexxsaa.h>
#include <stdio.h>

char vn[] = "VERSION";
char vd[256];
SHVBLOCK shvblk;

shvblk.shvnext = NULL;
shvblk.shvcode = RXSHV_PRIV;
shvblk.shvname.strptr = vn;
shvblk.shvname.strlength = strlen(vn);
shvblk.shvvalue.strptr = vd;
shvblk.shvvalue.strlength = sizeof(vd); /* size of buffer */
rc = RexxVariablePool(&shvblk);
if (rc == 0)
  printf("vardata: %s\n",vd);
```

16.7.6 RXSHV_SET (RXSHV_SYSET) – Set Variable

The contents of the shvvalue field are assigned to the variable shvname. The following variables must be set:

shvcode	RXSHV_SET or RXSHV_SYSET
shvname.strptr	pointer to name string
shvname.strlength	length of name
shvvalue.strptr	pointer to value string
shvvalue.strlength	length of value

Example:

The sample program fragment sets the REXX variable A to contain 123.

```
#define INCL_RXSHV /* SHVBLOCK definitions */
#include <rexxsaa.h>

char vn[] = "A"; /* variable name */
char vd[] = "123"; /* variable data */
SHVBLOCK shvblk;
shvblk.shvnext = NULL;
shvblk.shvcode = RXSHV_SET;
shvblk.shvname.strptr = vn;
shvblk.shvname.strlength = strlen(vn);
shvblk.shvvalue.strptr = vd;
shvblk.shvvalue.strlength = strlen(vd);
RexxVariablePool(&shvblk);
```

16.8 MACROSPACE

A macrospace is a REXX-maintained internal storage area (shared memory) used to contain command files (REXX execs and functions). Application-specific macrospaces can improve performance for frequently used routines by avoiding file access to external (disk) storage. Only a single macrospace exists at any one time, although multiple macrospaces can be stored as named disk files.

The macrospace interface supports the functions:

RexxAddMacro	Add exec to the macrospace.
RexxClearMacroSpace	Remove all execs from the macrospace.
RexxDropMacro	Remove exec from the macrospace.
RexxLoadMacroSpace	Load all (or selected execs) to the macrospace from a disk file.
RexxQueryMacro	Test whether exec is contained in the macrospace.
RexxReorderMacro	Change the search order of an exec.
RexxSaveMacroSpace	Save all (or selected execs) from the macrospace to a disk file.

The search order of individual execs in the macrospace can be set relative to registered functions and other external command files:

RXMACRO_SEARCH_BEFORE   Functions will be located in the macrospace before registered functions and external command files.

RXMACRO_SEARCH_AFTER   Registered functions and external command files will be used in preference to such functions in the macrospace.

The preprocessor declarative #define INCL_RXMACRO includes the macrospace definitions from the <rexxsaa.h> header file.

The macrospace functions issue one of the function return values:

RXMACRO_OK (0)   Successful processing.

RXMACRO_NO_STORAGE (1)   Insufficient main-storage.

RXMACRO_NOT_FOUND (2)   The function name not found in the macrospace.

RXMACRO_EXTENSION_REQUIRED (3) The macrospace file requires an extension; e.g., .DAT.

RXMACRO_ALREADY_EXISTS (4)   The function name already exists in the macrospace (duplicate function names are not allowed).

RXMACRO_FILE_ERROR (5)   An error occurred while processing the macrospace file.

RXMACRO_SIGNATURE_ERROR (6)   The macrospace file has an incorrect format.

RXMACRO_SOURCE_NOT_FOUND (7) Source file not found.

RXMACRO_INVALID_POSITION (8)   Invalid position (correct values are RXMACRO_SEARCHBEFORE and RXMACRO_SEARCH_AFTER).

Figure 16.10 shows the schematic processing for macrospace administration.

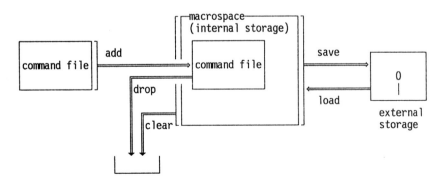

Figure 16.10. Macrospace administration.

16.8.1 RexxAddMacro – Add Exec to Macrospace

The RexxAddMacro function adds an exec (command file) to the macrospace.

Prototype:
```
APIRET APIENTRY RexxAddMacro(
  PSZ FuncName,
  PSZ FileName,
  ULONG Position);
```

FuncName (PSZ)

Function name. The name with which a function is called.

FileName (PSZ)

Name of the file that contains the function.

Position (ULONG)

Search position: RXMACRO_SEARCH_BEFORE or RXMACRO_SEARCH_AFTER.
The search position specifies whether the macrospace is searched for the exec before or after other sources.

Example:
```
RexxAddMacro("alpha","a:\\x1.xxx",RXMACRO_SEARCH_BEFORE);
```

This code fragment adds the command file a:\x1.xxx to the macrospace, and assigns it the function name alpha.

16.8.2 RexxClearMacroSpace – Remove All Execs from Macrospace

The macrospace is cleared of all loaded execs.

Prototype:
```
APIRET APIENTRY RexxClearMacroSpace(VOID);
```

Example:
```
RexxClearMacroSpace();
```

This code fragment removes all entries from the macrospace.

16.8.3 RexxDropMacro – Remove Exec from Macrospace

The specified exec (function name) is removed from the macrospace.

Prototype:
```
APIRET APIENTRY RexxDropMacro(PSZ FuncName);
```

FuncName (PSZ)

    Function name. The name with which the function is called.

Example:

```
RexxDropMacro("alpha");
```

This code fragment removes the function named alpha from the macrospace.

16.8.4 RexxLoadMacroSpace – Load Macrospace Execs

Selected (or all) execs are loaded into the macrospace from a disk file that contains previously saved macrospace execs.

Prototype:

```
APIRET APIENTRY RexxLoadMacroSpace(
    ULONG FuncCount,
    PSZ *FuncNames,
    PSZ FileName);
```

FuncCount (ULONG)

    The number of entries in the function names list (**FuncNames**). 0 = load all functions from the saved macrospace file.

FuncNames (PSZ)

    List of function names to be loaded. NULL – entry not used (all functions are to be loaded).

FileName (PSZ)

    File that contains the saved macrospace.

Example 1:

```
RexxLoadMacroSpace(0,NULL,"a:\\ms.dat");
```

This code fragment loads the previously saved macrospace file a:\ms.dat.

Example 2:

```
PSZ pc[] = {"alpha","beta"};
RexxLoadMacroSpace(2,pc,"a:\\ms.dat");
```

This code fragment loads the two functions alpha and beta from the previously saved macrospace file a:\ms.dat.

16.8.5 RexxQueryMacro – Test Whether Exec Is Contained in the Macrospace

The RexxQueryMacro function tests whether the specified function (name) is contained in the macrospace, and, if present, returns its search order.

Prototype:
```
APIRET APIENTRY RexxQueryMacro(
    PSZ FuncName,
    PUSHORT Position);
```

FuncName (PSZ)
Function name.

Position (PUSHORT)
Pointer to returned position:
RXMACRO_SEARCH_BEFORE (1)
RXMACRO_SEARCH_AFTER (2).

Example:
```
USHORT rc, position;
rc = RexxQueryMacro("alpha",&position);
if (rc == 0) printf("function:%s loaded:%hd\n",fn,position);
```

This code fragment tests whether the macrospace function alpha is available. If present, its search order is displayed.

16.8.6 RexxReorderMacro – Change the Search Order of an Exec
The search order of a macrospace exec can be altered. The RexxAddMacro function describes the significance of the search order.

Prototype:
```
APIRET APIENTRY RexxReorderMacro(
    PSZ FuncName,
    ULONG Position);
```

FuncName (PSZ)
Function name.

Position (ULONG)
position: RXMACRO_SEARCH_BEFORE or RXMACRO_SEARCH_AFTER.

Example:
```
RexxReorderMacro("alpha",RXMACRO_SEARCH_AFTER);
```

This code fragment sets the search order for the macrospace function alpha.

16.8.7 RexxSaveMacroSpace – Save Macrospace Execs

Selected (or all) macrospace execs are written to a disk file. Macrospace execs from this file can be subsequently loaded with the RexxLoadMacroSpace function.

Prototype:
```
APIRET APIENTRY RexxSaveMacroSpace(
    ULONG FuncCount,
    PSZ *FuncNames,
    PSZ FileName);
```

FuncCount (ULONG)
> The number of entries in the function names list (**FuncNames**). 0 = save all functions from the macrospace in the file.

FuncNames (PSZ)
> List of function names to be saved.

FileName (PSZ)
> File that is to contain the saved macrospace.

Example 1:
```
RexxSaveMacroSpace(0,NULL,"a:\\ms.dat");
```

This code fragment saves the complete macrospace in the file a:\ms.dat.

Example 2:
```
PSZ pc[] = {"alpha","beta"};
RexxSaveMacroSpace(2,pc,"a:\\ms.dat");
```

This code fragment saves the two macrospace functions alpha and beta in the macrospace file a:\ms.dat.

16.8.8 Macrospace Example

This sample code loads the saved macrospace file g:\pgm\ms.dat and tests whether the function gamma is present in the macrospace.

```
#define INCL_RXMACRO /* macrospace definitions */
#include <rexxsaa.h>
USHORT rc;
USHORT position;
char fn[] = "alpha";
RexxLoadMacroSpace(0,NULL,"g:\\pgm\\ms.dat");
rc = RexxQueryMacro(fn,&position);
if (rc == 0)
  puts("function loaded");
```

16.8.9 Invocation of Macrospace Execs

Macrospaces can be used in two ways:

- directly (the name of the macrospace exec is specified in the RexxStart call)
- indirectly (the macrospace is searched for external execs – the search order is specified when execs are added to the macrospace)

16.8.9.1 Use of the Macrospace with RexxStart. The name of macrospace exec can be explicitly specified in the RexxStart function call. The macrospace exec name is that with which the exec was added to the macrospace (see RexxAddMacro function). The **instore** array set to contain two NULL RXSTRINGs indicates that a macrospace call is to be made.

Example:
The program fragment explicitly invokes the macrospace exec alpha.

```
#include <rexxsaa.h>
RXSTRING Instore[2];
RXSTRING Result;
char str[256];
SHORT rc;
Instore[0].strptr = NULL; /* use macrospace */
Instore[1].strptr = NULL;
MAKERXSTRING(Result,str,sizeof(str));
RexxStart(0, NULL, "alpha", Instore, NULL, RXCOMMAND, NULL, &rc, &Result);
```

16.9 SYSTEM EXITS

System exits are application-defined exit handlers that are activated when a user exec is invoked with the RexxStart function.

A system exit handler can:

- process the condition (return status RXEXIT_HANDLED)
- return to the REXX interpreter to let it perform the standard processing (return status RXEXIT_NOT_HANDLED)
- set an error indicator (return status RXEXIT_RAISE_ERROR)

The names of the handler exits (and the exit types that they process) are specified in the **exit list** of the RexxStart function invocation. The system exit type code determines when the exit is invoked and which arguments are passed to the exit handler. Figure 16.11 shows the schematic processing for a system exit.

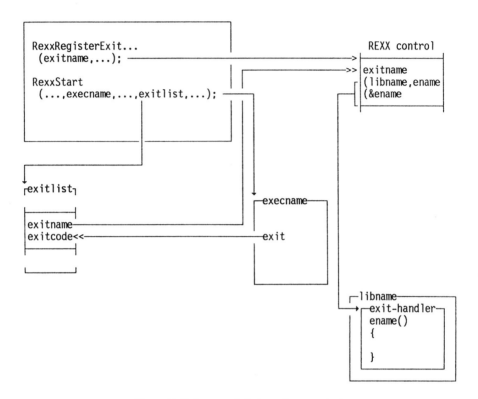

Figure 16.11. System exit (schematic processing).

16.9.1 Invocation Parameters

A system exit has a function prototype of the form:

```
typedef LONG RexxExitHandler(
    LONG ExitNumber,
    LONG SubFunction,
    PEXIT ParmBlock);
```

ExitNumber (LONG)

The function code specifies the exit type:

RXCMD   subcommand call
RXFNC   external function call
RXHLT   halt processing
RXINI   initialization processing
RXMSQ   external data queue
RXSIO   standard input and output
RXTER   termination processing

RXTRC   **trace processing.SubFunction**(LONG)
The subfunction code specifies the exit event type.

ParmBlock(PEXIT)
The exit parameter list is exit-specific. PEXIT is a generic pointer (to char). Each exit description specifies the form of its **ParmBlock**.

The exit handler return value indicates its execution status (the RC variable in the invoking exec):

RXEXIT_HANDLED (0)   Ok.
RXEXIT_NOT_HANDLED (1)   The exit handler did not process the exit call.
RXEXIT_RAISE_ERROR (-1) A fatal error occurred in the exit handler.

The REXX interpreter processes exits that return status RXEXIT_NOT_HANDLED and raises error condition 48 for exits that return status RXEXIT_RAISE_ERROR.

16.9.2 Exit Registration

REXX has four functions for registering and using system exits:

RexxRegisterExitDll   Register DLL function.
RexxRegisterExitExe   Register EXE function.
RexxDeregisterExit   Deregister function.
RexxQueryExit   Test function status.

The function return value indicates the exit registration status (the corresponding numeric value is shown in parentheses):

RXEXIT_OK (0)   Successful processing.
RXEXIT_DUP (10)   Ok, exit handler already registered.
RXEXIT_NOTREG (30)   Exit handler not registered.
RXEXIT_NO_CANDROP (40) Exit handler has been registered as not droppable.
RXEXIT_NOMEM (1002)   Insufficient memory to process function.
RXEXIT_BADTYPE (1003) Program not recognized as an exit handler.

16.9.2.1 RexxRegisterExitDll – **Register DLL Exit Handler.** The RexxRegisterExitDll function registers an exit handler that resides in a DLL module.

Prototype:

```
APIRET APIENTRY RexxRegisterExitDll(
    PSZ ExitName,
    PSZ ModuleName,
    PSZ EntryPoint,
    PUCHAR UserArea,
    ULONG DropAuth);
```

ExitName (PSZ)
> Name of the exit as used in the exit list.

ModuleName (PSZ)
> The name of the DLL file that contains the exit handler.

EntryPoint (PSZ)
> The name of the exit handler in the DLL.

UserArea (PUCHAR)
> An 8-byte area for user-defined data. NULL if not used.

DropAuth (ULONG)
> Drop authority:
> RXEXIT_DROPPABLE   any process can deregister the exit
> RXEXIT_NONDROP   only a thread in the same process as that which registered
>   the exit can deregister it

Example:
```
RexxRegisterExitDll("FEXIT","URXEXIT","XFUNCT",NULL,RXEXIT_DROPPABLE);
```

16.9.2.2 `RexxRegisterExitExe` – **Register EXE Exit Handler.** The
RexxRegisterExitExe function registers an exit handler that resides within the application code.

Prototype:
```
APIRET APIENTRY RexxRegisterExitExe(
    PSZ ExitName,
    PFN EntryPoint,
    PUCHAR UserArea);
```

ExitName (PSZ)
> Name of the exit as used in the exit list.

EntryPoint (PFN)
> The address of the exit handler EXE-code.

UserArea (PUCHAR)
> An 8-byte area for user-defined data. NULL if not used.

Example:
```
#define INCL_RXSYSEXIT /* system exit definitions */
#include <rexxsaa.h>
#include <stdio.h>
```

```
#include <string.h>
RXSTRING retval;
RXSYSEXIT sysexit[2];
RexxExitHandler fsysexit; /* function prototype */

main()
{
  char cmdname[] = "a:\\x2.cmd";
  SHORT rc;
  char str[250];

  RexxRegisterExitExe("FEXIT",(PFN)fsysexit,NULL);/* register local func. */
  /* initialize system exit block */
  sysexit[0].sysexit_name = "FEXIT";
  sysexit[0].sysexit_code = RXTRC; /* exit function */
  sysexit[1].sysexit_code = RXENDLST; /* end-of-list */
  /* invoke REXX interpreter with system exit */
  MAKERXSTRING(retval,str,sizeof(str));
  RexxStart(0, NULL, cmdname, NULL, NULL, RXCOMMAND,
            sysexit, &rc, &retval);
}
/* internal function */
LONG fsysexit(
  LONG  ExitNumber,
  LONG  SubFunction,
  PEXIT ParmBlock)
{
union {
  PEXIT           pexit;
  RXTRCTST_PARM *pparm;
} u;
static int count = 0;

  u.pexit = ParmBlock;
  if (++count > 3) /* increment and test count */
    u.pparm->rxtrc_flags.rxftrace = 1; /* set trace active */
  return RXEXIT_HANDLED; /* function RC */
}
```

16.9.2.3 RexxDeregisterExit – **Deregister Exit Handler.** The RexxDeregisterExit function deregisters an exit handler.

Prototype:
```
APIRET APIENTRY RexxDeregisterExit(
  PSZ ExitName,
  PSZ ModuleName);
```

ExitName (PSZ)

Name of the exit as used in the exit list.

ModuleName (PSZ)

The name of the DLL file that contains the exit handler. If **ModuleName** is NULL, the EXE for the current process will be searched first. If the entry is not found, the global exit list will be searched.

Example:
```
RexxDeregisterExit("FEXIT","URXEXIT");
```

16.9.2.4 RexxQueryExit – **Test Exit Status**. The RexxQueryExit function returns the status of an exit handler.

Prototype:
```
APIRET APIENTRY RexxQueryExit(
  PSZ ExitName,
  PSZ ModuleName,
  PUSHORT Flag,
  PUCHAR UserArea);
```

ExitName (PSZ)

Name of the exit as used in the exit list.

ModuleName (PSZ)

The name of the DLL file that contains the exit handler. If **ModuleName** is NULL, the EXE for the current process will be searched first. If the entry is not found, the global exit list will be searched.

Flag (PUSHORT)

Exit registration status:

| 0 | exit handler not registered |
| 1 | exit handler registered |

UserArea (PUCHAR)

The address of an 8-byte user area to contain any user information saved with the RexxRegisterExitDll or RexxRegisterExitExe function. NULL – do not return any information.

Example:

```
#define INCL_DOSPROCESS /* process and thread definitions */
#include <os2.h>
#define INCL_RXSYSEXIT /* system exit definitions */
#define INCL_RXARI /* halt and trace definitions */
#include <rexxsaa.h>
#include <stdio.h>
#include <string.h>
#define EXITNAME "FEXIT"
#define CMDNAME "x4.cmd"

RXSTRING retval;
RXSYSEXIT sysexit[2];

typedef struct {
  TID tid;
  PID pid;
} SX;

typedef union {
  SX     *psx;
  PUCHAR puc;
} UX;

SHORT rc;
char str[250];

RexxExitHandler fsysexit; /* function prototype */

main()
{
  PTIB pptib;
  TIB2 *ptib2;
  PPIB pppib;
  SX id;
  UX arg = &id;

  /* get thread, process IDs */
  DosGetInfoBlocks(&pptib, &pppib);
  ptib2 = pptib->tib_ptib2;
  id.pid = pppib->pib_ulpid;
  id.tid = ptib2->tib2_ultid;
  /* register local function */
  RexxRegisterExitExe(EXITNAME,(PFN)fsysexit,arg.puc);
```

```
    /* initialize system exit block */
    sysexit[0].sysexit_name = EXITNAME;
    sysexit[0].sysexit_code = RXINI; /* exit function */
    sysexit[1].sysexit_code = RXENDLST; /* end-of-list */
    /* invoke REXX interpreter with system exit */
    MAKERXSTRING(retval,str,sizeof(str));
    RexxStart(0, NULL, CMDNAME, NULL, NULL, RXCOMMAND,
              sysexit, &rc, &retval);
}
/* internal function */
LONG fsysexit(
  LONG ExitNumber,
  LONG SubFunction,
  PEXIT ParmBlock)
{
  union {
    SX    id;
    UCHAR User;
  } u;
  USHORT Flag;
  PUCHAR PUser = &u.User;

  RexxQueryExit(EXITNAME,NULL,&Flag,PUser);
  if (Flag != 0) /* exit registered */
    RexxSetTrace(u.id.pid,u.id.tid); /* set trace */
  return RXEXIT_HANDLED;
}
```

16.9.3 System Exit Definitions
REXX has eight system exits – some of which have subtypes (parenthesized subtypes exist for completeness, but are not used to distinguish the call):

RXCMD	subcommand call
	(RXCMDHST)
RXFNC	external function call
	(RXFNCCAL)
RXHLT	halt processing
	RXHLTCLR – clear halt indicator
	RXHLTTST – test halt indicator
RXINI	initialization processing
	(RXINIEXT)

RXMSQ	external data queue
	RXMSQPLL – pull a line from the external queue
	RXMSQPSH – place a line on the external queue
	RXMSQSIZ – return the number of entries on the external queue
	RXMSQNAM – set the external queue name
RXSIO	standard input and output
	RXSIOSAY – SAY processing
	RXSIOTRC – TRACE processing
	RXSIOTRD – PULL processing
	RXSIODTR – read a debug line
RXTER	termination processing
	(RXTEREXT)
RXTRC	trace processing
	(RXTRCTST)

16.9.3.1 RXCMD **– Subcommand Call.** RXCMD is called on invocation of a subcommand.

Parameter list:
```
    typedef struct {
      RXCMD_FLAGS rxcmd_flags;
      PUCHAR      rxcmd_address;
      USHORT      rxcmd_address1;
      PUCHAR      rxcmd_dll;
      USHORT      rxcmd_dll_len;
      RXSTRING    rxcmd_command;
      RXSTRING    rxcmd_retc;
    } RXCMDHST_PARM;
```

rxcmd_flags (RXCMD_FLAGS)
> Error/failure flags (each one bit) set by the subcommand handler to TRUE (1) if the condition is satisfied:

rxcmd_flags.rxfcfail	command failure
rxcmd_flags.rxfcerr	command error

rxcmd_address (PUCHAR)
> Pointer to address name.

rxcmd_address1 (USHORT)
> Length of address name.

rxcmd_dll (PUCHAR)
> DLL name for command.

rxcmd_dll_len (USHORT)
>   Length of DLL name – 0 indicates an EXE file.

rxcmd_command (RXSTRING)
>   Command string.

rxcmd_retc (RXSTRING)
>   Pointer to return buffer.

Example:

The sample exit handler is invoked before a command exit is processed. The environment and command are displayed.

```
define INCL_RXSYSEXIT /* system exit definitions */
#include <rexxsaa.h>
#include <stdio.h>
#include <string.h>

LONG fsysexit(
  LONG  ExitNumber,
  LONG  SubFunction,
  PEXIT ParmBlock)
{

union {
  PEXIT           pexit;
  RXCMDHST_PARM *pparm;
} u;

  char str[256];

  u.pexit = ParmBlock;
  strcpy(str,u.pparm->rxcmd_address);
  printf("ADDRESS:%s\n",str); /* environment name */
  if (RXSTRLEN(u.pparm->rxcmd_command) != 0)
    strcpy(str,RXSTRPTR(u.pparm->rxcmd_command));
    printf("CMD:%s\n",str); /* command */
  else /* no command, set error */
    u.pparm->rxcmd_flags.rxfcerr = 1;
  return RXEXIT_HANDLED; /* function RC */
}
```

16.9.3.2 RXFNC – **External Function Call.** RXFNC is called on invocation of an external function (subroutine).

Parameter list:
```
typedef struct {
  RXFNC_FLAGS rxfnc_flags;
  PUCHAR      rxfnc_name;
  USHORT      rxfnc_namel;
  PUCHAR      rxfnc_que;
  USHORT      rxfnc_quel;
  USHORT      rxfnc_argc;
  PRXSTRING   rxfnc_argv;
  RXSTRING    rxfnc_retc;
} RXFNCCAL_PARM;
```

rxfnc_flags (RXFNC_FLAGS)

Function flags (each one bit) set to TRUE (1) if the condition is satisfied:

rxfnc_flags.rxfferr	invalid call to routine (set by function handler)
rxfnc_flags.rxffnfnd	function not found (set by function handler)
rxfnc_flags.rxffsub	called using the REXX CALL instruction (passed to the function handler)

rxfnc_name (PUCHAR)

Pointer to the name of the called function.

rxfnc_namel (USHORT)

Length of function name.

rxfnc_que (PUCHAR)

Current queue name.

rxfnc_quel (USHORT)

Length of queue name.

rxfnc_argc (USHORT)

Number of arguments in list.

rxfnc_argv (PRXSTRING)

Pointer to argument list.

rxfnc_retc (RXSTRING)

Return value. This is optional for a function called as a subroutine (rxfnc_flags.rxffsub TRUE).

Example:

The sample exit handler is invoked before a function exit is processed. The function name, number of arguments, and the arguments are displayed. The string "gamma" is returned, unless the function is called as a subroutine.

```
#define INCL_RXSYSEXIT /* system exit definitions */
#include <rexxsaa.h>
#include <stdio.h>
#include <string.h>

LONG fsysexit(
  LONG  ExitNumber,
  LONG  SubFunction,
  PEXIT ParmBlock)
{
union {
  PEXIT           pexit;
  RXFNCCAL_PARM *pparm;
} u;
char str[256];
static char result[] = "gamma";
PRXSTRING prxstr;

  u.pexit = ParmBlock;
  strcpy(str,u.pparm->rxfnc_name);
  printf("FNC:%s\n",str); /* function name */
  printf("ARGC:%hd\n",u.pparm->rxfnc_argc); /* number of arguments */
  if (u.pparm->rxfnc_argc != 0)
  {
    prxstr = u.pparm->rxfnc_argv;
    strcpy(str,RXSTRPTR(*prxstr));
    printf("ARGV:%s\n",str); /* arguments */
  }
  /* test whether subroutine - no return value */
  if (u.pparm->rxfnc_flags.rxffsub != 1)
    MAKERXSTRING(u.pparm->rxfnc_retc,result,strlen(result));
  return RXEXIT_HANDLED; /* function RC */
}
```

16.9.3.3 RXHLT – **Halt Processing.** RXHLT is called for halt processing. If activated, this exit will be called after each REXX instruction, with a consequent performance degradation. The RexxSetHalt function can also be used to perform REXX halt processing without causing this exit handler to receive control.

The RXHLT exit has two subfunctions:

RXHLTTST (1) Test for halt condition.
RXHLTCLR (2) Clear halt condition.

Subfunction RXHLTTST (test for halt condition) parameter list:

```
typedef struct {
  RXHLT_FLAGS rxhlt_flags;
} RXHLTTST_PARM;
```

rxhlt_flags (RXHLT_FLAGS)

Halt flag (one bit) set to TRUE (1) if the condition is satisfied:
rxhlt_flags.rxfhhalt – set if halt occurred (the RexxVariablePool RXSHV_EXIT operation can be used to return an explanatory text string, which can be subsequently retrieved with the CONDITION("D") built-in function).

Subfunction RXHLTCLR (clear halt condition) has no parameters.

Example:
The sample exit handler is invoked before each statement is processed. A counter is maintained. The halt indicator is set after three statements have been processed.

```
#define INCL_RXSYSEXIT /* system exit definitions */
#include <rexxsaa.h>

LONG fsysexit(
  LONG  ExitNumber,
  LONG  SubFunction,
  PEXIT ParmBlock)
{
union {
  PEXIT            pexit;
  RXHLTTST_PARM *pparm;
} u;
static int count = 0;
  u.pexit = ParmBlock;
  if (++count > 3) /* increment and test count */
    u.pparm->rxhlt_flags.rxfhhalt = 1; /* set halt active */
  return RXEXIT_HANDLED; /* function RC */
}
```

16.9.3.4 RXINI – **Initialization Processing.** The initialization exit is called at the end of program initialization. It does not receive any parameters.

16.9.3.5 RXMSQ – **External Data Queue.** RXMSQ is called for queue processing.

The RXMSQ exit has four subfunctions:

    RXMSQPLL (1) Pull entry from queue.
    RXMSQPSH (2) Push entry on queue.
    RXMSQSIZ (3) Return the current queue size.
    RXMSQNAM (20) Set current queue name.

Subfunction RXMSQPLL (pull entry from queue) parameter list:
```
      typedef struct {
        RXSTRING rxmsq_retc;
      } RXMSQPLL_PARM;
```

rxmsq_retc (RXSTRING)
    Pointer to dequeued entry buffer.

Subfunction RXMSQPSH (push entry on queue) parameter list:
```
      typedef struct {
        RXMSQ_FLAGS rxmsq_flags;
        RXSTRING    rxmsq_value;
      } RXMSQPSH_PARM;
```

rxmsq_flags (RXMSQ_FLAGS)
    LIFO/FIFO flag (one bit) set to TRUE (1) if the condition is satisfied:
    rxmsq_flags.rxfmlifo – the stack entry is processed LIFO (last in/first out).

rxmsq_value (RXSTRING)
    The entry to be set into the queue.

Subfunction RXMSQSIZ (return the current queue size) parameter list:
```
      typedef struct {
        ULONG rxmsq_size;
      } RXMSQSIZ_PARM;
```

rxmsq_size (ULONG)
    Number of lines in the queue.

Subfunction RXMSQNAM (set current queue name) parameter list:
```
      typedef struct {
        RXSTRING rxmsq_name;
      } RXMSQNAM_PARM;
```

rxmsq_name (RXSTRING)
>   RXSTRING containing the queue name.

Example:
The same queue processing handler displays the passed queue entry.

```
#include <stdio.h>
#define INCL_RXSYSEXIT
#include <rexxsaa.h>

LONG APIENTRY xqueue(
  LONG    ExitNumber,
  LONG    SubFunction,
  PEXIT   ParmBlock)
{
union {
  PEXIT           pexit;
  RXMSQPSH_PARM *pmsq;
} u;

  u.pexit = ParmBlock;
  switch (SubFunction) /* test whether PUSH (QUEUE) subfunction */
  {
    case RXMSQPSH:
      /* display queue entry */
      printf("queue entry:%s\n",u.pmsq->rxmsq_value.strptr);
      return RXEXIT_HANDLED; /* end of exit processing /
    default:
      return RXEXIT_NOT_HANDLED; /* perform default processing */
  }
}
```

16.9.3.6 RXSIO – **Standard Input/Output.** RXSIO is called for standard input/output processing.

The RXSIO exit has four subfunctions:

>   RXSIOSAY (1) Perform SAY clause.
>   RXSIOTRC (2) Write trace output
>   RXSIOTRD (3) Read input from the terminal.
>   RXSIODTR (4) Read debug input from the terminal.

Subfunction RXSIOSAY (perform SAY clause) parameter list:
```
typedef struct {
  RXSTRING rxsio_string;
} RXSIOSAY_PARM;
```

rxsio_string (RXSTRING)
    String to be displayed.

Subfunction RXSIOTRC (write trace output) parameter list:
```
typedef struct {
  RXSTRING rxsio_string;
} RXSIOTRC_PARM;
```

rxsio_string (RXSTRING)
    Trace line to be displayed.

Subfunction RXSIOTRD (read input from the terminal) parameter list:
```
typedef struct {
  RXSTRING rxsiotrd_retc;
} RXSIOTRD_PARM;
```

rxsiotrd_retc (RXSTRING)
    RXSTRING for output.

Subfunction RXSIODTR (read debug input from the terminal) parameter list:
```
typedef struct {
  RXSTRING rxsiodtr_retc;
} RXSIODTR_PARM;
```

rxsiodtr_retc (RXSTRING)
    RXSTRING for output.

The PARSE LINEIN instruction, and the CHARIN, CHAROUT, CHARS, LINEIN, LINEOUT, and LINES functions do not invoke the RXSIODTR system exit handler.

Example:
The sample exit handler is invoked before the standard input/output commands are processed. This exit handler processes only the RXSIOSAY and RXSIOTRD subfunctions. For SAY the parameter string is displayed (with the prefix SAY:). For terminal input the fixed text "input text" is returned.

```
define INCL_RXSYSEXIT /* system exit definitions */
#include <rexxsaa.h>
#include <stdio.h>
#include <string.h>
```

```
LONG fsysexit(
  LONG  ExitNumber,
  LONG  SubFunction,
  PEXIT ParmBlock)
{
char str[256];
static char text[] = "input text";
union {
  PEXIT            pexit;
  RXSIOSAY_PARM *psay;
  RXSIOTRD_PARM *ptrd;
} u;

  u.pexit = ParmBlock;
  switch (SubFunction)
  {
    case RXSIOSAY:
      strcpy(str,RXSTRPTR(u.psay->rxsio_string));
      printf("SAY:%s\n",str);
      break;
    case RXSIOTRD: /* read from standard input */
      MAKERXSTRING(u.ptrd->rxsiotrd_retc,text,strlen(text));
      break;
     default:
       return RXEXIT_NOT_HANDLED; /* function RC */
  }
  return RXEXIT_HANDLED; /* function RC */
}
```

16.9.3.7 RXTER – **Termination Processing.** The termination exit is called at the start of program termination. It does not receive any parameters.

16.9.3.8 RXTRC – **Test External Trace Indicator.** RXTRC is called to test the external trace indicator. If activated, this exit will be called after each REXX instruction, with a consequent performance degradation. The RexxSetTrace function can also be used to activate REXX tracing without causing this exit handler to receive control.

Parameter list:
```
    typedef struct {
      RXTRC_FLAGS rxtrc_flags;
    } RXTRCTST_PARM;
```

rxtrc_flags (RXTRC_FLAGS)
  External trace status flag rxtrc_flags.rxftrace (one bit):
  1 (TRUE) Activate external trace.
  0 (FALSE) Deactivate external trace.

Example:
The sample exit handler is invoked before each statement is processed. A counter is
maintained. The trace indicator is set after three statements have been processed.

```
#define INCL_RXSYSEXIT
#include <rexxsaa.h>

LONG fsysexit(
  LONG  ExitNumber,
  LONG  SubFunction,
  PEXIT ParmBlock)
{
union {
  PEXIT           pexit;
  RXTRCTST_PARM *pparm;
} u;
static int count = 0;

  u.pexit = ParmBlock;
  if (++count > 3) /* increment and test count */
    u.pparm->rxtrc_flags.rxftrace = 1; /* set trace active */
  return RXEXIT_HANDLED; /* function RC */
}
```

16.9.4 Substructures
Some system exit parameter block structures use the further substructures:

RXCMD_FLAGS   command status
RXFNC_FLAGS   function status
RXHLT_FLAGS   set halt status
RXMSQ_FLAGS   queue LIFO flag
RXTRC_FLAGS   set external trace status

16.9.4.1 RXCMD_FLAGS.
```
typedef struct {
  unsigned rxfcfail : 1; /* command failed */
  unsigned rxfcerr  : 1; /* command ERROR occurred */
} RXCMD_FLAGS;
```

16.9.4.2 RXFNC_FLAGS.

```
typedef struct {
  unsigned rxfferr  : 1; /* invalid call to routine */
  unsigned rxffnfnd : 1; /* function not found */
  unsigned rxffsub  : 1; /* called as a subroutine */
} RXFNC_FLAGS ;
```

16.9.4.3 RXHLT_FLAGS.

```
typedef struct {
  unsigned rxfhhalt : 1; /* set if halt occurred */
} RXHLT_FLAGS;
```

16.9.4.4 RXMSQ_FLAGS.

```
typedef struct {
  unsigned rxfmlifo : 1; /* stack entry LIFO if set */
} RXMSQ_FLAGS;
```

16.9.4.5 RXTRC_FLAGS.

```
typedef struct {
  unsigned rxftrace : 1; /* set to run external trace */
} RXTRC_FLAGS;
```

16.9.5 Sample System Exit

Main program to register exit, and to execute its invoking exec (x1.cmd):

```
#define INCL_RXSYSEXIT /* system exit definitions */
#include <rexxsaa.h>
#define EXITNAME "CMD"
#define EXITMODNAME "URX"
#define EXITPROCNAME "XQUEUE"
char str[250];
SHORT rc, frc;
RXSTRING *argv, retval;
RXSYSEXIT sysexit[2];

main()
{
  /* register exit */
  rc = RexxRegisterExitDll(EXITNAME,EXITMODNAME,EXITPROCNAME,
      NULL,RXEXIT_DROPPABLE);
  /* initialize system exit block */
  sysexit[0].sysexit_name = EXITNAME;
  sysexit[0].sysexit_code = RXMSQ; /* manipulate queue function */
  sysexit[1].sysexit_code = RXENDLST; /* end-of-list */
```

```
       /* invoke REXX interpreter with system exit */
       frc = RexxStart(0, argv, "a:\\x1.cmd", NULL, NULL, RXCOMMAND,
              sysexit, &rc, &retval);
   }
```

x1.cmd exec:

```
       /* x1.cmd exec */
       PUSH "alpha"
```

System exit program:

```
       #include <stdio.h>
       #define INCL_RXSYSEXIT
       #include <rexxsaa.h>

       union {
         PEXIT           pexit;
         RXMSQPSH_PARM *pmsq;
       } u;

       RexxExitHandler xqueue; /* function prototype */

         LONG APIENTRY xqueue(
         LONG    ExitNumber,
         LONG    SubFunction,
         PEXIT   ParmBlock)
       {
         u.pexit = ParmBlock; /* point to common (MSQ) structure */
         switch (SubFunction)
         {
           case RXMSQPSH: /* process PUSH (QUEUE) subfunction */
             /* display queue entry */
             printf("queue entry:%s\n",u.pmsq->rxmsq_value.strptr);
             return RXEXIT_HANDLED; /* end of exit processing */
           default:
             return RXEXIT_NOT_HANDLED; /* perform default processing */
         }
       }
```

16.10 HALT AND TRACE FUNCTIONS

In addition to the halt and trace system exits, REXX has also a group of halt and trace functions that are usually invoked from an asynchronous routine. Whereas the REXX interpreter invokes the halt and trace system exits for each statement, the halt and trace functions are called only when required – with a consequent reduction in the processing overhead.

The following three functions are available:

RexxSetHalt	Raise the halt condition.
RexxSetTrace	Activate interactive trace mode.
RexxResetTrace	Deactivate interactive trace mode.

These functions require the process and thread identifier of the target REXX exec. The OS/2 DosGetInfoBlocks function can be used to get this information (see Appendix G.5).

The preprocessor directive
```
#define INCL_RXARI
```
includes the halt and trace definitions.

The functions return one of the values:

RXARI_OK (0)	Successful processing.
RXARI_NOT_FOUND (1)	The REXX exec was not found (e.g., invalid process or thread identifier).
RXARI_PROCESSING_ERROR (2)	Processing error.

16.10.1 RexxResetTrace – Deactivate Interactive Trace Mode

The RexxResetTrace function deactivates the interactive trace mode for the target REXX exec.

Prototype:
```
APIRET APIENTRY RexxResetTrace(
   PID ProcessId,
   TID ThreadId);
```

ProcessId (PID)

The process id of the target REXX exec. **ProcessId** is that of the application process that called the RexxStart function to invoke the exec.

ThreadId (TID)

The thread id of the target REXX exec. **ThreadId** is that of the application process which called the RexxStart function to invoke the exec.

16.10.2 RexxSetHalt – Raise the Halt Condition

The RexxSetHalt function terminates the target REXX exec.

Prototype:
```
APIRET APIENTRY RexxSetHalt(
    PID ProcessId,
    TID ThreadId);
```

ProcessId (PID)

The process id of the target REXX exec. **ProcessId** is that of the application process which called the RexxStart function to invoke the exec.

ThreadId (TID)

The thread id of the target REXX exec. **ThreadId** is that of the application process which called the RexxStart function to invoke the exec.

Example:
```
RexxSetHalt(27,1);
```

16.10.3 RexxSetTrace – Activate Interactive Trace Mode

The RexxSetTrace function activates the interactive trace mode for the target REXX exec.

Prototype:
```
APIRET APIENTRY RexxSetTrace(
    PID ProcessId,
    TID ThreadId);
```

ProcessId (PID)

The process id of the target REXX exec. **ProcessId** is that of the application process which called the RexxStart function to invoke the exec.

ThreadId (TID)

The thread id of the target REXX exec. **ThreadId** is that of the application process which called the RexxStart function to invoke the exec.

16.10.4 Asynchronous Sample Program

The sample program performs the following processing:

- Get the process and thread identifier of the current (main) program (with the DosGetInfoBlocks function).
- Create a new thread for the current process with the DosCreateThread function. Pass the address of a structure containing the process and thread identifier. This asynchronous routine waits for user terminal input to control a parallel-running REXX exec. Any terminal input initiates interactive debugging.
- Start a REXX exec with the RexxStart function.

Figure 16.12 shows the schematic processing involved.

Sample program:

```
#define INCL_DOSPROCESS /* process and thread definitions */
#include <os2.h>

#define INCL_RXARI /* halt and trace definitions */
#include <rexxsaa.h>
#include <stdio.h>

typedef struct {
  TID tid;
  PID pid;
} SX;

typedef union {
  ULONG dummy;
  SX   *psx;
} UX;

FNTHREAD asynch; /* function prototype */

main()
{
  PTIB pptib;
  TIB2 *ptib2;
  PPIB pppib;
  TID newtid;
  PFNTHREAD afptr;

  SX id;
  UX arg;
  arg.psx = &id;

  char str[250];
  char cmdname[] = "g:\\pgm\\x3.cmd";
  SHORT rc;
  RXSTRING retval;

  /* get thread, process IDs */
  DosGetInfoBlocks(&pptib, &pppib);
  ptib2 = pptib->tib_ptib2;
  id.pid = pppib->pib_ulpid;
  id.tid = ptib2->tib2_ultid;
```

```
/* start asynchronous thread */
afptr = (PFNTHREAD)asynch;
DosCreateThread(&newtid, afptr, arg.dummy, 0L, 4096);
/* invoke REXX interpreter */
MAKERXSTRING(retval,str,sizeof(str));
RexxStart(0, NULL, cmdname, NULL, NULL, RXCOMMAND,
        NULL, &rc, &retval);
}

/* asynchronous function */
VOID asynch(ULONG parm)
{
  UX arg;

  arg.dummy = parm;
  puts("hit any key for debug");
  getchar();
  RexxSetTrace(arg.psx->pid,arg.psx->tid);
  DosExit(0L, 0L); /* terminate thread */
}
```

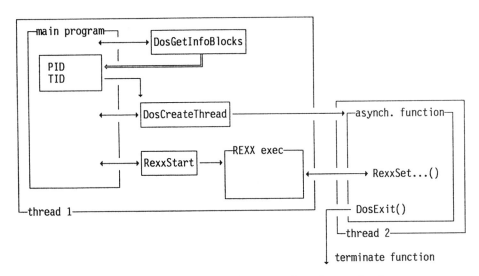

Figure 16.12. Schematic processing for the use of asynchronous functions.

16.11 QUEUE INTERFACE

This section is included for completeness as, with the exception of the RXMSQ system exit, OS/2 REXX does not have an API function to access the REXX queue. Although queue elements may only be placed at the head or tail of a queue, the inability to name elements can be mitigated by using named queues (only one queue is concurrently active) or assigning a tag to the queue elements. The worked example in Chapter 18 illustrates this technique.

If a program requires PUSH, PULL, or other similar services, a REXX exec must be invoked to perform the appropriate processing. An efficient means of doing this is to implement the exec as an in-store procedure, and so avoid the overhead of loading the exec from an external file. The QueuePush and QueuePull functions show how this can be done. The definition of a static Instore structure causes the tokenized image to be used on subsequent invocations, thus saving the time that would otherwise be required to reprocess to source exec.

Sample QueuePush and QueuePull functions:
The QueuePush function places the specified element at the head of the current queue. The equivalent processing to place an element at the tail (end) of the current queue can be performed by replacing the PUSH instruction with a QUEUE instruction.
The QueuePull function retrieves the next element from the head of the current queue. A null element is returned if the queue is empty (the QUEUED() function returns the value 0). To simplify processing, the result buffers have a maximum length of 100 characters.

```
#define INCL_RXSUBCOM /* Subcommand interface definitions */
#include <rexxsaa.h>
#include <string.h>

void QueuePush(char *pc)
{
  static char exec[] = "PARSE ARG qelem\r"\
                       "PUSH qelem\r"\
                       "RETURN qelem\r";

  static RXSTRING Instore[2] = { sizeof(exec)-1, exec,
                                 0, NULL };

  SHORT rc;
  LONG Argc = 1; /* number of arguments */
  RXSTRING Argv;

  MAKERXSTRING(Argv,pc,strlen(pc));
  RexxStart(Argc, &Argv, "queue", Instore, NULL, RXCOMMAND,
            NULL, &rc, NULL);
  return;
}
```

```
char *QueuePull(void)
{
  static char exec[] = "IF QUEUED() = 0 THEN RETURN ''\r"\
                        "PARSE PULL qelem\r"\
                        "RETURN qelem\r";

  static RXSTRING Instore[2] = { sizeof(exec)-1, exec,
                                 0, NULL };

  short rc, frc;
  RXSTRING Result;

  #define LEN 100
  char buf[LEN];
  static char str[LEN];

  /* preassign result buffer */
  MAKERXSTRING(Result,buf,sizeof(buf));
  frc = RexxStart(0, NULL, "queue", Instore, NULL, RXCOMMAND,
              NULL, &rc, &Result);
  if (frc == 0) /* REXX interpreter successfully invoked */
  {
    /* create C-processable result */
    str[sizeof(str)-1] = 0x00; /* preset terminating null character */
    strncpy(str,RXSTRPTR(Result),sizeof(str)-1);
    /* free result buffer, if interpreter-allocated */
    if (RXSTRPTR(Result) != buf)
      DosFreeMem(RXSTRPTR(Result));
  }
  return str;
}
```

Sample test program to enter an element into the queue, and retrieve and display the element:

```
#include <stdio.h>
/* function prototypes */
void QueuePush(char *);
char *QueuePull(void);

void main(void)
{
  char *pc;
  QueuePush("alpha beta");
  pc = QueuePull();
```

```
    printf("queue elem:%s",pc);
}
```

16.12 OTHER LANGUAGE SUPPORT

Although all the examples have been shown in C, REXX support is not restricted to the C language. Other 32-bit programming languages that support compatible C function-calling sequence can be used. In particular, PL/I Package 2 provides limited support for REXX APIs, although no function declarations are currently available.

16.12.1 PL/I External Function

The PL/I program RxFExe invokes the REXX interpreter RexxStart to execute the GOEX.CMD exec that calls the external programmed function RXFCON. Two arguments are passed to RXFCON: alpha and beta. RXFCON concatenates the received parameters, and returns this result string.

If the result string exceeds the allocated size (here 256 characters), the RXFCON function terminates with a function invocation error (REXX error 40).

```
RXFEXE.PLI
     *Process LANGLVL( SAA2 );
     *Process LIMITS( EXTNAME( 31 ));


     RxFExe: Proc Options( Main );

     dcl RexxStart entry( fixed bin(31),
                          pointer,
                          pointer,
                          pointer,
                          pointer,
                          fixed bin(31),
                          pointer,
                          pointer,
                          pointer)
               returns( fixed bin(31) )
               options( byvalue      /* pass parameters by value */
                        linkage(system));/* use system linkage   */
                                     /* convention.              */

     dcl RexxRegisterFunctionExe entry( pointer,
                             entry)
               returns( fixed bin(31) )
               options(byvalue linkage(system));
```

```
dcl fptr entry variable,
        (RXFCON) entry;

dcl FuncName char(9);

dcl Argc fixed bin(31);
dcl 1 Argv(2),
      2 strlength fixed bin(31),
      2 strptr ptr;
dcl ProcName char(16);
dcl EnvName char(8) init('USER');
dcl 1 SysExits(1),
      2 sysexit_name ptr,
      2 sysexit_code fixed bin(31);
dcl ReturnCode fixed bin(15);
dcl 1 Result,
      2 strlength fixed bin(31),
      2 strptr ptr;

dcl RxCommand fixed bin(31) init(0);
dcl RxEndLst fixed bin(31) init(0);

dcl rc fixed bin(31);
dcl charstring char(256) based(p);
dcl ResultString char(256) varying;
dcl p pointer;

dcl p1 char(5) init('alpha'); /* arguments */
dcl p2 char(4) init('beta');

FuncName = 'RXFCON'||'00'x; /* external function name */
fptr = RXFCON; /* address of local function */
rc = RexxRegisterFunctionExe( addr(FuncName), fptr);
Argc = 2; /* no. of arguments */
Argv(1).strptr = addr(p1);
Argv(1).strlength = length(p1);
Argv(2).strptr = addr(p2);
Argv(2).strlength = length(p2);
SysExits(1).sysexit_code = RxEndLst;
Result.strlength = 0; /* zeroize result */
ProcName = 'GOEX.CMD'||'00'x;
rc   = RexxStart(Argc,
                 addr(Argv(1)),
                 addr(ProcName),
```

```
                        NULL(),
                        addr(EnvName),
                        RxCommand,
                        addr(SysExits(1)),
                        addr(ReturnCode),
                        addr(Result));
        put list('RxStart: ', rc);
        put list('ReturnCode: ', ReturnCode);
        p = Result.strptr;
        ResultString = substr(charstring,1,Result.strlength);
        put list('Result: ', ResultString);
        return;

    end RxFExe;

RXFCON.PLI
        *Process LANGLVL( SAA2 );
        *Process LIMITS( EXTNAME( 31 ));

        RXFCON: Proc (FunctionName,
                        Argc,
                        PArgv,
                        QueueName,
                        RetVal)
                        returns(fixed bin(31))
                        options(byaddr linkage(system));

            dcl FunctionName char(8);
            dcl Argc fixed bin(31) byvalue;
            dcl PArgv ptr byvalue;
            dcl 1 Argv(1) based(PArgv), /* dimension is placeholder */
                2 strlength fixed bin(31),
                2 strptr ptr;
            dcl QueueName char(8);
            dcl 1 RetVal,
                2 strlength fixed bin(31),
                2 strptr ptr;

            dcl result char(256) static;
            dcl rc fixed bin(31);
            dcl (i,j,l) fixed bin(31);
            dcl p ptr;
            dcl charstring char(256) based(p);
```

```
        i = 1; /* initialize result index */
        /* concatenate passed parameters */
        do j = 1 to Argc;
          l = Argv(j).strlength;
          p = Argv(j).strptr;
          if (i+l > length(result)) /* test bounds */
             then return (40); /* function error return */
          substr(result,i,l) = substr(charstring,1,l);
          i = i+l;
        end;
        /* return result */
        RetVal.strlength = i-1; /* result length */
        RetVal.strptr = addr(result);
        return (0); /* function return code */
      end RXFCON;
```

GOEX.CMD
```
      PARSE ARG p1, p2
      x = RXFCON(p1, p2)
      SAY 'x:' x /* function result */
      return 4;
```

16.12.2 PL/I Subcommand

The PL/I program RxCEnv is a simple subcommand handler implemented as a DLL module. RxCEnv returns the passed command string as subcommand return value.

The GOCMD.CMD exec registers the subcommand handler, which is assumed to be in RXFUNCT.DLL.

RXCENV.PLI
```
      *Process LANGLVL( SAA2 );
      *Process LIMITS( EXTNAME( 31 ));

      /* command environment */
      RXCENV: Proc ( PCommand,
                     Flags,
                     RetVal)
                     returns(fixed bin(31))
                     options(byaddr nodescriptor linkage(system));

      dcl Flags fixed bin(15);
      dcl 1 RetVal,
            2 strlength fixed bin(31),
            2 strptr ptr;
```

```
dcl PCommand pointer byvalue;
dcl 1 Command based(PCommand),
      2 strlength fixed bin(31),
      2 strptr ptr;

dcl p ptr;
dcl charstring char(256) based(p);
dcl CommandString char(256) static;

/* get command */
p = Command.strptr;
CommandString = substr(charstring,1,Command.strlength);
/* return passed command */
Retval.strlength = Command.strlength;
Retval.strptr = addr(CommandString);
return (0); /* subcommand return code */
end RXCENV;
```

GOCMD.CMD
```
"RXSUBCOM REGISTER user rxfunct rxcenv" /* register function handler */
SAY 'RC:' RC
ADDRESS user
"gamma delta"
SAY "return:" RC
```

16.13 EXAMPLE

Chapter 18 contains a comprehensive worked example that illustrates many API facilities.

17

Service Routines

17.1 INTRODUCTION

Service routines (commands and functions) are available to perform many of the services provided by APIs at the handler registration level. These service routines are used directly from REXX execs.

REXX has four service routines:

RXSUBCOM   Register, deregister, load, and query subcommand handlers (command).

RXFUNCADD   Register an external function (function).

RXFUNCDROP   Deregister an external function (function).

RXFUNCQUERY   Test the registration status of an external function (function).

Table 17.1 shows the equivalent API. Note that there is no equivalent API for RXSUBCOM LOAD.

```
RXSUBCOM
   REGISTER      RexxRegisterSubcomDll
   DROP          RexxDeregisterSubcom
   QUERY         RexxQuerySubcom
   LOAD          -
RXFUNCADD        RexxRegisterFunctionDll
RXFUNCDROP       RexxDeregisterFunction
RXFUNCQUERY      RexxQueryFunction
```

Table 17.1. Correspondence between built-in service and equivalent API.

17.2 RXSUBCOM COMMAND

The RXSUBCOM command registers, deregisters, loads, and queries subcommand handlers. Each of these operations is specified as a subcommand.

The command return code (RC variable) indicates the function processing status:

0	Successful processing.
10	Ok, duplicate subcommand handler registered.
30	Subcommand handler not registered.
50	The DLL could not be loaded.
1002	Insufficient memory to process function.
-1	Parameter missing or invalid.

17.2.1 RXSUBCOM REGISTER – Register a DLL Subcommand Handler

The RXSUBCOM REGISTER command registers a subcommand handler that resides in a DLL module.

Syntax:
```
►►──RXSUBCOM REGISTER SubcomName ModuleName ProcName──►◄
```

SubcomName
> Name of the subcommand environment; i.e., the name used in the ADDRESS instruction.

ModuleName
> The name of the Dynamic Link Library (DLL) that contains the processing program (procname) for the environment. **ModuleName** is specified without the .DLL extension.

ProcName
> The name of the subcommand handler in the DLL.

Example:
```
"RXSUBCOM REGISTER user urx fuser"
```

This example registers the program fuser in the urx.dll DLL library as handler for subcommands in the user environment.

17.2.2 RXSUBCOM DROP – Deregister Subcommand Handler

The RXSUBCOM DROP command deregisters a subcommand handler.

Syntax:
```
►►──RXSUBCOM DROP SubcomName──┬──────────────┬──►◄
                             └─ ModuleName ─┘
```

SubcomName
> Name of the subcommand environment; i.e., the name used in the ADDRESS instruction.

ModuleName
> The name of the DLL file that contains the subcommand handler. If **Module-Name** is omitted, the global subcommand list will be searched.

Example:
```
"RXSUBCOM DROP user"
```

17.2.3 RXSUBCOM QUERY – Test Subcommand Status
The RXSUBCOM QUERY command returns the status of a subcommand handler.

Syntax:

SubcomName
> Name of the subcommand environment; i.e., the name used in the ADDRESS instruction.

ModuleName
> The name of the DLL file that contains the subcommand handler. If **Module-Name** is omitted, the global subcommand list will be searched.

Example:
```
"RXSUBCOM QUERY user urx"
IF RC = 0 THEN SAY "environment registered"
```

This example tests whether the user environment (contained in urx.dll) has been registered.

17.2.4 RXSUBCOM LOAD – Load Subcommand
The RXSUBCOM LOAD command loads a subcommand handler.

Syntax:
```
►►──RXSUBCOM LOAD SubcomName──┬──────────────┬──►◄
                             └─ ModuleName─┘
```

SubcomName
> Name of the subcommand environment; i.e., the name used in the ADDRESS instruction.

ModuleName
> The name of the DLL file that contains the subcommand handler. If **Module-Name** is omitted, the LIBPATH environment variable specifies the library search order.

Example:
```
"RXSUBCOM LOAD user urx"
```
This example loads the user environment from urx.dll.

17.3 EXTERNAL FUNCTION SERVICES

External function services are external (built-in) REXX functions to register, deregister, and query external function handlers:

RXFUNCADD	Register an external function.
RXFUNCDROP	Deregister an external function.
RXFUNCQUERY	Test the registration status of an external function.

The function return code indicates the function processing status:

0	Successful processing.
10	Ok, function already registered.
20	Insufficient memory to process function.
30	Function not registered.
40	DLL module name not found.
50	Entry point not found in DLL module.

17.3.1 RXFUNCADD – Register Function
The RXFUNCADD function registers an external function.

Syntax:
```
►►──frc = RXFUNCADD(FunctionName,ModuleName,ProcName)──►◄
```

FunctionName
> External function name – the name used to invoke the function.

ModuleName
> The name of the DLL file that contains the function handler.

ProcName
> The name of the function handler in the DLL.

Example:
```
     IF RXFUNCQUERY('SQLEXEC') = 0
        THEN RXFUNCADD('SQLEXEC','SQLAR','SQLEXEC');
```
registers SQLEXEC, if it is not currently registered.

17.3.2 RXFUNCDROP – Deregister Function
The RXFUNCDROP command deregisters (remove registration) a function.

Note: A function is deregistered for all REXX execs operating in the invoking session.

Syntax:
```
 ⊢──frc = RXFUNCDROP(FunctionName)──►
```

FunctionName
        External function name – the name used to invoke the function.

Example:
```
     IF RXFUNCQUERY('SQLEXEC') = 0
        THEN RXFUNCDROP('SQLEXEC');
```
deregisters SQLEXEC, if it is currently registered.

17.3.3 RXFUNCQUERY – Test Whether Function Is Not Registered
The RXFUNCQUERY function determines whether the function is not currently registered.
The value 0 (false) is returned if the function is currently registered.

Syntax:
```
 ⊢──frc = RXFUNCQUERY(FunctionName)──►
```

FunctionName
        External function name – the name used to invoke the function.

Example:
```
     IF RXFUNCQUERY('SQLEXEC') = 0
        THEN RXFUNCDROP('SQLEXEC');
```
tests whether SQLEXEC is registered.

18

Worked Example (Programmed Implementation)

18.1 INTRODUCTION

This chapter shows a programmed implementation of the exec shown in Chapter 13. The programmed implementation is realized as a subcommand, which is the form implemented for MVS and VM/CMS.

FEXECIO is a high-level file-oriented input/output routine that can process a complete file with a single call, whereas a loop is required for the standard line-mode input/output functions (LINEIN, etc.) to achieve the same result.

18.2 IMPLEMENTATION

The subcommand processor FEXECIO performs the mainline processing in two phases:

- analysis phase (MakeExec function)
- processing phase (PerformIO function)

To simplify the processing logic, an in-store exec is used to analyse the input command. The keyword values are set into a user queue. A local system exit (FQueueExit) intercepts the PUSH processing to place the queue entry into the UserQueue array (the keyword is used as index) – this approximates stem variable processing.

The processing phase tests which keywords have been set, and invokes the GetVar or GetQueue function to get the compound variables or queue entries accordingly. Because there is no program interface to the queue (other than as system exit), the GetQueue function is implemented as a small in-store exec to retrieve the next queue entry. To reduce the processing time, the tokenized exec is used for all invocations other than the first. The second (token) in-store array entry requires the attributes *static* and *initialized* to ensure that it is only invalidated for the initial call.

Note: To avoid overcomplicating the program, error checking is restricted to that directly connected with the processing logic. In particular, only limited bounds checking is performed.

Because the program logic parallels that of the exec shown in Chapter 13, the program is somewhat longer than it would otherwise be. Similarly, the use of native parsing-functions (e.g., sscanf) could reduce the program's execution time, but at the cost of increased complexity.

The program illustrates the use of a wide range of REXX programming techniques:

- a practical subcommand
- use of in-store procedures (to utilize powerful REXX facilities, such as parsing and queue processing)
- a system exit (to intercept PUSH queue requests)
- shared variable pool services
- RXSTRING manipulation

18.2.1 Program Code

```
1       #define INCL_RXSUBCOM /* Subcommand interface definitions */
        #define INCL_RXSYSEXII /* system exit definitions */
        #define INCL_RXSHV /* SHVBLOCK definition */
        #include <rexxsaa.h>

        #include <stdio.h>
        #include <string.h>

        #define EXITNAME "FEXIT"

2       #define NQ 5 /* no. of keywords */
        #define _OP "0"
        #define _LINES "1"
        #define _FILENAME "2"
        #define _VARNAME "3"
        #define _FINIS "4"
        #define OP 0
        #define LINES 1
        #define FILENAME 2
        #define VARNAME 3
        #define FINIS 4

3       RXSTRING Instore[2];
4       RXSYSEXIT Sysexit[2];
```

```
          /* function prototypes */
          void MakeExec(void);
          int RegLocalFunc(void);
          int PerformIO(void);
          char *GetQueue(void);
          char *GetVar(char *stem);
          RexxExitHandler FQueueExit;

          /* global variables */
5         char UserQueue[NQ][80]; /* parsed keyword array */
          char rcstr[3]; /* exec (numeric) result */
          char vd[256]; /* variable data */

          short rc, frc;
          int n; /* compound variable index */

6         ULONG APIENTRY FEXECIO(
            PRXSTRING  Command,
            PUSHORT    Flags,
            PRXSTRING  RetVal)
          {
            int i;

            for (i = 0; i < NQ; i++)
              memcpy(UserQueue[i],"",1); /* initialize array */
7           frc = RegLocalFunc(); /* register local system exit */
            if (frc == 0)
            {
              RXSTRING Result;

8             MakeExec(); /* create analysis exec */
9             MAKERXSTRING(Result,rcstr,sizeof(rcstr)); /* define result area */
              /* invoke REXX interpreter with system exit */
10            rc = RexxStart(1, Command, "EXECIO", Instore, NULL, RXCOMMAND,
                      Sysexit, &frc, &Result);
              if (frc == 0 && rc == 0)
11              frc = PerformIO();
            }
12          sprintf(rcstr,"%d\0",frc); /* format result */
13          MAKERXSTRING(*RetVal,rcstr,strlen(rcstr));
14          *Flags = RXSUBCOM_OK;
15          return 0;
          }

16        int RegLocalFunc() /* register local (PUSH) exit */
          {
            PFN afptr;
```

```
17          afptr = (PFN)FQueueExit; /* address of exit handler */
18          rc = RexxRegisterExitExe(EXITNAME,afptr,NULL);
            /* initialize system exit block */
19          Sysexit[0].sysexit_name = EXITNAME;
            Sysexit[0].sysexit_code = RXMSQ; /* exit function */
            Sysexit[1].sysexit_code = RXENDLST; /* end-of-list */
            return rc;
          }

20      void MakeExec() /* create analysis exec */
          {
21        static char exec[] =
          "PARSE UPPER ARG cmd lines op filename linenum '(' parm ')'\r"\
          "IF cmd <> 'EXECIO' THEN RETURN 1\r"\
          "IF lines = '' THEN RETURN 3\r"\
          "IF filename = '' THEN RETURN 3\r"\
          "SELECT\r"\
            "WHEN op = 'DISKW' THEN DO\r"\
              "PARSE VAR parm kywd parm\r"\
              "SELECT\r"\
                "WHEN kywd = 'STEM' THEN DO\r"\
                  "PARSE VAR parm varname finisparm .\r"\
                  "IF varname = '' THEN RETURN 5\r"\
                  "PUSH "_VARNAME" varname\r"\
                  "PUSH "_FINIS" finisparm\r"\
                "END\r"\
                "WHEN kywd = 'FINIS' THEN\r"\
                  "PUSH "_FINIS" kywd\r"\
                "WHEN kywd = '' THEN NOP\r"\
                "OTHERWISE\r"\
                  "RETURN 4\r"\
              "END\r"\
            "END\r"\
            "OTHERWISE\r"\
              "RETURN 2\r"\
          "END\r"\
          "PUSH "_FILENAME" filename\r"\
          "PUSH "_OP" op\r"\
          "PUSH "_LINES" lines\r"\
          "RETURN prc\r";

22        Instore[0].strptr = exec;
          Instore[0].strlength = strlen(exec);
          Instore[1].strptr = NULL;
          }
```

```
23      LONG APIENTRY FQueueExit(
          LONG    ExitNumber,
          LONG    SubFunction,
          PEXIT   ParmBlock) /* QUEUE system exit */
        {
          union {
            PEXIT            pexit;
            RXMSQPSH_PARM *pmsq;
          } u;

          char parm[80];
          int n;
24        u.pexit = ParmBlock;
25        switch (SubFunction)
          {
            case RXMSQPSH: /* process PUSH subfunction */
              /* parse input line */
26            sscanf(u.pmsq->rxmsq_value.strptr,"%d %s",&n,&parm);
27            strcpy(UserQueue[n],parm);
28            return RXEXIT_HANDLED; /* end of exit processing /
            default:
29            return RXEXIT_NOT_HANDLED; /* perform default processing */
          }
        }
30      int PerformIO() /* create file */
        {
          unsigned long ct;
          char *pc;
          FILE *fp;
31        if (strcmp(UserQueue[LINES],"*"))
            sscanf(UserQueue[LINES],"%ld",&ct);
          else
            ct = 999999; /* set high-value */
32        if (strcmp(UserQueue[OP],"DISKW"))
            return -1; /* unsupported operation */
33        fp = fopen(UserQueue[FILENAME],"wb");
          if (fp == NULL) return 1; /* open error */
34        for (n = 1; n <= ct ; n++) /* process each input line */
          {
            if (strlen(UserQueue[VARNAME]) != 0)
35            pc = GetVar(UserQueue[VARNAME]);
            else
36            pc = GetQueue();
```

```
37          if (pc == NULL) break;
38          strcat(pc,"\r\n\0"); /* set end-of-line */
            fwrite(pc,strlen(pc),1,fp); /* write line */
          }
39        fclose(fp); /* close file unconditionally */
          return 0;
        }
40      char *GetVar(char *stem) /* get compound variable */
        {
          char vn[256];
          char str[10];
          int rc;
41        SHVBLOCK shvblk;

          /* create compound name */
42        sprintf(str,"%d\0",n);
          strcpy(vn,stem);
          strcat(vn,str);
          /* build SHVBLK */
43        shvblk.shvnext = NULL;
          shvblk.shvcode = RXSHV_FETCH;
          shvblk.shvname.strptr = vn;
          shvblk.shvname.strlength = strlen(vn);
          shvblk.shvvalue.strptr = vd;
          shvblk.shvvalue.strlength = sizeof(vd);
44        rc = RexxVariablePool(&shvblk);
          if (rc != 0) return NULL; /* no data returned */
          return vd; /* return variable */
        }
45      char *GetQueue() /* get queue entry */
        {
46        static char exec[] = "IF queued() = 0 THEN RETURN ''\r"\
                        "PARSE PULL line\r"\
                        "RETURN line\r";
          static RXSTRING Instore[2] = {sizeof(exec), exec, 0, NULL};

          RXSTRING Result;
          short rc, frc;

          MAKERXSTRING(Result,vd,sizeof(vd)); /* define result buffer */
          frc = RexxStart(0, NULL, "EXECIO", Instore, NULL, RXCOMMAND,
                        NULL, &rc, &Result);
47        if (frc != 0) return NULL; /* interpreter error */
          if (rc != 0) return NULL; /* in-store command error */
```

```
48          if (RXSTRLEN(Result) == 0)
              return NULL; /* no queue entry */
49          else
            {
              /* create standard C string */
              vd[RXSTRLEN(Result)] = 0x00; /* set string-end */
              return vd; /* return result */
            }
          }
```

18.2.3 Program Explanation

1   Include the required <rexxsaa.h> definitions.

2   Define manifest constants. These (keyword) constants are the linkage between the analysed data stored in the queue and the associated processing. Each queue entry is prefixed with the appropriate code value. NQ specifies the number of keyword constants (used in the UserQueue array).

3   Define the global RXSTRING array Instore to contain the in-store exec information. In-store arrays always have two elements.

4   Define the global RXSYSEXIT array SysExit to contain the system exit information. In this example the SysExit array requires two elements: one element for the system exit, and one element for the end-of-array flag.

5   Define an array to contain the key code with its associated argument.

6   FEXECIO subcommand handler entry-point.

7   Call RegLocalFunc to register the local system exit.

8   Call MakeExec to create an in-store analysis exec.

9   Define result buffer into which the invoked exec can return its result. Because this invoked exec returns only a numeric result to indicate the processing status, a 3-byte string suffices.

10   Invoke the REXX interpreter (RexxStart) to process the internal exec referenced by Instore with the system exit defined in Sysexit activated.

11   Call the PerformIO function to write to the specified file.

12   Format the processing result as a character value.

13   Convert this value to a RXSTRING that is returned as the subcommand handler result.

14   Set Flags to indicate that the subcommand handler has successfully completed processing. The actual processing result is returned in RetVal.

15   Indicate that the subcommand handler was successfully invoked.

16   Register a local exit to process PUSH instructions.

17   Set the address of the local exit handler.

18   Call RexxRegisterExitExe to register the local exit handler. EXITNAME is the internal reference to the system exit.

19   Initialize the system exit control block. sysexit_name links to the handler; sysexit_code contains the exit type identifier (in this case RXMSQ – queue processing). The RXENDLST code indicates the last entry in the control block.

20   Function to create the in-store analysis exec.

21   The definition of the in-store analysis exec statements. Each statement must be terminated with \r (end-of-line).

22   Initialize the in-store control block. The first array element describes the source file (length and address). The second array element contains the equivalent information for the tokenized source. This tokenized source is intermediate code that can be more efficiently processed. This entry must be invalidated prior to the first call to stop spurious processing being performed.

23   FQueueExit system exit.

24   Set the address of the parameter block.

25   Process PUSH (QUEUE) subfunction.

26   Parse the input string into numeric code value and argument. The code value is used as index to the UserQueue array.

27   Set the corresponding argument into the UserQueue array.

28   Terminate the function with the RXEXIT_HANDLED condition to indicate that the exit was processed; otherwise, the exit condition would be processed by the REXX interpreter.

29   Terminate the function with the RXEXIT_NOT_HANDLED condition to indicate that the REXX interpreter must process the instruction.

30   Function to write the file.

31   Test whether the line count parameter (_LINES) contains *; if not the specified value is set into the ct variable, and otherwise ct is set to high-value (999999).

32   Terminate if the DISKW operation has not been specified.

33   Open the output file (write binary mode) with the specified file name. Terminate if the open fails.

34   Process each input line.

35   Test whether a stem variable has been specified (the _VARNAME entry is nonnull). If so, call the GetVar function with this stem variable to get the next compound variable.

36   Otherwise, call the GetQueue function to retrieve the next queue entry.

37   Both the GetVar and the GetQueue functions return a pointer to the read entry. NULL indicates no entry was found; i.e., the end of the input data.

38   Set "\r\n\0" at the end of the retrieved line, and write the line to the output file.

39   Unconditionally close the file at the end of processing.

40   GetVar function to retrieve the next compound variable. The global variable n contains the compound variable number.

41   Define shvblk as a SHVBLOCK entry.

42   Create the compound variable name (vn) from the stem variable name and the variable number.

43   Build the SHVBLOCK entry.

44   Call the RexxVariablePool function to retrieve the specified compound variable.

45   GetQueue function to get the next queue entry.

46   Use an in-store exec to perform queue processing. Define the exec with the static attribute so that the tokenized source can be used on subsequent calls.

47   Return a NULL pointer if an interpreter error was signalled.

48   Return a NULL pointer if no queue entry exists.

49   If no queue entry has been returned, create a standard C string by appending 0x00 at the end of the returned result, because the RexxStart interpreter does not place a terminating zero at the end of the result. The RXSTRLEN(Result) macro obtains the length of the result, which could possibly contain embedded 0x00s.

18.2.3 Program Preparation

The FEXECIO subcommand program would usually be invoked as a self-contained routine; i.e., a dynamic link library (DLL) module. The following sample program preparation statements assume:

USER	the subcommand environment name (the name used in the ADDRESS instruction)
URXLIB	the name of the DLL file that contains the program
FEXECIO	the name of the program (entry-point) in the DLL file

The following commands are required to prepare this program:

```
ICC /c /Ge- fexecio.c
LINK386 fexecio,urxlib.dll,,REXX,fexecio.def
```

The corresponding definitions file (fexecio.def) is:

```
LIBRARY URXLIB
DESCRIPTION 'EXECIO subcommand handler'
PROTMODE
DATA MULTIPLE NONSHARED LOADONCALL
EXPORTS FEXECIO
```

18.2.4 Sample Program Invocation

The FEXECIO subcommand handler must first be registered before it can be used. The following sample exec has both the registration and invocation – such system-like routines would normally be registered from the system startup routine (STARTUP.CMD procedure).

```
/* REXX */
/* register FEXECIO subcommand handler */
"RXSUBCOM REGISTER USER URXFUNCT FEXECIO"
/* set data */
B.1 = 'delta'
B.2 = 'epsilon'
B.3 = 'beta'
ADDRESS USER "EXECIO * DISKW data.txt (stem b."
IF RC = 0 THEN SAY "write ok"
```

Part 3

REXX Applications

19

Database Manager Interface

19.1 INTRODUCTION

Database Manager (renamed DB2/2 to emphasize its commonality with DB2) is IBM's relational database management system for OS/2.

REXX has three interfaces to Database Manager:

SQLDBS   Invoke Database Manager service.
SQLEXEC   Process SQL (Structured Query Language) request.
DSQCIX   Query Manager Callable Interface command.

Query Manager itself has one further interface:

DSQSETUP   Establish Query Manager application variables in REXX variable pool.

Application programs (REXX execs) use SQL statements to access a database (insert records, delete records, retrieve records, and so on). Database Manager services are required to administer the Database Manager environment for the application program. Query Manager is the standard dialogue-oriented user interface to Database Manager databases. Application programs can use the Query Manager Callable Interface to make use of Query Manager services (e.g., run a predefined query).

19.2 PROGRAMMING CONSIDERATIONS

The Database Manager interface functions (SQLDBS, SQLEXEC, DSQCIX, and DSQSETUP) must be registered before they can be used by REXX execs.

Table 19.1 contains the registration parameters for the REXX Database Manager
functions; the **module name** is the name of the DLL (Dynamic Link Library) that contains the function, and **proc name** is the entry point name.

Function Name	Module Name	Proc Name
DSQCIX	DSQCIX	DSQCIX
DSQSETUP	DSQCIX	DSQSETUP
SQLDBS	SQLAR	SQLDBS
SQLEXEC	SQLAR	SQLEXEC

Table 19.1. REXX Database Manager function registration parameters.

Note: The DSQRGSTR command can also be used to register DSQCIX; i.e., the command
sequences

    DSQRGSTR

and

    RXFUNCADD('DSQCIX','DSQCIX','DSQCIX');

are equivalent.

Example

    IF RXFUNCQUERY('SQLEXEC') <> 0
       THEN RXFUNCADD('SQLEXEC','SQLAR','SQLEXEC');

registers SQLEXEC if it is not currently registered.

19.3 DATABASE MANAGER ENVIRONMENT

A program that uses SQL services must run within the Database Manager environment. Three steps are required to activate the Database Manager environment:

- Identify the user (LOGON command).
- Initiate a Database Manager session (STARTDBM command).
- Connect the program to the appropriate database (START USING DATABASE routine).

Figure 19.1 illustrates this processing. There are corresponding stop commands
(LOGOFF, STOPDBM, STOP USING DATABASE) to terminate the action.

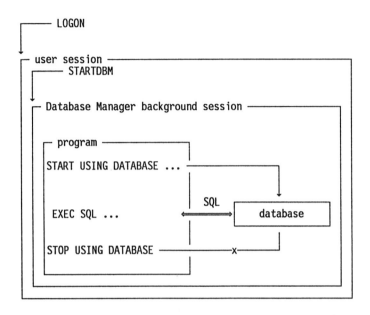

Figure 19.1. Interrelationship between program and Database Manager environment.

19.4 DATABASE MANAGER COMMANDS

Database Manager commands are invoked from either the OS/2 command prompt or a REXX exec.

This book describes only those Database Manager commands that are of direct interest to REXX applications:

LOGOFF	Disconnect user.
LOGON	Connect user.
STARTDBM	Start Database Manager.
STOPDBM	Stop Database Manager.

Equivalent Database Manager routines, which may be called directly from a program, are available for most of these commands. Table 19.2 hows the correspondence between Database Manager (DBM) commands and routines. A description of all the Database Manager commands is contained in the IBM manual: *Database Manager Programming Reference*.

DBM command	DBM routine
LOGOFF	UPMGLGN
LOGON	UPMGLGFF
STARTDBM	SQLGSTAR
STOPDBM	SQLGSTDM

Table 19.2. Equivalent Database Manager commands and routines.

19.5 SERVICE ROUTINES

There are three groups of service routines that can be invoked by programs:

- those routines concerned with Database Manager
- routine for the invocation of the Query Manager Callable Interface
- general routines

The Database Manager routines can be divided into two groups:

- those routines that are equivalent to the commands mentioned in Section 19.4
- routines required to make Database Manager services available to the invoking program; e.g., START USING DATABASE

19.6 DATABASE MANAGER ROUTINES

Various Database Manager routines are available to perform functions directly concerned with the Database Manager environment. SQL queries process the physical content of Database Manager entities (tables).
REXX supports all the Database Manager routines with exception of:

```
ALTER DATABASE PASSWORD
LOGOFF*
LOGON*
```

This book describes only those Database Manager routines that are of interest to the REXX application developer:

```
SQLGEXP      export
SQLGIMP      import
SQLGINTP     retrieve message
SQLGREST     restart database
SQLGSTAR     start Database Manager
SQLGSTDM     stop Database Manager
SQLGSTPD     stop using database
```

---

* The corresponding OS/2 command can be invoked from a REXX exec.

```
SQLGSTRD    start using database
UPMGLGFF    disconnect user
UPMGLGN     connect user
```

A description of all the Database Manager routines is contained in the IBM manual: *Database Manager Programming Reference*.

Table 19.3 lists the routine names and the equivalent REXX command. The two commands enclosed within parentheses are the equivalent OS/2 commands.

Routine	REXX Command
SQLGEXP	EXPORT
SQLGIMP	IMPORT
SQLGINTP	GET MESSAGE
SQLGREST	RESTART DATABASE
SQLGSTAR	START DATABASE MANAGER
SQLGSTDM	STOP DATABASE MANAGER
SQLGSTPD	STOP USING DATABASE
SQLGSTRD	START USING DATABASE
UPMGLGFF	(LOGOFF)
UPMGLGN	(LOGON)

Table 19.3. Routine names with equivalent REXX commands.

19.6.1 SQLGEXP – Export
The SQLGEXP routine exports to an OS/2 file the data produced by running an SQL query.

Syntax:

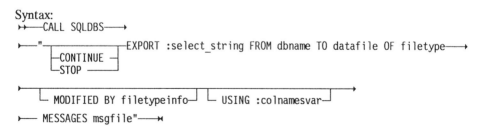

The **action** is specified as operation:

```
EXPORT              initial call
CONTINUE EXPORT     continue processing
STOP EXPORT         terminate processing
```

select_string
    SQL select statement string specifies the data to be extracted from the database.

dbname

Name of the database from which the data are to be exported.

datafile

Specification of the OS/2 file that is to contain the exported data.

filetype

Format of the OS/2 file to be produced:

DEL   delimited ASCII
WSF   work-sheet format
IXF   integration exchange format

IXF should be chosen if the exported data is to be subsequently loaded into a database.

colnamesvar

Compound variable containing the alternative column names.

colnamesvar.0   number of column names specified
colnamesvar.1   first column name
colnamesvar.2   second column name, and so on.

msgfile

Specification of the file to contain any messages produced by the export processor.

NUL   output suppressed.

filetypeinfo

Structure containing additional information appropriate for the specified **filetype**. The **filetypeinfo** entry is not used for IXF format files.

Example:

```
select_string = "SELECT PNO,PNAME FROM PERS";
CALL SQLDBS,
 "EXPORT :select_string FROM testdb",
 " TO a:expfile OF IXF MESSAGES a:msgfile";
```

19.6.2 SQLGIMP – Import

The SQLGIMP routine imports data from an OS/2 file into a Database Manager database.

Syntax:

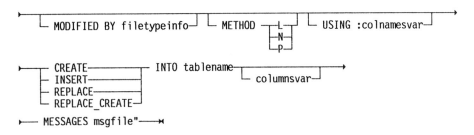

The **action** is specified as operation:

IMPORT	initial call
CONTINUE IMPORT	continue processing
STOP IMPORT	terminate processing

dbname

    Name of the database into which the data are to be imported.

datafile

    Specification of the OS/2 file that contains the data to be imported

filetype

    Format of the OS/2 file to be imported:

ASC	nondelimited ASCII
DEL	delimited ASCII
WSF	worksheet format
IXF	integration exchange format

METHOD

    Keyword denoting the method to be used to select columns:

L	locations
N	names
P	positions

colnamesvar

    Compound variable containing the names to be assigned to the columns in the table.

colnamesvar.0   number of column names specified
colnamesvar.1   first column name
colnamesvar.2   second column name, and so on.

msgfile

> Specification of the file to contain any messages produced by the import pro-
> cessor.
>
> NUL   output suppressed

filetypeinfo

> Structure containing additional information appropriate for the specified **file-
> type**.

Example:

```
CALL SQLDBS,
 "IMPORT TO testdb FROM a:expfile OF IXF",
 " CREATE INTO px MESSAGES a:msgfile";
```

19.6.3 SQLGINTP – Retrieve Message

The SQLGINTP routine retrieves the message text that applies to the current SQLCODE in
the specified SQLCA; this message text may contain supplementary information pertaining to the SQLCODE. Figure 19.2 shows the structure of the message area.

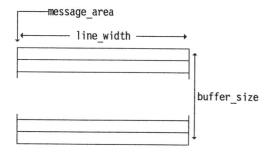

Figure 19.2. Structure of message buffer.

Syntax:

```
►►──CALL SQLDBS "GET MESSAGE INTO :msgvar──────────────────"──►◄
                                        └ LINEWIDTH width─┘
```

msgvar

> The variable into which the message text corresponding to the current value of
> SQLCA.SQLCODE is to be placed.

width

> The maximum line width for each text line, which is broken at word-end.
> Default: The text is not delimited.

One of the following return codes is set:

≥0   Successful execution. The value is the number of bytes returned in the message area.

-1   Insufficient main-storage is available for the message processing routine. No message is returned.

-2   The SQLCA did not contain a nonzero SQLCODE.

-3   The SQLCODE did not contain a valid message identifier.

-4   The **width** value is negative.

Example:
```
IF SQLCA.SQLCODE < 0 THEN DO;
  SAY "SQLCODE" SQLCA.SQLCODE SQLMSG;
  /* retrieve error message */
  CALL SQLDBS "GET MESSAGE INTO :msg LINEWIDTH 60";
END;
```

19.6.4 SQLGREST – Restart Database
The SQLGREST routine restarts a database that has been left in an uncommitted state.

Syntax:
```
►►──CALL SQLDBS "RESTART DATABASE dbname"──►◄
```

dbname
> The name of the database that is to be restarted.

19.6.5 SQLGSTAR – Start Database Manager
The SQLGSTAR routine starts the Database Manager background process. The SQLGSTAR routine and the STARTDBM command are equivalent.
Note: The SQLGSTAR routine is a global command that initiates the Database Manager for all processes.

Syntax:
```
►►──CALL SQLDBS "START DATABASE MANAGER"──►◄
```

19.6.6 SQLGSTDM – Stop Database Manager
The SQLGSTDM routine terminates the Database Manager background process. The SQLGSTDM routine and the STOPDBM command are equivalent.
Note: The SQLGSTDM routine is a global command that terminates the Database Manager for all processes.

Syntax:
```
►►──CALL SQLDBS "STOP DATABASE MANAGER"──►◄
```

19.6.7 SQLGSTPD – Stop Using Database

The SQLGSTPD routine disconnects the invoking program from the database to which it was connected.

Syntax:
```
►►──CALL SQLDBS "STOP USING DATABASE"──►◄
```

19.6.8 SQLGSTRD – Start Using Database

The SQLGSTRD routine connects the invoking program to the specified database.

Syntax:
```
►►──CALL SQLDBS "START USING DATABASE dbname──►
►──────────────────────────"──►◄
     └ IN ─┬─ EXCLUSIVE ─┬─ MODE ┘
           └ SHARED ─────┘
```

dbname
> The name of the database to which the program is to be connected.

19.7 THE SQL PROCESSOR

The SQL (Structured Query Language) processor is concerned with database data (e.g., retrieving data from a database).

Because the REXX procedural language is interpretive, programs written in REXX are directly executed (the precompilation, compilation, link, and bind required for conventional programs are not performed).

Embedded SQL statements are the statements in a REXX exec that interact with Database Manager. Embedded SQL statements are prefixed with EXEC SQL, and conform to usual the REXX syntax.

Embedded SQL statements can use:

* literals (character and numeric)
* database names
* host variables (prefixed by a colon (":"))

Host variables are REXX variables that supply the required data or contain returned data values. A special form of the host variable is an *indicator variable*, which contains a negative value if the corresponding database variable is null.

Character literals must be enclosed within quotes (e.g., 'alpha'). The colon is in many cases optional; it is only required to distinguish host variables from like-named Database Manager entries. However, it is good programming practice always to use a colon; consider the consequences of adding to a Database Manager table a column having the same name as a host variable.

The SQL Communication Area (SQLCA) is the compound variable SQLCA, and contains information returned by Database Manager to the invoking program; e.g., SQL return code. Table 19.4 describes the SQLCA format.

Because REXX is an interpretive language, programs written in it use dynamic SQL.

The SQLEXEC routine supports only a subset of the SQL DML (Data Manipulation Language):

```
CLOSE
COMMIT
DECLARE
DESCRIBE
EXECUTE
EXECUTE IMMEDIATE
FETCH
OPEN
PREPARE
ROLLBACK
```

Other statements (e.g., INSERT) can be invoked by means of the PREPARE and EXECUTE, or EXECUTE IMMEDIATE statements. REXX SQL statements can use only predefined statement and cursor names. Cursor names are C1 to C50 for cursors declared without HOLD, and c51 to c100 for cursors declared with HOLD. Statement names are S1 to S100.

REXX SQL statements have the syntax:

▸▸───CALL SQLEXEC *statement*───◂

statement
> The SQL statement to be invoked. **statement** conforms to the usual REXX syntax.

Example:
```
CALL SQLEXEC "EXECUTE s1 USING DESCRIPTOR :sqlda";
```

19.7.1 SQL Status

The status of each executable SQL statement after it has been processed is returned to the invoking program. Two status areas are set:

- the return code
- the SQLCA (SQL Communication Area)

The return code (REXX RC variable) contains general status as to whether the statement has been successfully processed:

0   Successful execution.
4   Warning, a positive SQLCODE has been set.
8   Error, a negative SQLCODE has been set.
12 Severe error.

Particular status information pertaining to the SQL query is stored as the return code in the SQLCODE variable of the SQLCA:

0   Successful execution (see following note).
>0   Warning.
<0   Error (-1 indicates an invalid SQLCA).

Note: If the SQLWARN0 field in the SQLCA is not blank, a warning condition has been set.

19.7.2 SQL Message Text

The message text associated with the current SQLCODE value can be retrieved with the SQLDBS GET MESSAGE routine, which formats the message contained in the SQLMSG variable – see Section 19.6.3.

19.8 REXX HOST VARIABLES

Host variables used in REXX execs are not explicitly defined; they are merely written in the SQL statement prefixed by the usual colon (:).

The REXX processor has predefined definitions for:

* statements (statement names S1 through S100)
* cursors (cursor names C1 through C100)

Example:
```
CALL SQLEXEC "DECLARE c1 CURSOR FOR s3";
```

19.9 REXX CONTROL VARIABLES

Database Manager routines set various REXX variables, as shown in Table 19.4.

```
RESULT              Operation Return Code

SQLCA.              compound variable containing the SQLCA
SQLCA.SQLCODE       SQL return code
SQLCA.SQLERRML      length of SQLCA.SQLERRMC data
SQLCA.SQLERRMC      error message tokens
SQLCA.SQLERRP       diagnostic information
SQLCA.SQLERRD.n     diagnostic information (n = 1 to 6)
SQLCA.SQLWARN.n     warning information (n = 1 to 6)

SQLISL              isolation level (CS, RR or UR)

SQLMSG              error message text

SQLFWREC            return data for ROLL FORWARD

SQLRIDA             default input SQLDA structure for
                    server procedures

SQLRODA             default output SQLDA structure for
                    server procedures

SQLRDAT             compound variable containing input data
                    passed from client application
```

Table 19.4. REXX control variables.

The SQLDA (SQL Descriptor Area) is represented as a compound variable with a user-specified stem name. Table 19.5 shows the structure of the SQLDA.

```
sqlda.              user compound variable containing the SQLDA
sqlda.SQLD          number of SQLVAR entries in the SQLDA

Each SQLVAR entry has the following format; n is the entry number

sqlda.n.SQLTYPE     data type
sqlda.n.SQLLEN      data length (see Note 1)
sqlda.n.SQLDATA     data value
sqlda.n.SQLIND      indicator variable
sqlda.n.SQLNAME     column name (see Note 2)
```

Table 19.5. REXX SQLDA structure.

Notes on Table 19.5:

1. *sqlda.n.*SQLLEN is a compound variable for a decimal data value; *sqlda.n.*SQLLEN.PRECISION is the precision, and *sqlda.n.*SQLLEN.SCALE is the scale factor.

2. *sqlda.n.*SQLNAME contains information only after a DESCRIBE or PREPARE statement.

19.9.1 RESULT Values

The REXX RESULT variable contains one of the following values:

n   n > 0, number of bytes in the formatted message returned by the SQLDBS GET MESSAGE routine.

0   The routine was executed successfully; SQLCA.SQLCODE contains the SQL status.

-1   Insufficient main-storage.

-3   SQLCA.SQLCODE contains an invalid value.

Other negative values are returned for miscellaneous error conditions.

19.10 REXX ISOLATION LEVEL

A bind file for REXX that is automatically generated during the creation of each database has Cursor Stability (CS) as the default isolation level. This isolation level can be changed with the SQLDBS CHANGE SQL ISOLATION LEVEL routine before the database is connected. The changed isolation level effects all REXX execs operating in the session.

Note: Each REXX exec should explicitly set its required isolation level, if there is a possibility that it has been changed by some other REXX exec.

19.10.1 CHANGE SQLISL – Change SQL Isolation Level

The REXX Database Manager routine CHANGE SQLISL is used to change the isolation level. The isolation level can only be changed before the database is connected.

Syntax:

```
►►──CALL SQLDBS "CHANGE SQLISL TO ─┬─CS─┬─"──►◄
                                   ├─RR─┤
                                   └─UR─┘
```

Example:

```
CALL SQLDBS "CHANGE SQLISL TO RR";
/* connect database */
CALL SQLDBS "START USING DATABASE testdb";
```

19.11 EMBEDDED SQL

The SQL statements in a program (exec) are called *embedded SQL statements*.

The SQL statements can be divided into two groups:

- those statements that return no or one result row
- those statements that return, or could return, more than one result row (this statement form is known as a *full-select*)

The first group contains all statements except for a full-select; the SELECT INTO statement returns only a single row, and so belongs to the first group. As REXX does not support the SELECT INTO statement, the REXX SQL statements can be simplified to those that return no data (non-SELECT) and those that return data (SELECT).

Non-SELECT SQL statements have two forms:

- PREPARE the SQL statement with a subsequent EXECUTE
- EXECUTE IMMEDIATE, which combines the PREPARE and EXECUTE statements

The first form is more efficient if the EXECUTE statements are to be performed more than once. Such EXECUTE statements can be parameterized.

The examples used in this section are based on the PERS table, in the TESTDB database, having the form:

```
PNO    PNAME
-------  ------------------------
1111   ALPHA
2222   BETA
3333   GAMMA
4444   -
```

Note: The PNAME entry for PNO 4444 is null.

PERS has the following table definition:
```
PNO SMALLINT NOT NULL,
PNAME VARCHAR(24)
```

Note: The program examples ignore or simplify error processing. The coding is illustrative of the use of embedded SQL, and does not necessarily depict good programming practice.

19.11.1 Non-SELECT Statement

The PREPARE statement takes the *host statement* as input, and produces an internal SQL statement identified by its *statement* name. The EXECUTE statement processes this statement. The functions of the PREPARE statement and the EXECUTE statement can be combined in a single EXECUTE IMMEDIATE statement.

The following non-SELECT example is equivalent to the SQL query:

```
INSERT INTO PERS (PNO,PNAME) VALUES(4444,'DELTA')
```

Example:

```
/* register Database Manager */
IF RXFUNCQUERY('SQLDBS') <> 0 THEN
  rcy = RXFUNCADD('SQLDBS','SQLAR','SQLDBS');
/* register SQLEXEC */
IF RXFUNCQUERY('SQLEXEC') <> 0 THEN
  rcy = RXFUNCADD('SQLEXEC','SQLAR','SQLEXEC');
/* connect database */
CALL SQLDBS "START USING DATABASE testdb";
/* initialize variables */
stmt = "INSERT INTO PERS (PNO,PNAME) VALUES(?,?)";
upno = 4444;
upname = "DELTA";
CALL SQLEXEC "PREPARE s1 from :stmt";
SAY "PREPARE SQLCODE:" SQLCA.SQLCODE;
CALL SQLEXEC "EXECUTE s1 USING :upno, :upname";
SAY "PREPARE SQLCODE:" SQLCA.SQLCODE;
/* disconnect database */
CALL SQLEXEC "CLOSE c1";
CALL SQLDBS "STOP USING DATABASE";
```

19.11.2 SQL SELECT with a Fixed Number of Columns

Database Manager (SQL) has no direct interface to host language tables. This means that SQL cannot directly return the values for more than one row to the calling program. SQL solves this by retrieving the selected rows into an internal work area, and then returning the individual rows. SQL uses an internal pointer called the *cursor* to maintain position to the current row.

The DECLARE statement produces an internal (host language) select statement, identified by the cursor, from the host statement. The OPEN statement uses this select statement to access the database to initialize an internal results table. The FETCH statement retrieves the next row from this results table; SQLCODE is set to +100 when the last row has been retrieved.

The example for static SQL performs a full selection with a fixed number of result columns equivalent to the SQL query:

```
SELECT PNO, PNAME FROM PERS
```

The content of PNO and PNAME for each row satisfying the selection criterion is to be displayed. The text NULL is displayed when PNAME contains no data (i.e., its indicator variable is negative).

Example:
```
/* register Database Manager */
IF RXFUNCQUERY('SQLDBS') <> 0 THEN
 rcy = RXFUNCADD('SQLDBS','SQLAR','SQLDBS');
/* register SQLEXEC */
IF RXFUNCQUERY('SQLEXEC') <> 0 THEN
 rcy = RXFUNCADD('SQLEXEC','SQLAR','SQLEXEC');
/* connect database */
CALL SQLDBS "START USING DATABASE testdb";
stmt = "SELECT PNO, PNAME FROM PERS";
CALL SQLEXEC "DECLARE c1 CURSOR FOR s1";
CALL SQLEXEC "PREPARE s1 from :stmt";
CALL SQLEXEC "OPEN c1";
DO WHILE SQLCA.SQLCODE < 100;
  CALL SQLEXEC "FETCH c1 INTO :upno, :upname:ipname";
  IF SQLCA.SQLCODE = 0 THEN DO;
    IF ipname >= 0
      THEN SAY upno upname;
      ELSE SAY upno "NULL";
  END;
END;
/* disconnect database */
CALL SQLEXEC "CLOSE c1";
CALL SQLDBS "STOP USING DATABASE";
```

19.11.3 SQL SELECT with a Variable Number of Columns

REXX execs do not have the usual problems encountered by conventional programs when used to process a variable number of columns (data values), namely the requirement that an SQLDA with the required number of column entries be defined and initialized with pointers to the corresponding data areas in the user-defined data buffer. In REXX, the DESCRIBE or PREPARE statement creates an SQLDA as a compound variable using the database information for the columns specified implicitly or explicitly in the host statement.

The data values and indicator variables are compound variables in the SQLDA. The variable SQLD specifies the actual (current) number of columns used in the SQLDA. The host variables from the SQLDATA (and SQLIND) are passed to the subsequent SQL statement (the USING DESCRIPTOR keywords indicate that an SQLDA is used). Figure 19.3 shows the schematic processing using the SQLDA.

Note: Figure 19.3 only shows that processing particular to the SQLDA; any other processing (e.g., EXECUTE) must be performed where appropriate.

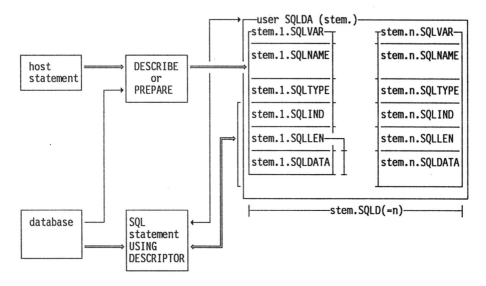

Figure 19.3. Processing using the REXX SQLDA.

The sample program illustrates the retrieval of a variable number of columns from a query entered from the terminal, and performs the following processing for each retrieved row:

- Prompt for the query by displaying the message "enter query".
- Process the query; for each retrieved row:
  - · display the column name
  - · display the maximum column width.
- Display the data content; a dash (-) is displayed for null fields.
- The SQLCODE is displayed should an SQL error occur.

The example processes three field types: CHAR, VARCHAR, and SMALLINT. Usually these field types suffice (e.g., DATE and TIME fields can also be displayed as character strings).

Example

```
/* register Database Manager */
IF RXFUNCQUERY('SQLDBS') <> 0 THEN
  rcy = RXFUNCADD('SQLDBS','SQLAR','SQLDBS');
/* register SQLEXEC */
IF RXFUNCQUERY('SQLEXEC') <> 0 THEN
  rcy = RXFUNCADD('SQLEXEC','SQLAR','SQLEXEC');
/* connect database */
CALL SQLDBS "START USING DATABASE testdb";
```

```
/* request query */
SAY "enter query"
PARSE PULL query;
/* process query */
CALL SelectStmt;
/* disconnect database */
CALL SQLDBS "STOP USING DATABASE";
EXIT; /* terminate exec */
SelectStmt:
  CALL SQLEXEC "DECLARE c1 CURSOR FOR s1";
  CALL TestSQLCODE;
  CALL SQLEXEC "PREPARE s1 INTO :sqlda FROM :query";
  CALL TestSQLCODE;
  /* save column names */
  DO j = 1 TO sqlda.SQLD;
    name.j = LEFT(sqlda.j.SQLNAME,18);
  END;
  IF SQLCA.SQLCODE >= 0 THEN DO;
    CALL SQLEXEC "OPEN c1";
    CALL TestSQLCODE;
    j = 0;
    DO i = 1 TO 999999;
      CALL SQLEXEC "FETCH c1 USING DESCRIPTOR :sqlda";
      CALL TestSQLCODE;
      IF SQLCA.SQLCODE <> 0 THEN LEAVE;
      DO j = 1 TO sqlda.SQLD;
        line = name.j;
        IF sqlda.j.SQLIND < 0
         THEN data = "-"
         ELSE data = RIGHT(sqlda.j.SQLLEN,5,'0') sqlda.j.SQLDATA;
        SAY line data;
      END;
    END;
  END;
  CALL SQLEXEC "CLOSE c1";
  CALL TestSQLCODE;
  RETURN;
TestSQLCODE:
  IF SQLCA.SQLCODE < 0
   THEN SAY "SQLCODE" SQLCA.SQLCODE SQLMSG;
  RETURN;
```

19.12 QUERY MANAGER CALLABLE INTERFACE

The Query Manager Callable Interface (DSQCI) can be called by applications to invoke Query Manager services. Query Manager is the standard dialogue program to process SQL requests. REXX fully supports the DSQCI with the DSQCIX command.

Each call to DSQCIX passes as parameter the Query Manager command that is to be executed (START must be the first command). Table 19.6 lists the start parameters; the **start parm** column lists the corresponding QUERYMGR command parameter.

Syntax:

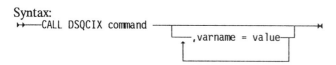

command

> The Query Manager command: GET, RUN, SET, START, etc. Each DSQCIX session must be initiated with the START command.

varname

> Variable name.

value

> Data value to be assigned to **varname**.

Example:

```
/* start DSQCIX session */
CALL DSQCIX "START","DSQSMODE='INTERACTIVE'","DSQSDBNM='TESTDB'";
IF DSQ_RETURN_CODE <> 0 THEN DO;
  SAY "return code" DSQ_RETURN_CODE;
  SAY "reason code" DSQ_REASON_CODE;
END;
```

Variable	Length	Start Parm	Description
DSQDSPLY	09		indicator for when screens are to be displayed, should be 'IMMEDIATE'
DSQSBUFF	02		work buffer size, default 35KB
DSQSCMD	08		name of the .CMD to invoke default: 'QRWEXECZ.CMD'
DSQSDBNM	08	/DATABASE	database name
DSQSMODE	11		mode 'INTERACTIVE' (dialogue) 'BATCH'
DSQSPOOL	04	/ROWBUFFER	pool size '0001' through '9999'
DSQSPROF	08	/PROFILE	profile name
DSQSQUAL	08	/DQUAL	list qualifier
DSQSRUN	27	/RUNPROC	name of procedure to be run
DSQSWDHD	03		is the window handle to be passed

Table 19.6. DSQCIX start parameters.

19.12.1 DSQCIX Status

DSQCIX sets status information for each call in status variables of the DSQCOMM (see Table 19.7).

DSQ_CANCEL_IND	command cancelled
DSQ_ERROR_ID	error id
DSQ_INSTANCE_ID	session identifier
DSQ_MESSAGE_ID	message id
DSQ_Q_MESSAGE_ID	query message id
DSQ_REASON_CODE	function reason code
DSQ_RETURN_CODE	function return code
DSQ_START_PARM_ERROR	parameter in error for START command

Table 19.7. DSQCIX status variables.

DSQ_CANCEL_IND
contains the cancel indicator:
0   command was not cancelled
1   command was cancelled

DSQ_ERROR_ID
contains further information pertaining to DSQ_REASON_CODE.

DSQ_MESSAGE_ID
contains the Query Manager message ID.

DSQ_REASON_CODE
contains reason code if an error has been signalled.

DSQ_RETURN_CODE
contains one of the following values:

0   successful
4   successful execution but warning issued
8   error
16   severe error, the Query Manager session is terminated.

Table 19.8 lists the Query Manager global status variables. The variables can be retrieved with the GET GLOBAL command; those variables directly associated with Query Manager objects (e.g., DSQAQNAM) may be changed with the SET GLOBAL command.

19.12.2 DSQSETUP – Establish Query Manager Application Variables in the REXX Variable Pool

The DSQSETUP function explicitly establishes Query Manager application variables in REXX variable pool. Because the first invocation of the DSQCIX function implicitly establishes these variables, the DSQSETUP function normally need not be called.

Syntax:

▸▸──CALL DSQSETUP──▸◂

Variable	Length	Description
DSQAAUTH	08	authorization ID
DSQADBNM	08	database name
DSQAQNAM	27	name of the last query edited
DSQAQTYP	03	type of the last query edited 'PQ ' = prompted query 'SQL' = SQL query
DSQAPANL	27	name of the last panel edited
DSQAMENU	27	name of the last menu edited
DSQAPROC	27	name of the last procedure edited
DSQAFORM	27	name of the last form edited
DSQATABL	27	name of the last opened table or view
DSQATTYP	01	type of object in DSQTABL: 'T' = table 'V' = view
DSQEQNAM	27	name of the last query executed
DSQEQTYP	03	type of the last query executed: 'PQ ' = prompted query 'SQL' = SQL query
DSQEPANL	27	name of the last panel executed
DSQEMENU	27	name of the last menu executed
DSQEPROC	27	name of the last procedure executed
DSQEFORM	27	name of the last form executed
DSQAPRNM	08	default printer name
DSQAMSGW	01	message text pending: '0' = no '1' = yes
DSQSQLEC		SQL return code
DSQAROWS		number of rows fetched
DSQAROWC	01	query-complete flag: '0' = no '1' = yes
DSQAMODE	01	execution mode '1' = interactive (dialogue) '2' = batch
DSQAWDHD		pointer to application window handle

Table 19.8. Query Manager status variables.

20

Personal REXX

20.1 INTRODUCTION

Quercus System's *Personal REXX* product is a complete replacement for the standard IBM version of REXX supplied with OS/2 described in the previous chapters of this book. This notwithstanding, *Personal REXX* applications can make use of PMREXX, the REXXUTIL function package, and the RXQUEUE command and function.

Personal REXX is designed to be compatible with IBM's REXX implementation. As such, applications should be able to run unchanged with *Personal REXX* (principal differences: the CHARIN, CHAROUT, LINEIN, and LINEOUT functions maintain independent read/write pointers; as defined in the REXX language specification; DBCS is not supported).

In addition to the standard features supplied by IBM, *Personal REXX* offers:

- an extensive function package, REXXLIB
- the RXWINDOW function package
- CMS-like utilities
- support program

The REXXLIB and RXWINDOW function packages are also available as standalone products.

20.2 REXXLIB FUNCTION PACKAGE

The REXXLIB function package contains an extensive range of functions. These functions can be grouped in the categories:

- mathematical functions (logarithmic, exponentiation, trignometrical, hyperbolic, statistical)

- array functions (*Personal REXX* defines a REXX array as being a stem variable with tail as numeric index)
- operating system information and services
- hardware information and access
- interprocess communication (semaphores, named pipes)

The function package contains the following functions:

ACOS	compute arc cosine
ARRAYCOPY	copy REXX array
ARRAYDELETE	delete one or more elements from a REXX array
ARRAYINSERT	insert elements into REXX array
CHARSIZE	return the height of text mode character box
CURSOR	position cursor
CURSORTYPE	return cursor type
ARRAYSORT	sort a REXX array
ASIN	compute arc sine
ATAN	compute arc tangent
ATAN2	compute arc tangent of quotient
COS	compute cosine
COSH	compute hyperbolic cosine
CVCOPY	copy compound variable
CVREAD	read compound variable from disk
CVSEARCH	search compound variable for specified pattern
CVTAILS	place selected tails of a variable into a REXX array
CVWRITE	write compound variable to disk
DATECONV	convert date format
DELAY	wait
DOSAPPTYPE	obtain application type
DOSBOOTDRIVE	obtain system boot drive id
DOSCD	return current directory
DOSCHDIR	set current directory
DOSCHMOD	change file attributes
DOSCOMMANDFIND	search for command file
DOSCREAT	create a new file
DOSDEL	delete a file
DOSDIR	return directory information
DOSDIRCLOSE	close DOSDIR search sequence
DOSDIRPOS	return DOSDIR position status
DOSDISK	return disk information
DOSDRIVE	return (set) current drive
DOSEALIST	obtain extended attributes
DOSEASIZE	obtain extended attributes size
DOSEDITNAME	generate string based on pattern
DOSENV	get environment variable

DOSENVLIST	return list of environment variables
DOSFDATE	change file date
DOSFILEINFO	obtain selected information for file
DOSFILESYS	obtain file system type
DOSFNAME	obtain fully-qualified file name
DOSFSIZE	obtain file size
DOSISDEV	determine whether name is a device
DOSISDIR	determine whether name is a directory
DOSISFILE	determine whether name is a file
DOSISPIPE	determine whether name is a named pipe
DOSKILLPROCESS	terminate process
DOSMAKEDIR	create directory
DOSMAXPATH	determine maximum (fully qualified) file size
DOSMKDIR	create directory (in an existing directory structure)
DOSPATHFIND	search path for file
DOSPID	obtain the process id (PID)
DOSPIDLIST	obtain process information
DOSPRIORITY	obtain priority information
DOSPROCINFO	obtain process information
DOSRENAME	rename directory or file
DOSRMDIR	delete directory
DOSSESSIONTYPE	obtain type of current session
DOSTEMPNAME	generate temporary file name
DOSVOLUME	obtain volume label
ERF	compute error function
ERFC	compute complement of error function
EVENTSEM_CLOSE	close event semaphore
EVENTSEM_CREATE	create event semaphore
EVENTSEM_POST	post event semaphore
EVENTSEM_QUERY	return information about event semaphore
EVENTSEM_RESET	reset event semaphore
EVENTSEM_WAIT	wait for event semaphore to be posted
EXP	compute exponential function
FILECRC	compute file CRC (cyclic redundancy check)
FILEREAD	read text file
FILESEARCH	search text file for specified pattern
FILEWRITE	write text file
GAMMA	compute gamma function
GREP	match pattern
INKEY	get character from keyboard
LOG	compute natural logarithm
LOG10	compute logarithm to base 10
LOWER	convert to lowercase
MACROADD	load procedure into the macrospace

MACROCLEAR	clear the macrospace
MACRODROP	remove a procedure from the macrospace
MACROLOAD	load procedure (procedures) from a saved macrospace
MACROQUERY	return the search position of a procedure in the macrospace
MACROREORDER	change the search position of a procedure in the macrospace
MACROSAVE	save macrospace procedure (procedures) in a file
MUTEXSEM_CLOSE	close mutual exclusion semaphore
MUTEXSEM_CREATE	create mutual exclusion semaphore
MUTEXSEM_QUERY	return information about mutual exclusion semaphore
MUTEXSEM_RELEASE	release mutual exclusion semaphore
MUTEXSEM_REQUEST	request mutual exclusion semaphore
NMPIPE_CALL	perform self-contained transaction on named pipe
NMPIPE_CLOSE	close named pipe
NMPIPE_CONNECT	connect named pipe
NMPIPE_CREATE	create named pipe
NMPIPE_DISCONNECT	disconnect named pipe
NMPIPE_OPEN	open named pipe
NMPIPE_READ	read data from named pipe
NMPIPE_TRANSACT	perform named pipe transaction
NMPIPE_WRITE	write data to named pipe
PCDISK	obtain disk information
PCFLOPPY	return the number of diskette drives
PCPARALLEL	return the number of parallel ports
PCRAM	return the RAM size
PCSERIAL	return the number of serial ports
PCVIDEOMODE	return screen mode information
PCCOPROCESSOR	test whether coprocessor installed
PCMODEL	obtain model number
PCSUBMODEL	obtain submodel number
POW	compute power function
REXXLIBDEREGISTER	deregister all REXXLIB functions
REXXLIBREGISTER	register all REXXLIB functions
REXXLIBVER	obtain REXXLIB version number
SCRBORDER	set screen border attributes
SCROLLDOWN	scroll text down
SCROLLLEFT	scroll text left
SCROLLRIGHT	scroll text right
SCROLLUP	scroll text up
SCRREAD	read text string from screen
SCRSIZE	return screen size
SCRWRITE	write text string to screen
SHIFTSTATE	return CapsLock, NumLoack, ScrollLock status
SIN	compute sine
SINH	compute hyperbolic sine

SOUND	beep
SQRT	compute square root
STRINGIN	read positioned string from terminal
TAN	compute tangent
TANH	compute hyperbolic tangent
TYPEMATIC	set typematic repeat rate
UPPER	convert to uppercase
VALIDNAME	test whether valid filename
VARDUMP	write selected variables to file
VARREAD	read selected variables from file
VARWRITE	write selected variables to file

20.3 RXWINDOW FUNCTION PACKAGE

The RXWINDOW function package contains functions for window processing. Although the RXWINDOW functions do not conform to IBM's CUA (Common User Access) standards for screen user interface, they enable REXX execs to create full-screen applications easily.

The function package contains the following functions:

W_ATTR	set screen attributes
W_BORDER	display border
W_CLEAR	clear window
W_CLOSE	close window
W_FIELD	define named input area
W_GET	read input from specified field
W_HIDE	suppress window display
W_ISFIELD	test whether name is a window field
W_ISWINDOW	test whether handle is an open window
W_KEYS	set cursor control keys
W_MOVE	move window position
W_OPEN	open a new window
W_PUT	display text string
W_READ	read input from fields
W_SCRPUT	write text to window
W_SCRREAD	read text to window
W_SCRWRITE	write text to window
W_SIZE	return height and width of window
W_UNFIELD	remove field definition
W_UNHIDE	restore hidden window

20.4 CMS-LIKE UTILITIES

Many OS/2 programmers have come from the IBM mainframe environment. To ease their transition to OS/2, *Personal REXX* provides versions of the following, frequently-used CMS commands:

EXECIO	perform file processing
GLOBALV	manipulate global variables
LISTFILE	list file information

Although the services provided by the EXECIO and LISTFILE commands are largely duplicated by other routines, GLOBALV increases the functionality of REXX by allowing interprogram access to variables.

20.5 SUPPORT PROGRAM

Personal REXX also has the utility program:

RXINFO	display information about a (*Personal REXX*) program

20.6 EXAMPLE

The following example uses the RXWINDOW function package to display in a scrollable window those files (with path) that match the specified file name. To simplify the processing, the scrollable window has only a single line.

Three keys control the display:

PGUP	up one line
PGDN	down one line
ESC	exit

```
/* REXX */
rc = rxfuncquery("w_register")
IF rc = 1 THEN DO /* register RXWINDOW package */
  call rxfuncadd "w_register", "RXWIN30", "rxwindow"
  call w_register
END
rc = rxfuncquery("SysLoadFuncs")
IF rc = 1 THEN DO /* register REXXUTIL package */
  call rxfuncadd "SysLoadFuncs", "REXXUTIL", "SysLoadFuncs"
  call SysLoadFuncs
END
/* find valid drives */
map = SysDriveMap()
```

```
DO i = 1 TO 99
  PARSE VAR map r.i ':' map
  r.i = STRIP(r.i)
  IF map = '' THEN LEAVE
END
r.0 = i-1 /* no. of entries */
/* "rxwindow" */
wh = w_open(5,5,20,60)
rc = w_field(wh,'fn',2,20,12)
rc = w_put(wh,2,2,"enter file name:")
rc = w_read(wh)
/* find files */
k = 0
DO i = 1 TO r.0
  rc = SysFileTree(r.i":\"fn,s.,"SO")
  IF rc = 0 THEN DO j = 1 TO s.0
    k = k+1
    b.k = TRANSLATE(s.j) /* convert to uppercase */
  END
END
rc = w_put(wh,4,20,k "files found")
rc = w_put(wh,3,2,"          file:")
b.0 = k
j = 0
key = 'PGDN' /* initialize */
DO WHILE k > 0 /* loop, if files found */
  IF key = 'PGDN' THEN DO
    j = j+1
    j = MIN(j,b.0)
    rc = w_put(wh,3,20,b.j,40)
  END
  IF key = 'PGUP' THEN DO
    j = j-1
    j = MAX(j,1)
    rc = w_put(wh,3,20,b.j,40)
  END
  rc = w_read(wh,,'F')
  key = _ACTIVATION_KEYNAME
  IF key = 'ESC' THEN DO
    rc = w_close(wh)
    EXIT
  END
END
```

21

Other Products

21.1 INTRODUCTION

REXX interfaces are increasingly being incorporated into other products. The OS/2 relational database product, Database Manager (see Chapter 19), is one example of a product that offers extensive REXX services. Other products are discussed briefly in this chapter:

- IBM's EHLLAPI (Emulator High-Level Language Application Programming Interface)
- *VisPro/REXX*
- *VX • REXX*
- *ObjectVision*
- macro languages

The sample examples are only illustrative, and do not show the all features of the respective products.

21.2 RXHLLAPI

RXHLLAPI is the REXX interface to EHLLAPI, which is a part of OS/2 Communications Manager that supplies program services to perform 3270 or 5250 emulation (EHLLAPI is also available for other software platforms). RXHLLAPI offers REXX support for most of the EHLLAPI functions.

The RXHLLAPI package consists of the SAAHLAPI.DLL executable file (DLL), which is included when the OS/2 Extended Services 3270 or 5250 emulation features are installed.

Two sources provide RXHLLAPI information:

- The RXHLLAPI.DOC documentation file contains information (and examples) on the use of the RXHLLAPI product.
- The IBM *OS/2 EHLLAPI Programming Reference* (S01F-0297) manual describes the use of EHLLAPI.

As with all external REXX functions, the RXHLLAPI package must be registered before it can be used. The following registration parameters are required:

```
HLLAPI        function name
SAAHLAPI      module name
HLLAPISRV     procedure name
```

For example,

```
IF rxfuncquery('hllapi')
   THEN CALL rxfuncadd 'hllapi','saahlapi','hllapisrv'
```

The RXHLLAPI services are provided by a single function (HLLAPI), with the specific service being requested by the first argument string (e.g., 'Connect').

HLLAPI can be invoked either as a function:

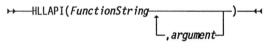

or as a subroutine:

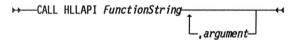

where **FunctionString** specifies the service to be performed:

Change_switch_name	set the name of the session shown on the OS/2 Task List
Connect	connect the REXX exec to the presentation space
Connect_PM	connect the REXX exec to the presentation space window
Convert_pos	convert row/column to presentation space position
Copy_field_to_str	return field data
Copy_OIA	return the Operator Information Area from the connected session.
Copy_PS	return the entire contents of the presentation space
Copy_PS_to_str	return data from the currently connected session
Copy_str_to_field	copy string to field
Copy_str_to_PS	copy string to position in the connected session
Disconnect	disconnect session
Disconnect_PM	disconnect session window

Find_field_len	return field length
Find_field_pos	return the position of field in the presentation space
Get_key	get keystroke
Get_window_status	return the current window status
Intercept_status	set intercept (reject) of keystrokes
Lock_PS	lock (unlock) presentation space
Lock_pmsvc	lock (unlock) presentation space window identified
Pause	pause for specified interval
Query_close_intercept	determine close request status
Query_cursor_pos	return cursor position
Query_field_attr	return field attributes
Query_host_update	determine whether presentation space has been updated.
Query_window_coord	return window coordinates
Query_session_status	return status information
Query_sessions	return session status information
Query_system	return system configuration status
Receive_file	transfer host file
Release	unlock keyboard
Reserve	lock keyboard
Reset_system	reset the system parameters
Search_PS	search presentation space for string
Search_field	search presentation space for a field containing the specified string
Send_file	transfer file to host
Sendkey	send keystroke(s)
Set_cursor_pos	set cursor position
Set_session_parms	set session parameters
Set_window_status	set window status
Start_close_intercept	trap host session close
Start_host_notify	trap host session screen update
Start_keystroke_intercept	intercept session keystrokes
Stop_close_intercept	end trapping of host session close request
Stop_host_notify	end trapping of host session screen update
Stop_keystroke_intercept	end trapping of session keystrokes
Wait	check session status

Note: The REXX exec must disconnect and reset the session on completion.

21.2.1 RXHLLAPI Example
The following example returns the current host time to the invoking exec.

```
/* set error exits */
SIGNAL ON HALT NAME quit
```

```
SIGNAL ON ERROR NAME quit
SIGNAL ON SYNTAX NAME quit

IF RXFUNCQUERY('HLLAPI') /* register HLLAPI */
  THEN CALL RXFUNCADD 'HLLAPI','SAAHLAPI','HLLAPISRV'
IF RC <> 0 THEN DO
  SAY 'rxfuncadd:' RC
  SIGNAL quit /* terminate */
END
RC = HLLAPI('Connect','A') /* connect session */
IF RC <> 0 THEN DO
  SAY 'connect:' RC
  SIGNAL quit /* terminate */
END

CALL HLLAPI 'Sendkey','@C' /* send clear key */
CALL HLLAPI 'Wait' /* wait */

CALL HLLAPI 'Sendkey','TIME @E' /* send TIME command */
CALL HLLAPI 'Wait' /* wait */

pos = HLLAPI('Search_ps','TIME-',1) /* search for TIME- string */
IF pos = 0 THEN DO
  SAY 'no time returned'
  SIGNAL quit /* terminate */
END

time = HLLAPI('Copy_ps_to_str',pos+5,8) /* copy time string */
SAY 'host time' time

quit:
  CALL HLLAPI('Disconnect')
  CALL HLLAPI('Reset_system')
```

21.3 VisPro/REXX

HockWare's *VisPro/REXX* is a product used to simplify the creation of applications with a graphical user interface (GUI) that make use the REXX language. *VisPro/REXX* incorporates an on-line testing facility to simplify the testing of the application. The completed application can be converted (built) into a self-contained EXE module that can be distributed to users without requiring a runtime library. *VisPro/REXX* applications can make full use of REXX facilities.

The *VisPro/REXX* interface uses the drag-and-drop programming technique to create applications. This is used to create both the screen formats and the associated processing logic. The usual Workplace Shell objects (push buttons, radio buttons, check boxes, list boxes, combination boxes) can be used. *VisPro/REXX* also offers draw (painting) and business graphic formatting services.

21.3.1 VisPro/REXX Example

The following simple example serves to illustrate the power and simplicity of *VisPro/REXX*. It also shows how standard REXX services can be incorporated into a *VisPro/REXX* application.

The sample application searches the named drives for files having the specified name. *Note*: This example is only illustrative, as there is a standard OS/2 service to perform this service.

Figure 21.1 shows the layout of the application's display mask (**form**). This display mask is created using *VisPro/REXX*'s screen painter. Each distinct item on the screen (including text fields) is an **object** that is assigned a unique identifier (number or symbol) – the sample example has the identifiers 1000 through 1007.

Note: For simplicity, the sample example has only a single display mask. Applications may use multiple linked forms.

Various form items can trigger **events** either implicitly or explicitly – for example, when the initial form is displayed, or when a field is selected. Such events (e.g. clicking a push button) result in some **behavior**, which is implemented as a REXX exec. *VisPro/REXX* has editor services to create and modify such execs.

Sample objects (shown in Figure 21.2 with their associated behavior execs):

- 1000 text: Enter Search Drives:
- 1001 multiple selection list box
- 1002 text: Found Files:
- 1003 list box
- 1004 text: File Name:
- 1005 entry field
- 1006 push button (default): Start
- 1007 push button: Cancel.

Notation:

```
┌──────┐
│      ║
└──────┘
```

```
┌nnnn─┐
└──────┘  represents the object with identifier nnnn
```

```
┌nnnn─┐
│      ┐  represents a text object with identifier nnnn
│
└────> associated event
```

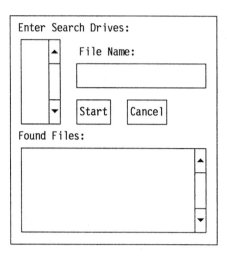

Figure 21.1. Application's display mask.

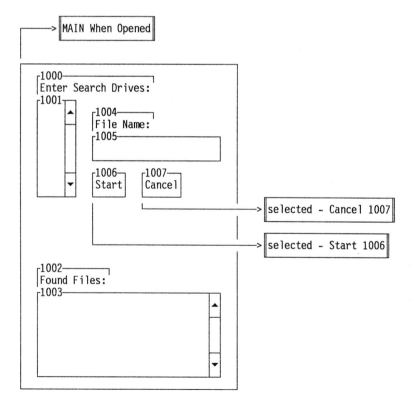

Figure 21.2. Objects with their associated behavior execs.

21.3.1.1 Behavior Execs. The sample example has three behavior execs:

- MAIN When Opened. This exec is executed before the initial form (the **main form**) is displayed; i.e., before any processing has been performed. It activates (register and load) the REXXUTIL function package; calls the SysDriveMap function to obtain the list of installed drives; and places the drive identifiers in a multiselection list box (object 1001).
- Selected - Start 1006. This exec performs the processing when the Start button is pressed: the file name (object 1005) is retrieved and tested to determine whether it is nonblank; the selected drive identifiers (from object 1001) are stored as the REXX R. stem variables; the SysFileTree function is called to search for the specified file name; the located files are set into the list box object 1003 (sorted in ascending order); and a message with the number of files is displayed on completion of the search operation.
- Selected - Cancel 1007. This exec performs the processing when the Cancel button is pressed: the window is closed.

The generated statements are written italicized. Some of the generated statements require minor modifications to better fit into the hand-coded REXX statements (e.g., application-oriented text in the messages).

MAIN When Opened

```
Arg window
/* activate REXXUTIL function package */
CALL RxFuncAdd 'SysLoadFuncs', 'RexxUtil', 'SysLoadFuncs'
CALL SysLoadFuncs
/* get installed drives */
map = SysDriveMap()
DO i = 1 TO 99
  PARSE VAR map r.i ':' map
  r.i = STRIP(r.i)
  /* Add item to end  List Box */
  CALL VpAddItem window,1001, 'END', r.i
  IF map = '' THEN LEAVE
END
```

Selected - Start 1006

```
Arg window self
/* get file name */
fn = VpGetItemValue(window,1005)
IF fn = '' THEN DO
  response=VpMessageBox(window,'','enter file name')
  CALL VpWindow window,'CLOSE'
END
/* get selected drives */
```

```
index = 0
DO i = 1 to 99
  /* Get index of next selected value  List Box */
  index=VpGetIndex(window,1001,'SELECTED',index)
  IF index = 0 THEN LEAVE
  /* Get item value at index  List Box */
  r.i=VpGetItemValue(window,1001,index)
END
r.0 = i-1 /* no. of selections */
/* find files */
ct = 0
DO i = 1 TO r.0
  path = r.i':\'fn
  rc = SysFileTree(path,s.,'SO')
  IF rc = 0 THEN DO j = 1 TO s.0
    value = TRANSLATE(s.j) /* convert to uppercase */
    /* Add item sorted ascending  List Box */
    CALL VpAddItem window,1003,'ASCENDING',value
    ct = ct+1 /* increment count */
  END
END
response=VpMessageBox(window,'search ended',ct 'files found')
```

Selected - Cancel 1007
```
Arg window self
CALL VpWindow window,'CLOSE'
```

21.4 VX • REXX

WATCOM's *VX-REXX* product is very similar to *VisPro/REXX* in that it is used to create a GUI which can make use the REXX language. *VX-REXX* incorporates an on-line testing facility to simplify the testing of the application. The completed application can be converted (built) into a self-contained EXE module, which, unlike *VisPro/REXX*, requires a licence-free runtime library (VROBJ.DLL) to be able to execute. *VX-REXX* applications can make full use of the standard REXX facilities.

VX-REXX uses the drag-and-drop technique to create the screen formats (objects) with their properties. Conventional techniques are used to create the associated processing logic.

21.4.1 VX • REXX Example
The following example shows the *VX-REXX* implementation of the same application as in Section 21.3 (and so serves as a comparison between the two tools).

VX-REXX uses the same display mask shown in Figure 21.1, but calls it a **window**. This display mask is created using *VX-REXX*'s screen painter. Each distinct item on the screen (including text fields) is an **object** that is assigned a unique identifier.

Each object has associated **properties, events,** and **methods**. The processing of an event is implemented as a REXX exec. *VX-REXX* has editor services to create and modify such execs.

Sample objects (shown in Figure 21.3 with their associated processing execs):

- DT_1   text: Enter Search Drives:
- LB_1   multiple selection list box
- DT_2   text: Found Files:
- LB_2   list box
- DT_3   text: File Name:
- EF_1   entry field
- PB_1   push button (default): Start
- PB_2   push button: Cancel

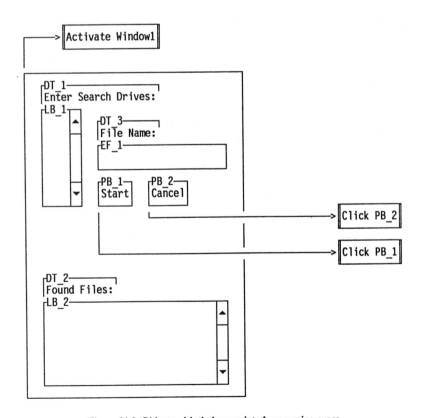

Figure 21.3. Objects with their associated processing execs.

21.4.1.1 Processing Execs. The sample example has three processing execs:

- Activate Window1. This exec is executed before the initial window is displayed; i.e., before any processing has been performed. It activates (register and load) the REXXUTIL function package; calls the SysDriveMap function to obtain the list of installed drives; and places the drive identifiers in a multiselection list box (object LB_1).
- Click PB_1. This exec performs the processing when the Start button is pressed: the file name (object EF_1) is retrieved and tested to determine whether it is non-blank; the selected drive identifiers (from object LB_1) are stored as the REXX R. stem variables; the SysFileTree function is called to search for the specified file name; the located files are set into the list box object LB_2; and a message with the number of files is displayed on completion of the search operation.
- Click PB_3. This exec performs the processing when the Cancel button is pressed: the window is closed.

The generated statements are written italicized.

Activate Window1

```
/*:VRX */
Window1_Activate:
/* activate REXXUTIL function package */
CALL RxFuncAdd 'sysLoadFuncs','RexxUtil','SysLoadFuncs'
CALL SysLoadFuncs
/* get installed drives */
map = SysDriveMap()
DO i = 1 TO 99
    PARSE VAR map r.i ':' map
    r.i = STRIP(r.i) /* remove surrounding blanks */
    IF map = '' THEN LEAVE
END
r.0 = (i-1) /* number of items */
CALL VRMethod 'LB_1','AddStringList','r.'
return
```

Click PB_1

```
/*:VRX */
PB_1_Click:
/* get file name */
fn = VRGet('EF_1','Value')
IF fn = '' THEN DO
    CALL VRMessage '','','enter file name','N'
    RETURN
END
/* get selected drives */
```

```
CALL VRMethod 'LB_1','GetSelectedStringList','r.'
ct = 0
DO i = 1 TO r.0
    path = r.i':\'fn
    rc = SysFileTree(path,s.,'SO')
    IF rc = 0 THEN DO
        DO j = 1 TO s.0
            s.j = TRANSLATE(s.j) /* convert to uppercase */
            ct = ct+1
        END
    CALL VRMethod 'LB_2','AddStringList','s.'
    END
END
CALL VRMessage '',ct 'files found','search ended','N'
window = VRWindow()
CALL VRSet window,'ShutDown',1
return
```

Click PB_2
```
/*:VRX */
PB_2_Click:
window = VRWindow() /* get window ID */
CALL VRSet window,'ShutDown',1 /* close window */
return
```

21.5 OBJECTVISION

Borland's *ObjectVision* is an object-oriented application generator that contains many services and functions. It has a REXX interface that enables both *ObjectVision* applications to be invoked from a REXX exec, and REXX execs (functions) to be used from *ObjectVision* applications.

ObjectVision supplies the VISION subcommand handler to process *ObjectVision* applications from a REXX exec. There are also two new functions to access *Object-Vision* variables from an exec: GETOVVALUE, and PUTOVVALUE.

REXX functions that are to be used from *ObjectVision* applications must be registered with the @REXXREGISTER *ObjectVision* function. Such REXX functions can be used to perform processing that is not available with native *ObjectVision*, for example, generate a random number. An *ObjectVision* debugging tool is available to assist with the testing of *ObjectVision* REXX functions in the *ObjectVision* environment.

21.6 MACRO LANGUAGES

Rather than having a proprietary language, an ever increasing number of products use REXX as their macro language. Command Technology Corporation's (CTC) SPF/2 is a typical example of a product that uses REXX as its macro language. IBM's Enhanced Editor (EPM) has its own macro language, but also permits the use of REXX macros. Macro languages usually combine REXX facilities with application-specific features (host command environment or functions).

21.6.1 SPF/2 Macro Language

SPF/2 uses a host command environment that it preregisters. This command environment processes the specified subcommands (prefixed with ISREDIT). SPF/2 macros have .SPF as extension. SPF/2's macro language supplies a wide range of editing operations (search, change, delete, insert, etc.). The full repertoire of REXX services can be used where the standard macro operations do not suffice.

Example:
```
/* SPF macro */
'ISREDIT MACRO'
SAY "enter program name"
PARSE PULL pgm
'ISREDIT LINE_AFTER 0 = DATALINE "/*"'
'ISREDIT LINE_AFTER 1 = DATALINE <1 "PGM:" 5 "'pgm'">'
str = DATE('L')
'ISREDIT LINE_AFTER 2 = DATALINE "DATE:'str'"'
'ISREDIT LINE_AFTER 3 = DATALINE "*/"'
```

This macro creates a C program header containing the program name (prompted) and the current date at the start of the program.

21.6.2 EPM REXX Macro Language

Although EPM's own macro language (E language) can be used to provide customized services, it needs to be learnt (EPM has a compiler to create optimized modules from E language macros), and REXX can often be used to provide equivalent functionality. REXX macros for EPM have .ERX as extension.

EPM provides a host command environment and functions as its REXX interface. Its host command environment can be used to extract internal EPM variables that are made available as REXX stem variables with the same name (for example, filename, getline (the current line)), and to create customized edit menus.

A subset of the EPM functions are available for REXX execs. These functions provide such services as line manipulation (delete, insert before, replace), set internal EPM variables, and set edit key.

Example 1:

This example performs similar processing to the SPF/2 macro example (the program name (file name), and current date are set into the program's prologue).

```
/* EPM REXX macro to create C program header */
"EXTRACT /filename"
pgmname = FILESPEC('NAME',filename.1)
CALL ETKInsertText "/*",1
CALL ETKInsertText "pgmname:" pgmname,2
str = DATE('L')
CALL ETKInsertText "Date:"str,3
CALL ETKInsertText "*/",4
```

Example 2:

This example creates a new menu item (UserMenu) that can be used to select the EPM DIR command (an EPM-frontend to the OS/2 DIR command).

```
/* EPM REXX macro to add a new menu */
'buildsubmenu default 10 UserMenu 0 0'
'buildmenuitem default 10 11 Directory 0 0 dir'
'showmenu default'
```

APPENDIX A

Instruction Syntax Summary

= – Assignment
⊢⊢——*symbol=expression;*——⊣

ADDRESS – Set Environment
⊢⊢——ADDRESS——...——;——⊣
  environment
  CMD ... *expression*
  VALUE *environment*
  (*environment*)

ARG – Fetch Argument
⊢⊢——ARG——...——;——⊣

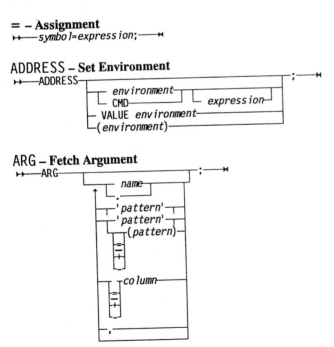

CALL – Invoke Routine

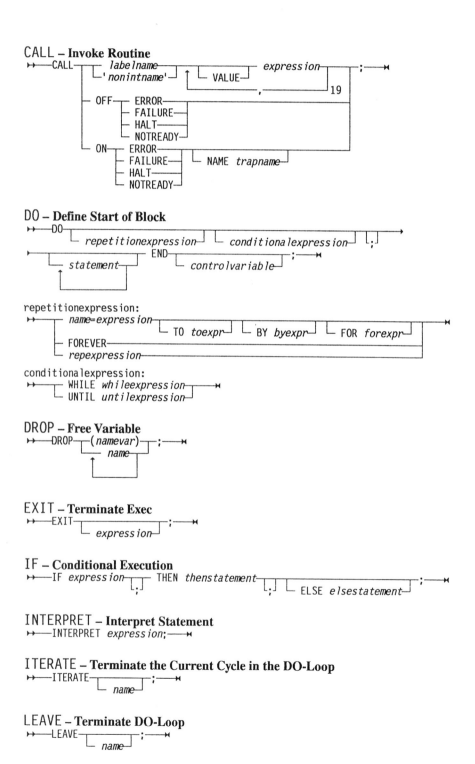

DO – Define Start of Block

repetitionexpression:

conditionalexpression:

DROP – Free Variable

EXIT – Terminate Exec

IF – Conditional Execution

INTERPRET – Interpret Statement

ITERATE – Terminate the Current Cycle in the DO-Loop

LEAVE – Terminate DO-Loop

NOP – No-Operation
⊢⊢——NOP;——⊣

NUMERIC – Define Numeric Format

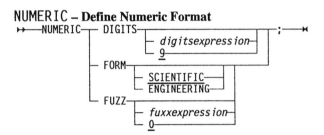

OPTIONS – Pass Special Parameters to the Language Processor
⊢⊢——OPTIONS *expression*;——⊣

PARSE – Assign Data

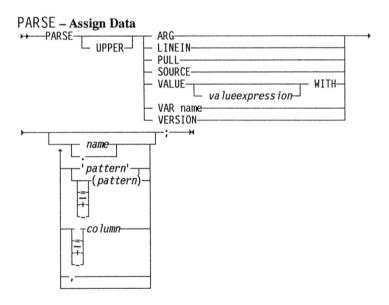

PROCEDURE – Define Internal Procedure

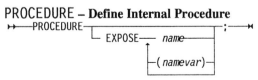

PULL – **Fetch Data Element from the Head of the Queue**

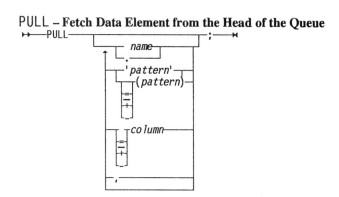

PUSH – **Set Data Element at the Head of the Queue**

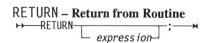

QUEUE – **Set Data Element at the Tail of the Queue**

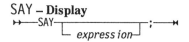

RETURN – **Return from Routine**

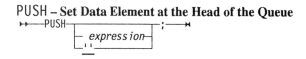

SAY – **Display**

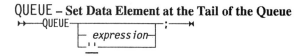

SELECT – **Conditional Execution of One Statement from a Group of Statements**

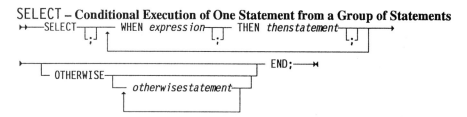

SIGNAL – **Enable (or Disable) an Exception Condition, or Cause Control To Be Passed to a Routine (or Label)**

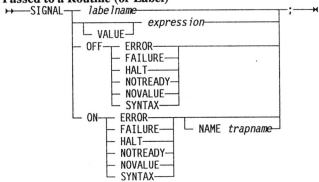

TRACE – **Set Debugging Options**

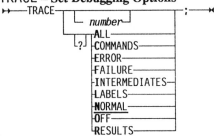

or

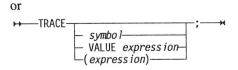

APPENDIX B

Syntax Notation

B.1 SYNTAX DIAGRAM

This book makes use of syntax diagrams to describe the syntax of expressions. Syntax diagrams are read left to right, top to bottom.

▸▸—   indicates the beginning of the statement

—▸◂   indicates the end of the statement

—▸   indicates that the statement is continued

▸—   indicates the continuation of the statement

— —   mandatory blank (one or more)

—   optional blanks

- Mandatory items cannot be branched around.

Examples:

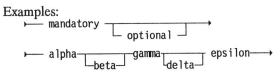

One or more blanks may be placed between alpha and beta. No blanks may be placed between gamma and delta, but one or more blanks must precede epsilon.

- If one of a number of mandatory items must be selected, then those items appear in a vertical stack. Example:

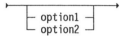

- Multiple options appear in a vertical stack; one of the specified options may be selected. Example:

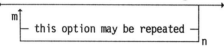

- Repetition is indicated by the following construction:

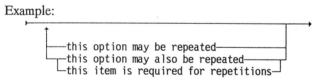

m, if present, specifies the number of times that the item must be repeated; n, if present, specifies the maximum number of times that the item may be repeated (the default value is unlimited).

- If the repeat arrow contains an item, then this item is mandatory for repetitions.

  Example:

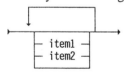

- Restricted repetition (each item from the list may occur at the most once) is indicated by the following construction:

- An item written in boldface may be used instead of the complete parameter. A default value is underlined. Example:

```
►── alpha ┬─────────────►
          ├─ BETA ─┤
          └─ GAMMA ─┘
```

The first item is mandatory and must be alpha; the second item is optional, with default value BETA – the short form B or G may be specified.

- If an item is written italicised, then this is a parameter, the definition of which follows (either as a syntax diagram or in the subsequent text). For example:

```
►── logicaloperator ──►
```

logicaloperator:

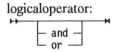

The parameter "logical-operator" may be replaced by one of the optional values: and or or.

A syntax diagram is formed by combining the simple elements defined in this appendix.

B.2 FONT
The sans serif font (e.g. ABBREV) is used to depict commands, keywords, variable names, etc. This convention is also adopted in the index.

Example:
The REXX function REXXSTART.

B.3 DIAGRAM CONVENTIONS
Diagrams in this book use the following conventions:
- ←——   pointer
- <——   build
- <<——   reference
- ⇐==   data transfer
- ↑   data item is a pointer

APPENDIX C

Bibliography

C.1 OS/2 2.x REXX IMPLEMENTATION

OS/2 2.0 Technical Library – Procedures Language 2/ REXX User's Guide
Contains short code examples on the use of REXX in the OS/2 implementation.

OS/2 2.0 Technical Library – Procedures Language 2/ REXX Reference
Describes the OS/2 REXX implementation – syntax and semantics. This manual includes brief descriptions of the system interfaces.

C.2 REXX LANGUAGE

SAA Common Programming Interface Procedures Language Level 2 Reference
Describes the SAA definition of the REXX language.

Michael Cowlishaw. (1990). *The REXX Language, A Practical Approach to Programming (Second Edition)*. Englewood Cliffs (NJ): Prentice-Hall.
The REXX author's description of the language.

Anthony Rudd. (1990). *Practical Usage of REXX*. Chichester (England): Ellis Horwood.
This book describes the REXX language and its usage in the MVS/TSO environment. The book contains an extensive description of the system interfaces – with examples in Assembler, COBOL and PL/I.

Gabe Goldberg and Phil Smith (editors). (1992). *The REXX Handbook*. New York: McGraw-Hill.
The REXX Handbook is a collection of tutorials on programming methods for a wide range of REXX implementations.

Charles Daney. (1992). *Programming in REXX*. New York: McGraw-Hill.
This book, written by the developer of Personal REXX, covers the REXX language with particular emphasis on efficiency and portability.

C.3 OS/2 2.x SUPPLEMENTARY MANUALS

OS/2 2.0 Technical Library – Application Design Guide
Contains an overview of the requirements of OS/2 application programs. In particular for REXX applications, detailed reference information on dynamic linking (DLLs), use of the System Object Model (SOM), and the Workplace programming interface.

OS/2 2.0 Technical Library – Programming Guide: Volume 1 – Control Programming Interface
Contains reference information for the base operating system. Volumes 2 and 3 contain reference information for Presentation Manager and graphics programming – topics not used in the examples shown in this book.

OS/2 2.0 Technical Library – Control Program Programming Reference
Contains detailed descriptions of the base operating system APIs.

Extended Services for OS/2 – Database Manager Programming Guide and Reference (Volume 4. Host Language Information)
Describes the REXX interfaces to Query Manager and Database Manager.

C.4 C PROGRAMMING

Brian Kernighan and Dennis Ritchie. (1988). *The C Programming Language (2nd Edition)*. Englewood Cliffs (NJ): Prentice-Hall.
The authoritive work on the C language, although the library functions are only mentioned in passing.

Anthony Rudd. (1993). *Mastering C*. Wellesley (MA): QED Publishing Group, 1993.
Mastering C is a combined reference and tutorial that explains C programming in detail. The book also pays special attention to common problems and difficulties encountered in the C language.

APPENDIX D

Glossary

alphabetic The set of characters containing the lower- and uppercase letters, together with the three national characters: #, @ and $.

alphanumeric The **alphabetic** characters, together with the ten numeric digits: 0 through 9.

ASCII American Standard Code for Information Interchange. The data code used primarily on personal computers.

boot Boot, used as a verb, means to start the computer system from scratch. Boot is derived from bootstrap in the context: to pull oneself up from one's own bootstraps.

built-in function A function that is defined in the REXX language.

clause In the REXX sense, the smallest grouping of tokens that form a subexpression.

CMS Conversational Monitor System. VM's user interface.

command An instruction that is neither a REXX keyword instruction nor a comment. Commands are passed to the currently active subcommand environment handler.

compiler A software component that converts a source program into an object module.

compound variable A variable consisting of a **stem** variable and one or more **tail** variables. Each variable is separated by a period (.).

Database Manager^{TM} IBM relational data base.

DBCS Double-Byte Character Set. A set of pairs of characters used to represent characters in Far-East languages (Chinese, Japanese, Korean, etc.).

DLL   Dynamic Link Library. A library of shareable functions that are accessed at execution-time.

DOS   Disk Operating System – the generic name for the two operating systems (MS-DOS and PC-DOS) used for the IBM Personal Computer and compatibles.

EBCDIC   Extended Binary Coded-Decimal Interchange Code. The data code used primarily on IBM mainframe computers.

environment   The host environment is an external subcommand handler that processes commands. The operating system command processor is the default environment.

exe   An executable program (.EXE extension).

exec   A synonym for a REXX program (usually .CMD extension).

extension   The low-level file name qualifier. REXX execs must have .CMD as their extension (this also applies to HPFS files), and a REXX comment as the first line. These restrictions do not apply to execs that are directly invoked with the REXX interpreter (REXXSTART function).

FAT   File Attribute Table. The original MS-DOS^{TM} file allocation system. *See HPFS*.

FIFO   First-in/First-out. Storage management concept where the elements are retrieved in the same order in which they were inserted – this is also known as **queue processing**.

filename   The identifier of a file. In the PC environment a fully qualified file name contains the drive (unit) identifier, and the directory (path), in addition to the file name.

hexadecimal   The coding scheme which uses sixteen as its base. The decimal values 10, 11, 12, 13, 14 and 15 are represented by A, B, C, D, E and F, respectively. One byte (8 bits) in hexadecimal notation can be presented by 2 digits, 00 through FF. The suffix operator X is used to denote a hexadecimal value; for example, '10'x represents decimal 16.

HPFS   High-Performance File System. The OS/2 (optional) file system that permits file names to have a maximum length of 255 characters. HPFS is optimised for high-capacity disks. Even when HPFS has been installed, FAT is used for diskette storage.

IBM^{TM} International Business Machines Corporation.

instruction   A self-contained expression: keyword instruction (e.g. DO), assignment or command.

internal routine   A routine (function or subroutine) contained in the same program as the invoking expression (function invocation or CALL instruction).

interpreter   A software component that directly executes a source program without producing an intermediate object module. An interpreter offers more flexibility than a compiler and usually has better diagnostics (the complete source code is available). However, this flexibility is bought at the cost of increased resource usage at runtime.

LIFO   Last-in/First-out. Storage management concept where the elements are retrieved in the reverse order in which they were inserted – this is also known as **push-down stack processing**.

Linker   Program to combine one or more object modules into an executable load module or DLL module.

load module   Machine-readable linker output in a form suitable for loading into storage for execution – synonymous with an exe module.

MVS^{TM} Multiple Virtual Systems operating system.

null clause   A clause that only consists of blanks or a comment.

object module   Machine-readable compiler output.

Operating System/2^{TM} also known as OS/2. The operating system originally announced for IBM PS/2 computers, but now supported for many non-IBM computers. OS/2 1.x runs on Intel 286 processors. OS/2 2.x requires an Intel 386 (or better) processor.

OS/2^{TM} See Operating System/2.

Personal REXX^{TM} Quercus Systems implementation of the REXX language for personal computers (DOS and OS/2 software environments).

phrase   In the REXX sense, one or more characters. A phrase is usually used as argument for a longer string.

REXX   Restructured Extended Executor.

SAA^{TM} Systems Application Architecture^{TM}. SAA is an IBM concept designed to provide a standard interface to the user (application developer).

SBCS   Single-Byte Character Set. The standard character set where one byte represents one character. See also **DBCS**.

session   In the OS/2 environment, a session is a self-contained process. OS/2 supports multiple parallel sessions.

source program   Input to a compiler. A source program constitutes the "computer instructions" produced by the programmer. Source programs can exist in a number of levels of detail. **Low-level** languages (e.g. Assembler) require that the programmer has an intimate knowledge of the machine instructions available on the computer on which the program will run. **High-level** languages (e.g. C) remove much of this burden from the programmer and enable him or her to be more concerned with the procedure required to solve the problem; such languages are often referred to as **procedure-oriented** languages. So-called **4th generation** languages (REXX offers certain features) are **problem-oriented**. Modern high-level languages offer structuring facilities.

startup   To initiate the operating system environment (*see* **boot**).

stem variable   The first name in a compound variable. The stem variable may not be assigned a value.

string   In the REXX sense, one or more characters.

tail variable   The following variable names in a compound variable. Tail variables are assigned values.

token   The lowest-level grouping of characters from which clauses are built. Tokens are literal strings, symbols, numbers, operators, and special characters.

TRL   Popular nickname for Mike Cowlishaw's book (*The REXX Language*).

TSO   Time Sharing Option, programming system to provide users with online access to the MVS computing system.

VM^{TM} Virtual Machine. Mainframe operating system that supports the concurrent operation of multiple operating systems. CMS is VM's user interface.

word   In the REXX sense, one or more nonblank characters.

word-list   In the REXX sense, one or more **words** separated by blanks.

APPENDIX E

Compatibility

This appendix summarizes the features available in various REXX implementations. The following legend is used in the tables:

s	SAA specification (Level 2)
x	extension for the implementation
+	additional feature
( )	implementation dependent
-	not available

E.1 REXX INSTRUCTIONS

	MVS/TSO-E	VM/CMS	OS/2 REXX	Personal REXX
= (assignment)	s	s	s	s
ADDRESS	s	s	s	s
ARG	s	s	s	s
CALL	s+	s	s	s
DO	s	s	s	s
DROP	s	s	s	s
EXIT	s	s	s	s
IF	s	s	s	s
INTERPRET	s	s	s	s
ITERATE	s	s	s	s
LEAVE	s	s	s	s
NOP	s	s	s	s
NUMERIC	s	s	s	s
OPTIONS	(s)	(s)	(s)	(s)
PARSE	s+	s	s	s
PROCEDURE	s	s	s	s
PULL	s	s	s	s
PUSH	s	s	s	s
QUEUE	s	s	s	s
RETURN	s	s	s	s
SAY	s	s	s	s
SELECT	s	s	s	s
SIGNAL	s+	s	s	s
TRACE	s	s	s	s
UPPER	x	x	-	-

E.2 BUILT-IN FUNCTIONS (SAA)

	MVS/TSO-E	VM/CMS	OS/2 REXX	Personal REXX
ABBREV	s	s	s	s
ABS	s	s	s	s
ADDRESS	s	s	s	s
ARG	s	s	s	s
BITAND	s	s	s	s
BITOR	s	s	s	s
BITXOR	s	s	s	s
B2X	-	-	s	-
CENTRE (CENTER)	s	s	s	s
CHARIN	-	-	s	s
CHAROUT	-	-	s	s
CHARS	-	-	s	s
COMPARE	s	s	s	s
CONDITION	s	-	s	s
COPIES	s	s	s	s
C2D	s	s	s	s
C2X	s	s	s	s
DATATYPE	s	s	s	s
DATE	s	s	s	s
DELSTR	s	s	s	s
DELWORD	s	s	s	s
DIGITS	s	-	s	s
D2C	s	s	s	s
D2X	s	s	s	s
ERRORTEXT	s	s	s	s
FORM	s	-	s	s
FORMAT	s	s	s	s
FUZZ	s	-	s	s
INSERT	s	s	s	s
LASTPOS	s	s	s	s
LEFT	s	s	s	s
LENGTH	s	s	s	s
LINEIN	-	-	s	s
LINEOUT	-	-	s	s
LINES	-	-	s	s
MAX	s	s	s	s
MIN	s	s	s	s
OVERLAY	s	s	s	s
POS	s	s	s	s
QUEUED	s	s	s	s
RANDOM	s	s	s	s
REVERSE	s	s	s	s
RIGHT	s	s	s	s
SIGN	s	s	s	s
SOURCELINE	s	s	s	s
SPACE	s	s	s	s
STREAM	-	-	s	-
STRIP	s	s	s	s
SUBSTR	s	s	s	s
SUBWORD	s	s	s	s
SYMBOL	s	s	s	s

cont.

E.2 BUILT-IN FUNCTIONS (SAA) (continued)

	MVS/TSO-E	VM/CMS	OS/2 REXX	Personal REXX
TIME	S	S	S	S
TRACE	S	S	S	S
TRANSLATE	S	S	S	S
TRUNC	S	S	S	S
VALUE	S	S	S	S
VERIFY	S	S	S	S
WORD	S	S	S	S
WORDINDEX	S	S	S	S
WORDLENGTH	S	S	S	S
WORDPOS	S	–	S	S
WORDS	S	S	S	S
XRANGE	S	S	S	S
X2B	–	–	S	–
X2C	S	S	S	S
X2D	S	S	S	S

E.3 BUILT-IN FUNCTIONS (NON-SAA)

	MVS/TSO-E	VM/CMS	OS/2 REXX	Personal REXX
BEEP	–	–	X	–
DIRECTORY	–	–	X	–
ENDLOCAL	–	–	X	–
EXTERNALS	–	X	–	–
FILESPEC	–	–	X	–
FIND	X	X	–	X
INDEX	X	X	–	X
JUSTIFY	X	X	–	–
LINESIZE	X	X	–	X
SETLOCAL	–	–	X	–
USERID	X	X	–	X

APPENDIX F

REXX Data Types

REXX APIs use many extended data types. Most of these definitions are not restricted to use by REXX applications, but are of general use. The definitions are contained in the os2.h (OS/2) and <rexxsaa.h> header (REXX-specific) files, and described in the *Procedures Language 2/REXX Reference* and *OS/2 Control Program Programming Reference* manuals.

CHAR   char
```
#define CHAR char
```

INT   integer
```
#define INT int
```

LONG   long
```
#define LONG long
```

PCHAR   pointer to char
```
typedef CHAR *PCHAR;
```

PFN   pointer to function
```
typedef int (* APIENTRY PFN) ();
```

PINT   pointer to integer
```
typedef INT *PINT;
```

PLONG   pointer to long
```
typedef LONG *PLONG;
```

PRXSTRING   pointer to REXX string
```
typedef RXSTRING *PRXSTRING; /* pointer to a RXSTRING */
```

PRXSYSEXIT   pointer to REXX system exit array

PSHORT   pointer to short
```
typedef SHORT *PSHORT;
```

PSZ   pointer to zero-terminated string
```
     typedef unsigned char *PSZ;
```

PUCHAR   pointer to unsigned char
```
     typedef UCHAR *PUCHAR;
```

PUINT   pointer to unsigned integer
```
     typedef UINT *PUINT;
```

PULONG   pointer to unsigned long
```
     typedef ULONG *PULONG;
```

PUSHORT   pointer to unsigned short
```
     typedef USHORT *PUSHORT;
```

RXSTRING   REXX string
```
     typedef struct {
       ULONG strlength; /* length of string */
       PCH   strptr;    /* pointer to string */
     } RXSTRING;
```

RXSYSEXIT   REXX system exit entry
```
     typedef struct {
       PSZ   sysexit_name; /* name of exit handler */
       LONG  sysexit_code; /* system exit function code */
     } RXSYSEXIT;
```

SHORT   short
```
     #define SHORT short
```

UCHAR   unsigned char
```
     typedef unsigned char  UCHAR;
```

UINT   unsigned integer
```
     typedef unsigned int UINT;
```

ULONG   unsigned long
```
     typedef unsigned long ULONG;
```

USHORT   unsigned short
```
     typedef unsigned short USHORT;
```

APPENDIX G

Control Program Services

The application program examples shown in this book make use of several control program services. To help in the understanding of these programs, a brief description of these APIs follows (the OS/2 *Control Program Programming Reference* manual contains a detailed explanation). The <os2.h> header file contains the definitions.

G.1 DosAllocMem – Allocate Memory

```
#define INCL_DOSMEMMGR
APIRET DosAllocMem(PPVOID PBaseAddress, ULONG ObjectSize, ULONG Flags)
```

PBaseAddress (PPVOID)

A pointer to the variable that will receive the base address of the allocated memory object.

ObjectSize (ULONG)

The size (in bytes) of the memory object to be allocated.

Flags (ULONG)

PAG_COMMIT	all pages initially committed
PAG_EXECUTE	execute access
PAG_READ	read access
PAG_WRITE	write access

+ other (specialised) settings.

G.2 DosCreateThread – Create an Asynchronous Thread

```
#define INCL_DOSPROCESS
APIRET DosCreateThread(PTID ptid, PFNTHREAD PThreadAddr, ULONG ThreadArg,
ULONG Flags, ULONG StackSize)
```

ptid (PTID)

Address of doubleword in which the thread identifier is to be returned.

PThreadAddr (PFNTHREAD)

Address of execution code.

ThreadArg (ULONG)

The argument to be passed to the thread routine.

Flags (ULONG)

0	Execute thread immediately.
1	Thread is created in suspended state.

StackSize (ULONG)

Stack size (in bytes).

G.3 DosExit – Terminate Thread

```
#define INCL_DOSPROCESS
VOID DosExit(ULONG ActionCode, ULONG ResultCode)
```

ActionCode (ULONG)

EXIT_THREAD (0)   Terminate the current thread.
EXIT_PROCESS (1) Terminate the current process.

ResultCode (ULONG)

The program completion code.

G.4 DosFreeMem – Free Allocated Memory

```
#define INCL_DOSMEMMGR
APIRET DosFreeMem(PVOID BaseAddress)
```

BaseAddress (PVOID)

The base address of a memory object to be freed.

G.5 DosGetInfoBlocks – Get the Addresses of Information Blocks

```
#define INCL_DOSPROCESS
APIRET DosGetInfoBlocks(PTIB ptib, PPIB ppib)
```

ptib (PTIB)

Pointer to the Thread Information Block (TIB).

ppib (PPIB)

Pointer to the Process Information Block (PIB).

APPENDIX H

RXSTRING Processing Routines

H.1 STANDARD RXSTRING PROCESSING ROUTINES

Two forms of standard routines are supplied to simplify the processing of RXSTRINGs:

- macros
- functions

H.2 RXSTRING PROCESSING MACROS

The <rexxsaa.h> header contains several useful macros for the manipulation of RXSTRINGs.

RXNULLSTRING	Test for a null RXSTRING.
RXZEROLENSTRING	Test for zero-length RXSTRING.
RXVALIDSTRING	Test for valid RXSTRING.
RXSTRLEN	Get length of RXSTRING data.
RXSTRPTR	Get address of RXSTRING data.
MAKERXSTRING	Create a RXSTRING from a string.

The following descriptions use the symbols:

r	RXSTRING
p	pointer to a null-terminated source string
l	length of the source string data

H.2.1 RXNULLSTRING(r) – Test for Null RXSTRING

The RXNULLSTRING macro tests whether an RXSTRING is NULL. RXNULLSTRING returns true (nonzero) if **r** is a null RXSTRING.

H.2.2 RXZEROLENSTRING(r) – Test for Zero-Length RXSTRING

The RXZEROLENSTRING macro tests whether the specified RXSTRING has a zero length. RXZEROLENSTRING returns true (nonzero) if **r** is a RXSTRING of zero length.

H.2.3 RXVALIDSTRING(r) - Test for Valid RXSTRING
The RXVALIDSTRING macro tests whether the specified structure is a valid RXSTRING. RXVALIDSTRING returns true (nonzero) if **r** is a valid RXSTRING.

H.2.4 RXSTRLEN(r) – Get Length of RXSTRING Data
The RXSTRLEN macro returns the data length of the specified RXSTRING.

Example:
```
long len;
RXSTRING retval;
len = RXSTRLEN(retval);
```

H.2.5 RXSTRPTR(r) – Get Address of RXSTRING Data
The RXSTRPTR macro returns the address of the data area of the specified RXSTRING.

Example:
```
char *pc;
RXSTRING retval;
pc = RXSTRPTR(retval);
```

H.2.6 MAKERXSTRING(r,p,l) – Create a RXSTRING from a String
The MAKERXSTRING macro sets the pointer and length of the specified string into the result RXSTRING.

Note: No copy of the source string is made.

Example:
```
static char source[10];
RXSTRING retval;
MAKERXSTRING(retval,source,strlen(source));
```

H.3 RXSTRING PROCESSING FUNCTIONS

The RXSTRING.LIB library contains many RXSTRING processing functions. Most of these functions perform analogue processing to the corresponding standard C string processing functions. The OS/2 Toolkit documentation contains a detailed description of the functions.

There are five groups of functions:

- numeric conversion functions
  ```
  INT    rxtoi(rxstr);
  LONG   rxtol(rxstr);
  ULONG  rxtoul(rxstr);
  ```

- file input/output functions
  ```
  VOID rxprint(rxstr);
  LONG rxread(file, prxstr);
  LONG rxwrite(file, rxstr);
  ```

- copy and conversion functions
  ```
  RXSTRING memcpy2rx(prxstr,buf,len);
  RXSTRING rxmemcpy(prxstr,prxstr2,len);
  RXSTRING rxstrcat(prxstr,prxstr2);
  RXSTRING rxstrcpy(prxstr,prxstr2);
  RXSTRING rxstrdup(rxstr);
  RXSTRING rxstrncat(prxstr,prxstr2,len);
  RXSTRING rxstrncpy(prxstr,prxstr2,len);
  RXSTRING strcat2rx(prxstr,str);
  RXSTRING strcpy2rx(prxstr,str);
  RXSTRING strdup2rx(buf,len);
  RXSTRING strncat2rx(prxstr,str,len);
  ```

- comparison and character functions
  ```
  LONG    rxmemcmp(rxstr,rxstr2,len);
  LONG    rxmemicmp(rxstr,rxstr2,len);
  PUCHAR  rxstrchr(rxstr,ch);
  LONG    rxstrcmp(rxstr,rxstr2);
  LONG    rxstricmp(rxstr,rxstr2);
  PUCHAR  rxstrrchr(rxstr,ch);
  ```

- miscellaneous functions
  ```
  RXSTRING rxalloc(len);
  VOID     rxfree(rxstr);
  RXSTRING rxreturn_value(prxstr,buf,len);
  RXSTRING rxset_length(prxstr,len);
  RXSTRING rxset_null(prxstr);
  RXSTRING rxset_zerolen(prxstr);
  ULONG    rxstrlen(rxstr);
  VOID     rxstrnset(rxstr,ch,len);
  PUCHAR   _make_hptr(rxstr);
  ```

These function prototypes use the data types:

```
HFILE file;
PRXSTRING prxstr
RXSTRING rxstr;
PSZ str;
PUCHAR buf;
UCHAR ch;
ULONG len;
```

APPENDIX I

Function Migration

OS/2 2.x is a 32-bit operating system. To take full advantage of this operating system, the OS/2 2.x Toolkit contains new 32-bit interfaces for REXX services, although the 16-bit REXX interfaces are still available. The following table serves as migration aid – the left-hand column lists the old 16-bit REXX interfaces with the equivalent 32-bit interface in the right-hand column.

OS/2 1.x	OS/2 2.x
REXXSAA	RexxStart
RxSubcomDrop	RexxDeregisterSubcom
RxSubcomExecute	RexxSubcomHandler
RxSubcomLoad	–
RxSubcomQuery	RexxQuerySubcom
RxSubcomRegister	RexxRegisterSubcomDll
	RexxRegisterSubcomExe
RxFunctionCall	RexxFunctionHandler
RxFunctionDeregister	RexxDeregisterFunction
RxFunctionQuery	RexxQueryFunction
RxFunctionRegister	RexxRegisterFunctionDll
	RexxRegisterFunctionExe

RxMacroChange	RexxAddMacro
RxMacroDrop	RexxDropMacro
RxMacroErase	RexxClearMacroSpace
RxMacroLoad	RexxLoadMacroSpace
RxMacroQuery	RexxQueryMacroSpace
RxMacroReorder	RexxReorderMacroSpace
RxMacroSave	RexxSaveMacroSpace
RxVar	RexxVariablePool
RxExitDrop	RexxDeregisterExit
RxExitQuery	RexxQueryExit
RxExitRegister	RexxRegisterExitDll
	RexxRegisterExitExe
RxHaltSet	RexxHaltSet
RxTraceSet	RexxTraceSet
RxTraceReset	RexxTraceReset

APPENDIX J

Program Preparation

J.1 INTRODUCTION

External programs must be compiled and linked (to form an EXE module or DLL entry) before they can be used.

All the examples in this book use the 32-bit IBM OS/2 development environment:

- C Set/2 (C compiler)
- Operating System/2 LX (Linear Executable) Linker

The samples shown in this book use separate commands to invoke the compiler and linker – depending on the options specified, the compiler and linker can be invoked with a single command.

The final section of this appendix gives introductory information for the use of the PL/I Package/2 product.

J.2 C COMPILATION

The C compiler creates an object module (object modules have the .OBJ extension) from the specified source program (C source programs have the .C extension).

The REXX interpreter does not require any specific C compiler options to be set. The options shown are the minimum required to generate executable code for the examples shown in this book. User-written application programs may, however, require or benefit from additional options (refer to the compiler manual or its on-line help for further information).

Syntax:

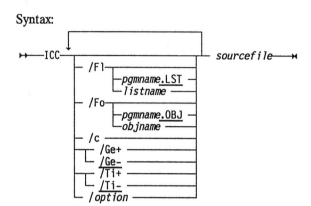

option

    A compiler option (e.g. /Fl produces a listing of the generated object code). Refer to the compiler reference manual for a full description of the allowed options.

/Fl

    Create a listing of the source file.
    Default: **pgmname.**LST.

/Fo

    Specify the output object file.
    Default: **pgmname.**OBJ.

/c

    The ICC command is only to compile the source; i.e., no implicit link is to be performed.
    Default: compile and link.

/Ge+

    Generate the object file in EXE-code format.

/Ge-

    Generate the object file in DLL-code format.
    Default: /Ge+.

/Ti+

    Generate debugging information.

/Ti-

    Generate no debugging information.

sourcefile
> The name of the source program (including the extension). **Pgmname** is **sourcefile** without its extension.

Example of C Set/2 invocation:
```
ICC /c /Ge- fconcat.c
```

The source file fconcat.c is to be compiled (/c option) to produce a DLL-format (/Ge-option) object module.

J.3 LINKER (LINK386)

The linker produces an executable program from the object output by the compiler. The linker includes any routines required for unresolved external addresses.

There are two forms of executable program:

- EXE
- DLL

An EXE-module can be directly executed (EXE = **executable module**). A DLL-module is a member of a Dynamic Link Library that contains functions that are shareable and accessed at execution-time; i.e., not directly combined with the EXE-module. DLLs can be accessed in two ways: at load-time or at runtime. Programs must explicitly load runtime loaded DLL routines.

EXE file generation does not require any link options to be set. However, the explicit setting of /PM:VIO will avoid a warning message being issued. To generate a DLL module, the linker must use a definition file, and the object file produced by the compiler must have been generated as DLL code (/Ge- option – /Ge+, the default, generates EXE code).

Syntax:

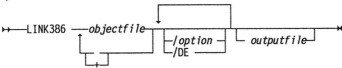

outputfile:

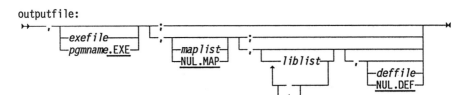

objectfile

The name of the object module produced by the compiler. Multiple object modules may be input to the linker – each such module name must be joined by either the plus character (+) or at least one blank. The object modules need not be written in the same programming language, provided that the interlanguage linkage conventions are observed.

Default extension: OBJ.

option

A link option (e.g. /PM:VIO – application compatible with PM; the default for EXE files). Refer to the linker reference manual for a full description of the allowed options. /PM:VIO (application is compatible with PM) is the default for EXE files, although a warning message will be issued if the option is not specified.

Note: The options may be positioned anywhere before the terminal semicolon (;) in the command line.

/DE

Include debugging information.

exefile

The name to be assigned to the load module produced by the linker. A DLL module has the .DLL extension. The **deffile** specifies the required additional information.

Default: The program name specified in **objectfile** (with .EXE as extension).

maplist

The name to be assigned to the link output listing.

Default: NUL.MAP; i.e., no output listing.

liblist

The list of names of the libraries containing modules needed by the object program. Multiple libraries may be specified, with each library name joined by either the plus character (+) or at least one blank.

The linker needs three sets of libraries; the first two are mandatory, the third depends on whether the program being linked requires external modules:

- C libraries
- REXX libraries (REXX.LIB)
- user libraries

The required C libraries are normally automatically generated when the compiler is installed.

deffile
>The name of the file containing definitions for the linker.
>Default: NUL.DEF; i.e., no definition file is present.

Sample syntax:
```
LIBRARY libname
DESCRIPTION 'description text'
PROTMODE
DATA MULTIPLE NONSHARED LOADONCALL
EXPORTS procname
```

>This syntax example shows typical entries of a definition file. The LIBRARY entry names the DLL. SINGLE or MULTIPLE specifies whether a unique data segment is to be created. PRELOAD or LOADONCALL specifies whether the data (code) is to be loaded when the DLL is accessed (PRELOAD) or as needed (LOADONCALL). The EXPORTS entry specifies the entry-point names.

libname
>The name of the DLL file (**libname**.DLL)

procname
>The program entry-point of the function (i.e., the name of the program function).

Example of LINK386 invocation:
```
LINK386 fconcat,urxfunc.dll,,REXX,fconcat.def
```

The linker is to produce urxfunc.dll as the output file from the input object file fconcat[.obj]. REXX[.LIB] is to be used for any unresolved external names. The definitions file is fconcat.def.

Note: The brackets ([]) indicate an optional item.

J.4 PL/I PACKAGE/2

The IBM PL/I Package/2 compiler provides limited support for REXX programs.

PL/I Package/2 has two components:

```
PLI.EXE       the PL/I compiler
PLICLINK.EXE  the PL/I linker (a modified version of LINK386, but with the same
              options) – two library files are required: CEELINK and IBMLINK.
```

Sample command file to perform a compile and link:

```
PARSE ARG name '(' opts
'PLI' name '(' opts
IF RC < 12 THEN DO
  "pliclink" name ,
  "/PM:VIO /DOSSEG /NOE /CO /STACK:5000000,,",
  "load.map,ceelink+ibmlink+rexx,nul.def"
END
```

Index

Entries written in a sans serif font are instructions, commands, function names, etc. Functions are written with parentheses (e.g., ABBREV()).